ERIC SLOANE'S AMERICA

ERIC SLOANE'S AMERICA

Written and Illustrated by
Eric Sloane

PROMONTORY PRESS

Originally published in three volumes as *American Barns and Covered Bridges;*
Our Vanishing Landscape; and *American Yesterday.*

A Promontory Press book
Published in the United States of America by
Galahad Books, Inc.
166 Fifth Ave
New York, NY 10010

Published by arrangement with Harper & Row, Publishers, New York.

Library of Congress Catalog Card Number 82-82851

ISBN 0-88394-061-2

Printed in the United States of America

CONTENTS

AMERICAN BARNS & COVERED BRIDGES

AMERICAN BARNS

and

COVERED BRIDGES

by

Eric Sloane

AUTHOR'S NOTE

THIS BOOK began one day when I was dismantling an old barn. The ironlike quality of the old wood and the cleanness of the adze cuts made me wonder what those times must have been like, and what sort of man the builder of this barn had been. For on lifting a timber from a part of the dry-wall, which had been plastered over on top and protected from two hundred years of weather by the covering of wood, I found the imprint of the builder's hand. Every callus and scar was there, and even the skin pores were visible. To me it was as though he had reached down across the years to greet me, and right then and there I knew I'd continue seeking to know better that first American, the Barn Builder.

As I sit now, drawing and writing amidst an array of long-disused tools and old almanacs and my sketches of rotting wooden structures, my children often confront me with the question, "What is an antique?" Anyone who has ever tried to explain a love for antique things to a child will understand my quandary. But one day my youngest answered the question when she said, "Is my teddy bear an antique?" Teddy Bear, I might explain, has one eye gone along with most of his fur which makes him related somewhat to my ancient and well-used barns and bridges. Teddy Bear certainly was an antique! He was a symbol of something past; but age had nothing to do with it and his condition was entirely beside the point. A love for antiques is not explained, it's something you acquire.

I'm not worried about my youngest. I think she might still have Teddy Bear when she is as old as I am; I think she will also be surrounded with the spiritual beauty and perhaps some of the tangible things that are the heritage of her forefathers. On the other hand, she might succumb to the modern habit of discarding old teddy bears, supplanting them with new ones of plastic. In any event, although there may well be not one ancient barn or original covered bridge left in America for her to see, there will still be this record.

Hand-hewn woods and barns are not confined to America, of course, but somehow the American pioneer gave to his craft something that has made his barn like no other barn in the world. The pioneer's love for wood and his skill in using it, together with the surviving examples of early American wooden architecture and artifacts, are fast disappearing. To revive an understanding and adoration for wood seems as hopeless as trying to bring back the horse and buggy. But to revive the eloquence of those times is indeed worth while. This book of sketches and comment is designed to lift the old barn and covered bridge out of the category of quaintness and the antique curiosity and to secure for them a rightful place in the story of architecture so that we may better see and feel the fine fabric of American development.

Things are never beautiful just because they are old. Let it become our duty to seek out and select the authentic beauty of the past and so keep it alive for the future. Goethe said it this way: "Whatever we come upon that is great, beautiful, significant, cannot be recollected. It must from the first be evolved from within us, be made to become a part of us, developed into a new and better self, and so, continuously created in us, live and operate as part of us. There is no Past that we can bring back by the longing for it, there is only an eternally new Now that builds and creates itself out of the elements of the Past as the Past withdraws."

So, rather than preserving things just because they are old or exulting in the fact that a Washington slept in its front bedchamber, one can take pride in the house that breathes the early American spirit by sheer dignity of form, purity of line, by a fine use of the right wood. Surely this is better than masquerading it in ancient costume by decorating it with antiques. The modern builder by the same means can borrow from colonial grace without resorting to patent nostalgia.

Those old structures were functional for reasons of life and death, whereas we wear our modern functional style too often as a uniform of distinction or as a decoration. There have always been fashions in architecture but the early American farmhouse style is an exception because it is never out of fashion. The farm and its barn buildings, in harmony with their setting, and simple in their Grecian plainness, do not seem subject to obsolescence. The Athenians built with marble, the Americans built with wood but the two architectural forms were founded on simplicity and—as with some ancient Greek ruins—I feel that I am in the presence of greatness when I happen upon a crumbling ruin of an early barn.

8

An architectural style is too often merely a criticism of some other style. The "revolt" trend in design reflects an unhealthy philosophy. When patriotism depends upon the hatred for another nation, or when one moves to the country because he hates the city or builds a traditional house because he hates the modern ranch-type, then there is snobbery in the making. The barn builder, in creating a new style, was being architecturally honest; he neither borrowed nor revolted against a foreign style, he was merely a serviceable carpenter creating a future. Which, by the way, is an inspiration for American thinking, architecturally and otherwise.

The great names of the American past have been well recorded but the country barn builder is anonymous. Those who would find the spirit of early America must look first in the country: in the city no one whistles yesterday's tunes. In the country the old tunes sound best; to those who can hear it, the song sung by old barns and wooden structures is precious music. It can be informative music too, for old houses speak as plainly as humans. An early barn or a hand-hewn bridge, though often regarded as a landmark or a curiosity, is better still a shrine. Beholding it is the closest thing to an intimate communion with the plain people who first kindled the American spirit and who evolved that architectural inheritance which has all but disappeared.

Sometimes echoes seem to be the loudest noises. I hope this book, like the sound of ax and adze across the countryside, will bring back some of the past and give a new importance to America's old barns and bridges and to all things that were once made only of wood.

I built those stalls and that shed there; I am barber, leech and doctor. I am a weaver, a shoemaker, farrier, wheelwright, farmer, gardener, and when it can't be helped, a soldier.
—FROM *Travels in the Confederation*, 1783.

The NEW ROOF

The WOOD

The log at the wood pile, the axe supported by it;
The sylvan hut, the vine over the doorway, the space cleared
for a garden,
The irregular tapping of rain down on the leaves, after the
storm is lull'd,
The wailing and moaning at intervals, the thought of the sea,
The thought of ships struck in the storm, and put on their
beam ends, and the cutting
away of masts;
The sentiment of the huge timbers of old fashion'd houses
and barns.
—Walt Whitman

The foundations of the American nation were laid with the building of its first barns. The hewn rafters of the first Plymouth barn were put in place and, with a prayer of thanksgiving, a small tree was lashed to the peak as part of the ceremony. Builders still put that symbolic tree on the rooftree of a new house without any particular reverence for wood itself, but just for "the luck of the house." The great importance of trees in the forming of an American philosophy seems almost lost in this plastic age.

You can't cut down a group of trees without being impressed by the characters of their wood. Some woods will accept the ax cleanly, some cut stubbornly, others will bounce an ax away unless the differences are allowed for. Just as a child today knows the differences between aluminum and spring steel, the early American child knew the differences in the softwoods and the hardwoods. Children today can point out any automobile and tell its make, but two hundred years ago they could point out any wood or

11

even smell it and call it by name. Without learning it in school or by book, it was perfectly natural for any American to know that black gum was for plowshares, oak for framing and pegs, apple for saw handles, chestnut for barrel hoops, cedar for pails, pine for kindling, and oak for heat. Even the plainest carpenter knew that a rocking chair needed at least four kinds of wood. Each wood did its specific job; there was pine for a soft seat, hickory for a springy back, walnut for strong legs, and oak for the fastening pegs. And any eighteenth-century farmer had the knack of making wooden hinges, locks, nails and spikes, hooks, plows, rakes; almost all his needs around the farm were satisfied with nothing more than a sharp tool and the right kind of wood.

Our forefathers were steeped in the romance and tradition of wood. The forest and its trees were part of their thinking and language. If a man were weak, strong, honest, or dishonest, he was likened to some kind of tree and although such a simile would not be very impressive today, it hit home then.

The old-timer interpreted man by likening humanity to the forest, saying: "There are warped and crooked trees that grow from poor soil. They just hold the soil together but they are neither beautiful nor useful and there are men just like that. There are trees like the dogwood that are just put on earth to be beautiful. There are fast-growing trees that crowd out everything but their own kind, that look like strong trees but are soft and weak inside. Some of their family are even poison to the touch and unfortunately there are men like that, attractive only from a distance. Then there are the tall hardwoods that become taller and stronger because of long, cold winters and high winds; broken limbs have left rough calluses along their trunks, but they stand out in the forest of trees like leaders. There are the soft, radiant woods which can be molded into useful things that become richer with age and smoother with usage; there are men like that too."

Asked to name something symbolic of America, we might first think of wheat, gold, silver, iron, or steel. Few of us would think of wood. Yet from the beginning, the greatest wealth of our country has been wood. Twenty years after their arrival, the Pilgrims were exporting American white pine as far as Madagascar in ships built of American trees. Scouts of "His Majesty's Woods" stalked through New England forests seeking suitable mast wood for Britain's Navy. Even as late as 1830, trees were seen with the King's "Broad Arrow" mark branding them as the property of England.

To think that the coming of iron eliminated some of the need for wood is wrong, for it was wood that made the Iron Age possible. Our greatest forest clearing was done to make charcoal which up until a century ago was the only fuel known for smelting iron. It might be argued that America's real growth came later with the steel railroads, but again wood enters the picture. One of the few things in America that has never changed with modern improvements is the railroad tie which is the same as it was when the first locomotive was made. Locomotives first used wood for fuel, but even today as the Twentieth Century flashes past at ninety miles an hour, it passes four thousand wood ties and a hundred wood telephone poles a minute. Stop now to think how much of the present American scene is composed of wood—books, newspapers, money, checks, bonds, documents, and deeds (even the page you are now reading was once a tree). Continue on with plastics, medicines, paints, houses, furniture, ships, and almost every conceivable necessity only to find in wood the source material. Even our coal and oil originated in ancient forests. America has been from the beginning a vast wood workshop.

The first settlers obtained sugar from maple trees; their soap came from fireplace ashes boiled with fat; charcoal went into their gunpowder; leather was tanned with oak bark and their medicine closet consisted of remedies derived entirely from the forest. Even colors for dyeing clothes came from the trees; there was butternut for brown, hickory bark for yellow, white maple for gray, sassafras bark for orange, and sumac for red. Almost all early American needs were filled by the wealth of the forests.

It seems strange that with all our modern methods, today's lumber is so very inferior to that used two hundred years ago. Even the best of modern kiln-dried wood cannot equal the keeping quality of wood as "prepared" by the early craftsmen. If you doubt this, try to buy an absolutely straight ruler today; hold any so-called straight-edged new piece of wood up to your eye and you will frequently find a curve that will increase with years. Yet some old houses have pine doors only a half inch thick by twenty-four inches wide that are as straight as the day they were cut, even without bracing. This was no accident, for the early settlers knew their wood. Their wood wisdom began from the moment the tree was cut. If cut at the right time, some insisted that lengthy "seasoning" was less important, often unnecessary. An old almanac states, "If you'd have your flatboards lay, hewe them out in March or Maye." During the "old moon of February" the New England woods rang with ax blows, for, according to belief, that was the right time for cutting timber that would stand forever straight and unwarped. It has even been suggested that the word "seasoned" as in "seasoned wood" has reference to wood having been cut during the proper season of the year. We are not in an age of folklore, but be it superstition or science, the results have certainly been interesting: the *New England*

13

Farmer says, "The moon has potential influence in the various parts of her orbits, that by cutting one tree three hours before the new moon and another of the same kind of tree six hours afterwards, a difference in the soundness of the timber would be noticed." "When the moon is new to full," reads an old almanac proverb, "timber fibers warp and pull." There were rules even for cutting firewood, for an entry for January 6, 1799, in an early Almanac advises, "At this quarter of the moon, cut fire wood to prevent it from snapping and throwing embers beyond the hearth."

Another proverb says "wood that lives with face away from sun, doesn't warp when sap has run." This suggests that wood cut from the north side of a tree (where the green moss is prevalent and where the sun shines the least) is less liable to warp from further dampness after milling. In the early days when pine flooring was cut, the log was first split in half. The northern half, according to custom, was kept for wide floorboards, while the southern side was quarter-sawed for lumber where warping might be less important.

It is quite true that almost every early builder had his own methods of seasoning and that each method was often so distinctive that one would contradict another. In all cases, the care and time taken to hew and turn the timbers by hand aided in the natural seasoning or drying of the wood. But the method used by the experts involved the presoaking with water; as logs were often moved from place to place by the simple means of floating in a stream or river, this alone might often have taken care of the soaking process. But let an early description in The *Builder's Handbook*, 1732, speak for the methods and the times of fine wood seasoning:

"There are some who keep their timber submerged in water to hinder the cleaving; this is good in fir, both for better stripping and seasoning; yea not only in fir but in other timber as well. Lay therefore your boards a fortnight in water (if running as in some mill-stream, the better) and there setting them upright in the sun and wind so it may pass freely through them, especially during the heats of summer which is the proper time for finishing buildings. Turn them daily. Thus treated, even newly sawn boards will season better than many years of dry seasoned methods. Let then the floorboards be tacked loosely for the first year and nailed for good and all the next year. Elm felled ever so green, for sudden use, if plunged for five days in salt water obtains admirable seasoning and may be immediately used. Water seasoning is not only a remedy against the worm but for its efficacy against warping and the distortions of timber. There are some who bury their timber in the earth, others in wheat. There are those who season by heating with fire, as for the scorching and hardening of piles. But for general seasoning and quick use, the soaking methods seem best.'"

14

Quarter-sawing was the practice of sawing boards so that the grain (when looking at the butt end of a board) runs as nearly at right angles with the width of the board as possible. Because warping is often caused by the grain "fighting against" a shape contrary to the grain's anatomy when the wood dries, it stands to reason that if you cut in harmony with the grain, you will then have less warping. Quarter-sawing is still being done, but the waste along with the necessity for huge logs and the resulting number of odd-sized widths makes quarter-sawing an expensive process. The dictionary will tell you that quarter-sawing is done to better "show the grain": how little were the settlers concerned about how the grain looked and how wrong the dictionary would have been two hundred years ago when quarter-sawing was done only to prevent warping! Actually many of the old buildings were built by plain farmers who were less concerned with carpentry than you might suppose and good wood took over where their poor carpentry left off. To say, "Ah, they built houses right in those days," does not explain why the house remarked about is found to contain all sorts of odd and erratic measurements that would be frowned upon today. Few rooms were actually square, ceilings were seldom the same height at the opposite side of the room and "random width" floorboards were more accidental than intentional. So what? Generally speaking, the materials were better than the carpentry, but the buildings were sounder, more pleasing, and more lasting.

In the beginning, well-seasoned timber was the result of simple convenience rather than of special effort. Dry wood burns better, cuts better, and weighs less, so it became perfectly natural to allow all wood to dry well before using it for any purpose. An old farmer's calendar reads: "It is said that a cord of green wood weighs about fifty-six hundred weight; a cord of dry, thirty-eight hundred weight. If then a farmer consumes thirty cords yearly and sleds it green, he sleds twenty-seven tons of water more than his neighbor who sleds it dry. Besides, if this wood is burned green, it requires wood enough in addition, to evaporate twenty-seven tons of water in order to obtain the same amount of heat. Using only dry wood is a saving of labor and expense."

Good seasoning of wood, which simply means proper drying, is regarded as a lost art or a matter of using more time than we have to spare now. Actually, the pioneer had much less time than we have today: he was in a hurry to get his barn or his house built, for the cold of winter would not wait. It is strange that, even with today's conveniences or so-called time-savers, we seem to have less than time permits. Good workmanship and the hand-made things of wood that have endured without rotting or warping are too often passed off with a wave of the hand and a remark about "people having more time to do things in the old days." How much less time they

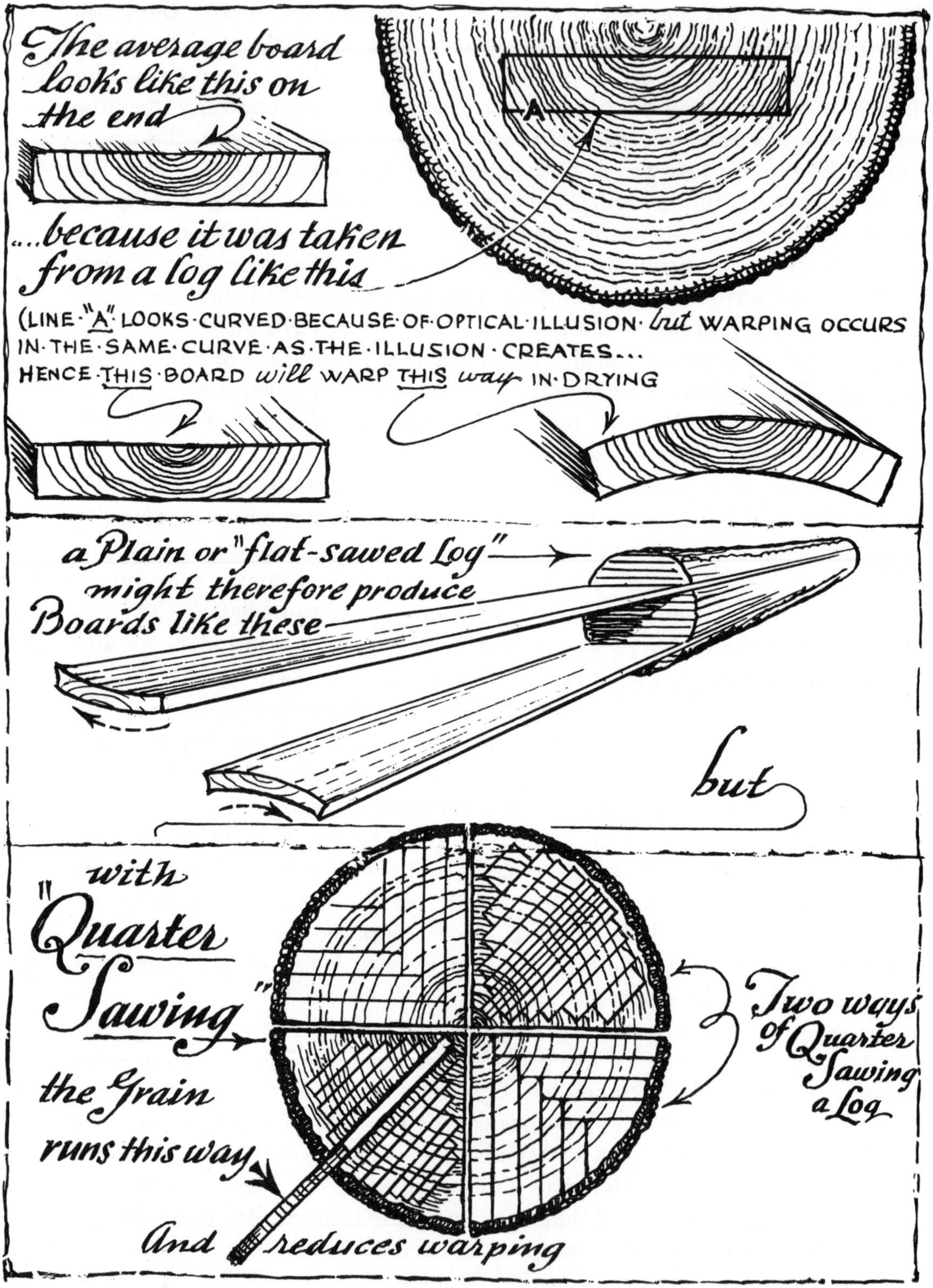

The average board
looks like this on
the end

...because it was taken
from a log like this

(LINE "A" LOOKS CURVED BECAUSE OF OPTICAL ILLUSION *but* WARPING OCCURS
IN THE SAME CURVE AS THE ILLUSION CREATES...
HENCE THIS BOARD *will* WARP THIS *way* IN DRYING

a Plain or "flat-sawed Log"
might therefore produce
Boards like these

but

"with
Quarter
Sawing"

the Grain
runs this way

Two ways
of Quarter
Sawing
a Log

And reduces warping

had is realized by remembering that the workday of a union carpenter now is not much longer than the chore time needed by the early backwoods carpenter before he even started his day of "work." Add to this the fact that there were only candles then, and when the sun went down the craftsman's day was over.

The time "saved" by mechanically-dried wood today is really lost many times over by having to paint-preserve it or even to discard or replace it a few years later. Furthermore, properly seasoned wood will harden with age and soft woods will often assume the properties of hardwood. It was the custom of match factories to buy large quantities of well-dried pine and so, when one factory heard that the old Ninth Street Bridge in Pittsburgh was being taken down, it put in a bid to buy all the white pine it contained. The factory regretted this move for the pine could not be made into matches; even an ax could not slice the once soft pine which had now become as tough as red gum or green sycamore.

The first settlers learned tree wisdom from the Indians. Cutting lower bark away for shelter and canoes, the Indians found that this operation killed most trees. So the art of girdling or killing a tree by cutting away the bark began. The usual practice was to girdle the trees that were on land to be farmed later. When the trees died, the summer sun reached through the naked branches and a garden could be hastily created even in the forest: later, as time permitted, the dried trees were felled and utilized as partly seasoned timber. A few years back, when America's chestnut trees were struck with a blight, several lumber firms bought quantities of the "dead" wood and found that the timber had seasoned nicely before it was even felled, making ideal warp-proof building material.

While girdled trees and quartered timbers were drying in the sun, there were always farm jobs, land clearing, rock wall building, and the thousand chores of everyday life to contend with. Hewing and chipping, cutting and setting, might take three months, although the actual raising of a barn often was accomplished in a single day. It was fortunate that the colonial builder was also a woodsman. What carpenter today knows his wood when it stands in the forest? But it all went together in those days, the clearing of land for raising food, the hewing of lumber, and the building of houses. The interrupted carpentry work probably gave some extra time for the wood to dry out.

In 1798, Isaac Weld of Dublin was in America making sketches and reports of the American way as seen through the eyes of a foreigner. Impressed by an ability to clear land, he commented that "these people have an unconquerable aversion to trees—to them the sight of a wheat field or a cabbage garden conveys pleasure far greater than the most romantic woodland views." Earlier, in his *Travels Through the States of North America, 1797*, he wrote: "The fact of the matter is, that from the face of the country being entirely overspread with trees, the eyes of the people become satiated with them. The ground cannot be tilled nor can the inhabitants support themselves until they are removed; they are looked upon as a nuisance and the man who can cut down the most of them and have the fields about the house clear of them, is looked upon as the most industrious citizen and the one who is making the most improvements in the country." Isaac was only twenty-one then and he was speaking as a fashionable member of the Irish gentry at a time when it was chic to wax romantic about the wonders of nature. He was "showing off" and being far too critical. If he had ridden through America seventy-five years earlier he would have known why the settlers were so proud of their clearings. Like Isaac, even now it is hard for us to realize the dangers of those early days, when pioneers, moving into the heart of a strange country with wild animals and savages at the door, valued the farm clearing as a safety "moat" between their homeplaces and the forest. But even a hundred years before Isaac's visit there were American conservationists; for back in 1681 William Penn decreed that one acre in every five be left in trees.

The clearing of land gave rise to one of the first industries in America. To clear the land much wood had to be burned and burned wood left ashes containing potash which was used for making soap. "Soap ashes" was the chief wealth of some of the first American settlements. Large quantities of wood ashes were tamped down in huge vats with holes underneath; water was poured in from the top and the residue contained lye salts which were boiled down and chiseled out of the pots when cool.

Large tree roots were found too difficult to burn and almost impossible to dispose of, so the "root fence" was devised. A stretch of roots with their tentacles turned upward made a menacing enclosure for cattle or for protection from Indian attack. There are still many root-fences in the north country and some in the far west. Generally speaking, however, the root-

18

a ROOT FENCE

fence was temporary, especially in New England where fence-consciousness became almost a form of fanaticism. An early copy of the *Christian Almanac* from Boston reads, "be tolerant of thy neighbor and be not jealous of the condition of his fences." A sound fence or stone wall became the rural sign-post of a good farm and any farmer insisted that he could glance at one and tell the character of the man who built it.

Those who have wondered why fences or walls in the city have a men-acing appearance that is entirely absent in the country, should remember that in the city fences keep things out while in the country fences keep things in. There is an almost human friendliness in the early stone walls of New England that makes you wonder what the people were like who built them. A hundred years ago a "no trespassing" sign in the country would be the signal of downright unfriendliness but "no hunting" was always permissible. Some of the old walls had an upraised flat rock here and there bearing the "no hunting" legend in white paint. Typical of New England friendliness is a sign done on a barn, at the farmer's insistence, by the sign-painter who did the patent-medicine advertisement on the opposite side. It read, "If you can't stop, wave as you go by."

Actually the walls are merely stones cleared from the fields and piled neatly to one side. But they happen to make fine enclosures. As a Connecticut farmer remarked, "They're better than wood fences because when they fall down you still have material to put them back again."

The Oriental philosophy of contemplation involves forsaking all work; the European does his meditating while relaxing from work, but the American seems to think things out best while working. So the stone walls of New England may be thought of as monuments to the thoughts that occurred while they were being built, for those were the days of great decision and profound planning. The thoughts one thinks while sawing a tree or making a stone wall are surprising. It is almost as if the mind becomes ashamed of the work the body is doing and starts doing a little "showing off" by itself. Lincoln said he did some of his deepest thinking while splitting rails. The plain farmer of two hundred years ago was weaving the fabric of a new nation and although there are no marble statues to his patriotism now, there are still his stone walls.

In the beginning no farmer attacked his land clearing alone but when the trees were felled and ready to be piled aside or burned, the whole country-side gathered for the "log-rolling." When they left, most of the heavy work had been done and only the smaller stone moving was left for the farmer and his oxen. Each participant was entitled to take home his load of special wood—young maple limbs for baking fuel, alder for gunpowder charcoal or whatever he needed most. Ashes in those days were valuable for what they

Fence Types.

Snake & Cross

Locust

Flat rock

Plain Snake
or Worm fence

Iron
rod

Post and rail (two types.)

contained and also what they did by way of preserving and insulating. Baking in the Dutch ovens was only possible by the even heat of clean ash; cooked meats were kept preserved within the insulating confines of maple and hickory ashes; the first wall insulation was a mixture of ashes and hay; bake-oven and fireplace ashes were not thrown away but kept till spring to use as fertilizer in the garden. Fifty years ago ashes from the kitchen stove were still being used for scouring dishes and cleaning knives. Every farm made its own soap from ashes at least once during the year. Near the barn there was a "leach barrel" filled with several layers of straw, lime, and ashes in that order; rain water was poured in daily from the top and what came out through a hole in the bottom was lye for soap. Six bushels of ashes plus twenty-four pounds of grease made one barrel of soap.

Another farm industry was the making of charcoal. Today we think of charcoal as being just something to cook and flavor the steaks with. Actually nothing has less flavor than charcoal which is tasteless. The settlers flavored their smoked meats with corncobs and hickory bark and not with charcoal. Charcoal does give much heat with little smoke and it is, therefore, an ideal fuel. Charcoal is wood that has been heated under cover, leaving just enough air to burn off the gases. What is left is almost pure carbon. Anyone old enough to remember the charcoal tablets which once were so widely used as a tooth whitener and as an aid for indigestion will recall how tasteless the stuff was.

Only a little over a century ago, charcoal was the basic industrial fuel for smelting iron. Each iron furnace drew its fuel from the surrounding hills and, although few of us realize it, the Iron Age did most to strip America of its early forests. One iron furnace would clear an average of two thousand acres of woodland annually for the production of charcoal and there were many hundreds of such furnaces. The J. and J. Rogers Company of Au Sable Forks averaged seven thousand acres of woodland each year.

The denser hardwoods such as beech, birch, maple, and oak were ideal for charcoal making and their wood was cut into four-foot lengths. The sticks were piled on end to form a hemispherical mound about ten feet high and twenty-five feet in diameter. This was covered with a flexible hood of ferns, hay, and sod, then fired from the top down through a hole in the middle. The slightest flow of air could cause an explosion that ruined days of labor nursing the slow manufacture of the charcoal. The work was, therefore, a twenty-four-hour-day job and the charcoal maker usually slept alongside his oven. Black and strange-looking from his unusual and lonely occupation, the charcoal maker was a colorful nineteenth century character of which little has been recorded. The simple life called for no mastery of the English language and as it was an existence not unlike that of mountain

Solid Zig-zag fence

WIRE

Solid Staked fence

a STONE

farming or sheepherding, many Europeans, particularly Russian and Swiss, came over to partake in the new America iron bonanza and became charcoal burners. The communities that grew up around the charcoal and iron industries were very much like the western towns that were to come later with the gold rush. A war was on and iron was the great necessity of the day. In Connecticut, the town of Salisbury became one of the cornerstones of the structure of the Continental Army; guns, anchors, chains, and field pieces of every sort were manufactured there. The anchor of the *Constitution* was forged at nearby Riga; fittings and chains for the entire fleet were forged there and for a while the Salisbury pits were putting out over thirty thousand tons of metal a year. In 1778, the famous Sterling Iron Works began a rush order to make a chain for stretching across the Hudson to keep the British fleet from going up the river. It is said that the complete chain, weighing 180 tons and each link being about four feet long, was finished in six weeks at a cost of four hundred thousand dollars. The wood burned into charcoal to smelt ore for that one chain probably leveled a small forest. Such towns became the little Pittsburghs of New England until something happened overnight. The Bessemer process and the use of coke was invented. Charcoal was a doomed industry.

22

After twenty years of trying to make a living from the ravaged forests and the petered-out charcoal deposits, the charcoal clan became hill squatters in sad little cabins, a hopeless and stranded population. Living on woodchuck and small game, most of them died of malnutrition but a few struggled on with their solitary charcoal pits. The infrequent visit to town was usually an event, for living in rattlesnake country, the latter-day charcoal men were addicted to the use of what they called "rattlesnake medicine," or moonshine whiskey. But the visits to town became fewer and fewer until finally the charcoal-wood wagons returned to the hills never to appear again and the clans of mountain colliers were soon forgotten. What remained were the commercial pits nearer town and the charcoal made there was used for medicine, polish, fertilizer, and gunpowder.

Another extensive use for firewood was in the lime kiln which every farmer owned or had access to. The kilns were usually built by "lime men" who were experts at kiln construction. The lime men traveled about the country making kilns for farmers, sometimes selling housewares and iron stoves as a sideline. The little stoves that are now sold in antique shops as toy stoves are often working models of real stoves which the agent brought to the housewife for demonstration. Stoves, incidentally, were about the only things that the farmer could not build for himself. Almost everything in the early days was made on the farm and every farmhouse had its own smokehouse, forge, and woodworking barn. The farmer was a jack-of-all-trades and there were few specialists.

But the increasing uses of wood called for European specialists and the New World always had room for those woodcraftsmen who were known as coopers. Although we never hear about it now, no ship would put out of port without having at least one good cooper. Several of the crew of the *Mayflower* were coopers. It is interesting to note that John Alden was accepted in the already-filled crew roster only because of his training as a cooper. The coopers of America were to be important people because dishes, hardware, containers for solid food and liquids, almost everything used as a container, had to be made of wood. In this trade of wood specialists there was the wet cooper—also known as a tight cooper—who made staved casks and barrels for all kinds of liquids; he was an expert with oak wood. The dry (or slack) cooper made barrels for sugar, flour, and meal. He was expert with maple, elm, and chestnut. Small tubs, butter churns, bowls, plates, and boxes were made by the white cooper who was expert with birch, beech, maple, and pine. All these things were called "treenware" from the early plural of trees. The cooper's shop was usually the busiest in town but during summer when his apprentice could take over, he took to the backroads, his wagon stocked with staves, hoops, and assorted treenware to call on his customers. A visit from the traveling cooper often lasted the day for there was always an abundance of wooden utensils to be repaired.

When the first coopers came over from England, they found much to be learned from the American Indian. The Indian had already devised an adze, almost exactly like the European shipwright's adze though the blade was made of flint. By burning fires in a log and adzing out the charred parts, the Indians made huge wooden canoes. This does not sound impressive to us, but it must have been so to the early settlers, for some of the canoes made by the Indians from one log were much longer than the boats in which the settlers themselves had come to America. It is quite natural that all early treenware should be influenced by American Indian design. This is most noticeable in treenware handles which were frequently designed in the Indian manner.

Sometime during visits to antique shops one comes across a wooden bowl of unusual hardness and extreme luster, having a wavy "bird's-eye maple" quality to the wood grain. That is a "burl" wood bowl, copied directly from similar bowls used by the Indians before the white man arrived. A burl is an abnormal wartlike growth occurring on the trunks of trees and is of hard and irregular grain. By cutting this lump from the tree and burning out the inside, an unusually beautiful and serviceable wooden eating-bowl was made that had no tendency to crack along the grain.

The use of particular woods to suit each need was the cooper's special art; chapters could be written about how each wood reacts to different liquids and how the cooper took this all into consideration, knowing how loose or tight to fasten each kind of wood and how to match up the right woods to make a perfect container. Consider the sap bucket. The hoops were hickory saplings with the bark left on; the staves were of maple to blend with the sap; the spiles or spouts which the sap ran through were sumac or basswood with the pith burned out by a heated wire; wooden pegs for fastening the hoops were made of birch.

At one time the only sugar available in America was from the maple tree and up until the 1800's many farms still derived sweetening from nothing but maple trees and the honey-bee. An average tree yields from five to fifteen pounds of sugar. "Sugarin' time" in the past must have been a wonderful event. The maple grove was usually a mile or so away from the farmhouse and in the middle of the grove there would be a sugar cabin where the whole family and perhaps a few hands would live the while sugaring went on. The children watched and emptied the sap buckets into large wooden sap barrels which were then collected on sugar sleds drawn by oxen. The fires were kept going for three days and three nights; the whole affair had a festive mood more of a frolic than the hard work it really was.

24

in The Cooperage trade there was

the Wet Cooper

who made
containers
for liquids

from
White oak
and Ash..

Liquids — Sap carriers

Tubs
and
Piggins

the Dry Cooper or "Slack-cooper"

used maple, oak, ash,
hickory, chestnut,
to make containers for... Sugar... Flour... Cakes, Grain

The White Cooper

used Pine, birch,
maple, ash

Nests of Boxes, Baskets

Pails, Bowls, Boxes etc.

The first run of sap made a pure white sugar which was hardened into cakes and, usually placed in the attic out of the children's reach, reserved for special cakemaking. Each run of sap became darker and made different qualities of "soft sugar," syrup, or maple-molasses and each product needed its special kind of treenware to hold it. For example, hard sugar takes on the flavor of whatever material it is enclosed in, so pine and similar odorous woods were avoided. Wherever there was a grove of sugar maples, there was work for the cooper.

In later years when coopers were scarce, it became the common thing to buy five-gallon tins from paint companies at wholesale rates and use them for storing syrups. There is a tale about a New York man who bought an old Vermont barn to remodel; he found ten five-gallon tins in the loft labeled "Fine Varnish" and upon opening them he found the contents to be still smooth and clear. But it wasn't until the handyman had scraped two rooms and finished them off that he realized he had been using maple syrup to "varnish" the floor.

At one time apple butter and apple cider were as evident at the dinner table as bread and butter are now. No tree was more important than the apple tree which offered raw fruit, vinegar for cooking and preserving, butter and drink, and wood for special tools. The use of apple wood for fuel was banned in several states and out of reverence for the many things apple trees have to offer, farmers still consider it unlucky to cut down old apple trees or sell the wood. Some of the toll-takers of the old covered bridges considered it unlucky to take money for apple-laden wagons on their way to the cider press. So it was the custom to have a basket of fruit ready beside the driver as payment for their way across the bridge.

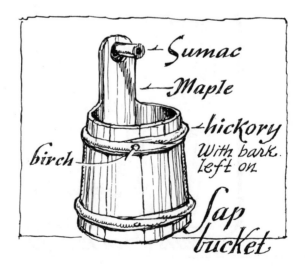

26

CEDAR was used as fence posts by all farmers because of its resistance to rot. Coffins were also made of cedar. There were cedar coopers who specialized in making tubs and pails. In Pennsylvania, cedar was used for making chests, which resulted in the present day "moth-proof" cedar closet.

CHESTNUT was first used for its bark which was cut in large squares and used as shingles on early barn roofs. Having an irregular wavy grain, its warp resistance, when properly seasoned, makes for fine wide flooring and for heavy cooperage.

HICKORY was used first by the Indians for an oily liquor which was pressed from pounded hickory nuts, and called "pawhiccorri," whence comes the name hickory. A few of the larger masts of early sailing vessels were made of hickory. The "summer beam" in early barns and houses was often hewn from one hickory tree; this beam was the horizontal beam taking the main burden of the whole structure and its name was originally "sumpter beam," so called from the sumpter or burden horse. The young hickory limbs, with bark usually left on, were used as barrel hoops. In the spring when the sap was running and the wood was, therefore, more porous, loads of hickory shoots and hickory strips were weighted and sunk in a pond to soak until ready for use. The Indians used hickory for basket splints and the settler soon learned to copy their technique, even improving upon it later by using steam instead of slow soaking. The Shakers became expert in using hickory splint for making chair bottoms, baskets, and sieves.

PINE was once considered as the emblem for America. More uses for pine were found than with any other wood. Light in weight, pine does not decay easily even when wet and it found its way into all kinds of early furniture, floors, and outside walls. Because the trees grew so straight and the wood was so well suited and light, America traded ship and mast pine for everything from Haitian sugar to African slaves. Many distant countries thought for a while that pine was the only thing growing in America. Tar taken from pitch pine was an important "first industry" and pitch-pine splinters were used as tapers for matches. Pitch-pine knots were collected and stored in barns to be used as emergency torches for out-of-doors lighting and night-time hunting. Pine was the standard covering for both barns and bridges.

BIRCH was rated second among the hardwoods. It was a mainstay with the white cooper and it made perfect material for both lye-ash and charcoal. Both tanning-oil and wine were made from birch sap by the Indians and later by the settlers.

Notice how this Indian tomahawk resembles this old Wooden

water DIPPER

& stirring SPOON

& basswood SCOOPS

a SHAKER Apple Butter SCOOP →

and an Iroquois scoop

a Connecticut NOGGIN →

like an INDIAN PITCHER →

Oak was the heaviest native wood and chosen first for framing barns and houses. Having no odor and bending easily, it was used by the wet cooper for barrel staves. Treenails or "trunnels" were made of oak. Because it was important in those days for fireplace wood to last throughout the night and also not to throw sparks, an oak log was always reserved for bedtime firelighting.

Spruce was abundant in the north and it was used in framing barns and in building bridges. Because it was the lightest yet strongest wood, spruce was reserved for long spans and bridge arches.

Ash has much of the quality of oak and, being a fast growing tree, it was considered a cash crop for the early farmer who sold the young ash trees for splint and barrel-hoop material. Many barns are framed entirely with ash although the fastening pins were always of oak.

These were the woods that made America a rich place. Richness to the European was something created so it was difficult for those across the sea to regard the New World as having wealth or culture of its own. As the European was a connoisseur of wine and perfume, the American took to his heart the aroma of good wood and the richness of pioneer life. To this day, few Americans find anything more invigorating than the smell of burning leaves, hickory-smoked hams, coffee on the stove, or the fragrance of pine. Who but an American would name an after-shave lotion "old spice," "pine chips," "sportsman," or "bayberry"?

No matter how "modernized" we are, somewhere out of the past will come a remembrance of wood, perhaps the crinkling of oak leaves in an autumn wind, perhaps the smell of a certain Christmas tree or of an old chunk of apple wood ending its life in your fireplace—and we share with the first settlers a reverence for wood.

The Burl Bowl

The TOOLS

The Carpenter who builds a good House to defend us from
Wind and Weather, is far more serviceable than the curious
Carver who employs his art to please his Fancy. . . .
— FROM A Pamphlet of 1719

THE FIRST TOOL to be devised by man was the ax. But it met its greatest
test in America. The ax has had more to do with the building of our country
than any other tool. Within twenty years after the first settlement, the ax
had improved to the design we still use today. The settler used his ax to
a great degree of efficiency, from felling a tree to sharpening a twig of wood
in penknife fashion. He could hold the axhead in the palm of his hand and
smooth wood as we do now with a plane. He marked the handle with nicks
at every inch for measuring timber, and, by striking the axhead with a maul,
he had an improvised chisel.

Hidden out of the way in many old barns may still be found those
flat axhandle-shaped pieces of wood that were patterns for the making of
new handles. Their lines are simple, graceful, subtle, serviceable. Although
all axhandles look alike to the uninitiated, each man knew well the curves
and proportions of his own ax. They were as individual as his fingerprints,
as identifying as his signature. Once in ancient times, a murder was solved
by tracing the murder ax to the axhandle pattern in the murderer's barn.

The metal end of a tool is a cold and heartless thing, but the wooden
handle seems to assume something of the user's character. Whether it is
imagination or tradition, the good carpenter knows well the almost human
capacity of wood to "fight back" against pressure and its ability to improve
with age. Why a well-played violin or a correctly used tool is better for its
age is impossible to explain scientifically, but wood has that quality. The
handle, according to carpenters, is what has the "heft" or "feel" of a fine tool.

30

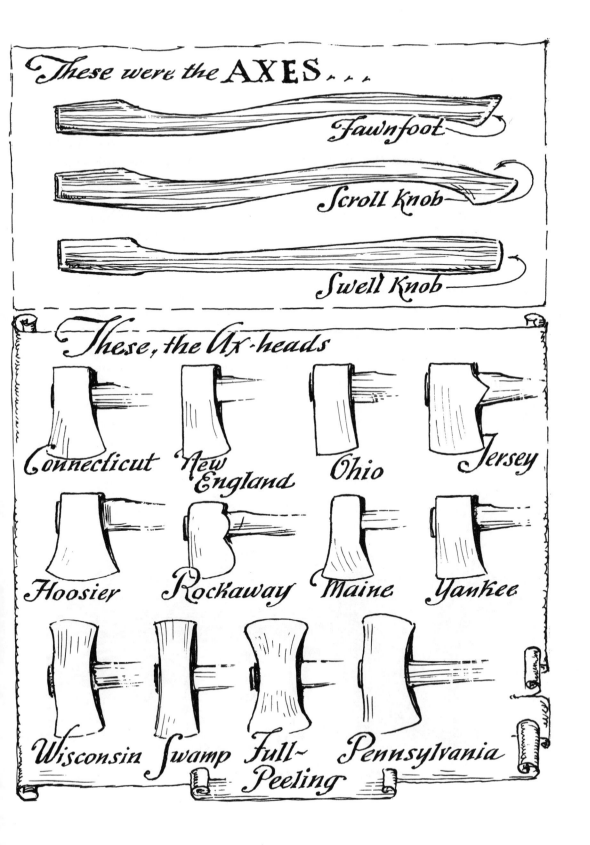

These were the AXES . . .

Fawnfoot

Scroll Knob

Swell Knob

These, the Ax-heads

Connecticut New England Ohio Jersey

Hoosier Rockaway Maine Yankee

Wisconsin Swamp Full-Peeling Pennsylvania

The story of early American tools is more one of adoption than invention, because almost all woodworking tools had been invented in ancient times and had changed little since the time of the Romans. The chisel, for example, has never changed nor has the way of using it changed. Some people gush over the chiseled numbers at the joints of old barn timbers, saying, "See—they are done in Roman numerals, the way our forefathers printed." Yet when they mark their own modern screens and windows to match, those same people use Roman numerals too, because they are the only numerals that a straight-edged chisel can make.

The first ax brought over from England was heavy and it had a battle-ax appearance. But as the ax became more important and the axman more proficient in its use, a subtle variety in design evolved.

There were two kinds of American axes, the pole-ax and the double-bit ax: the pole-ax has a flat head and the double-bit ax two cutting blades. The axheads are as different in design as the axhandles, but, whereas the handle identified the man, the axhead told where he came from. Certain axheads were typical of Pennsylvania, Ohio, Michigan, Jersey, and so on.

Long before the time of the so-called Americana that we see in the average antique shop, all hardware and tools were made in the farmer's forge barn, which was a small house near the barn with a stone forge and chimney in it. Very often you will notice a toolshed with vestiges of a chimney and wonder why the farmer might have wanted fire or heat in such a place. When hard-

the forge barn

32

Pattern kept for making new Ax handles

ware became available without the usual British tax on it and tools could be made at the nearest blacksmith, the farmer's forge was usually dismantled and the forge barn became just a toolshed. But the fact that the earliest tools were hand-made at home and were skilfully used somewhat explains the very clean adzemarks and sharp mortise cuts that are often seen in the old hand-hewn barn beams. Many of the private forge barns had bellows over six feet long and were made from the hide of a complete moose or deer.

Spikes and nails were fashioned by hand in the forge barn until 1796, when a nail cutting-and-heading machine was devised and patented by G. Chandlee. Nails at one time were so expensive and in such demand that it was customary for the owner to burn down an abandoned building in order to recover his nails. In 1645 the colonial authorities in Virginia offered to pay the owner of an abandoned building the worth of its nails if he would not resort to burning the structure.

Symbolic of the Yankee carpenter, who is a fanatic about letting no one use his tools but himself, was a sign found in an old forge barn. "Using your neighbor's tools," it reads, "is like wearing his clothes." An old-timer who always made his own tools was once given one of those newfangled iron-handled hammers. "It's a fine tool," he said, "but it ain't a hammer. It don't sound like a hammer and it don't feel like a hammer. It's a fine tool but it ain't no hammer."

"Watching an axman," an early letter to England reads, "is like watching magic. These men of the woods sleep with their axes under their beds at night and every minute of the day they are swinging their blades with such sure strokes that they can just look at a tree and know how many strokes will fell it." A little later, a surveyor in New Hampshire tells how ". . . the axmen were identified from the surveyors by their type of headgear; bowlers are the standard headgear of the gentleman surveyor, while stocking caps are that of the axmen. The axmen go ahead as fast as one

33

can manage to walk behind them, clearing the way as a ballet dancer might brush aside parlor chairs out of the way of his dance. Their axes are unbelievably small but they seem to cut twice as fast as anything that we have ever seen."

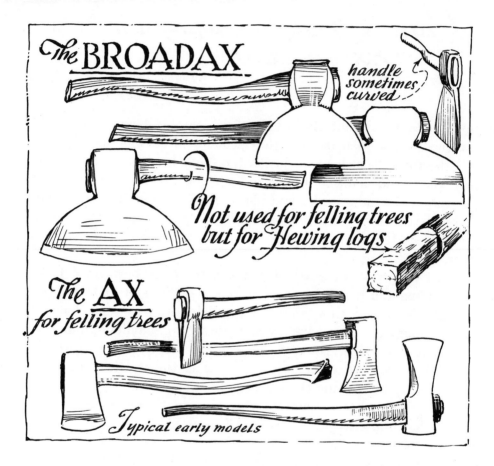

Although most people think that the early American broadax was used for cutting down trees, this short-handled monster was more a "carpenter-shop tool" than a woodsman's. Straight from the Middle Ages and weighing close to ten pounds, the broadax had one purpose and that was to make already felled, rough logs into serviceable building timbers; the process was called hewing. Here even the dictionary often goes wrong for, if you were to say that you "hewed a tree down" as some dictionaries say is correct for "felling a tree," your language to a seventeenth century person would be strange and incorrect. "The ax that fells a tree," goes an ancient proverb, "has not the wisdom of the broadax that hews the timber."

Each hewer had his own method of using a broadax. As it was beveled on only one side and the handle was often curved to "hug" the log that was being worked on, there were both right- and left-handed broadaxes. The general method of hewing was to go down the rounded top of a felled log with deep notches; then, with the beveled edge of the broadax up, the wood between each notch was hacked out. This went on until the rounded surface became flat; when four sides had been done, the result was a square beam.

A similar hewing instrument, but used for smaller logs, was the adze. All adze heads had square eyes or openings upon which the head slid. There were as many adze styles and combinations of handles as there were users. Because the adze was used on a timber that the hewer straddled, and the blade swept past between his legs, few old-timers went long without serious scars on both legs. The Indians had adzes of their own but they were flint blades and without a long handle. The Indian adze was really a knife-like scoop and, before using it, the wood to be hollowed out was usually softened by burning. During Indian raids, the settlers' adzes were sought for making into tomahawks and many of the so-called "Indian war hatchets" displayed at museums throughout the country are really remodeled adzes stolen from the whites. From the drawing it may be seen that adze handles were unusually graceful, also that the heads are loose and not anchored on by an inserted wedge as in the case of the hammer and ax. The mattock and grubbing hoe of today are really earth-digging versions of the adze. The adze, as it used to be, still exists in the shipbuilding business.

Shingles were not cut; they were split or cleaved, or "rived" and the instrument used for making them was called a froe. It was one of the few tools that could be used sitting down, so Grandpa of a hundred years ago enjoyed riving shingles in the toolshed when there was nothing else to do; there was usually a large overstock of shingles on hand for roof repairs. A good dry piece of pine, cedar, or oak was used, and the froe was placed blade down and with the grain, on a cross section of a chunk of log. With one blow of a maul or a wooden mallet, the froe would split thin sections or "shakes" from the chunk. Making a smooth and nearly finished piece of wood by just one blow is a fascinating operation and one can understand why Grandpa enjoyed his "riving" only second best to whittlin' or crackin' hickory nuts. There is nothing attractive about a froe. The blade isn't even sharp and the handle is just any old piece of round wood that was handy. The art of "riving" was a trick that needed no skill so there was no pride or dignity reflected in the design or construction of the tool. Even the maul that went with it lacked in grace; it was just a round "hunk of wood with a handle on it."

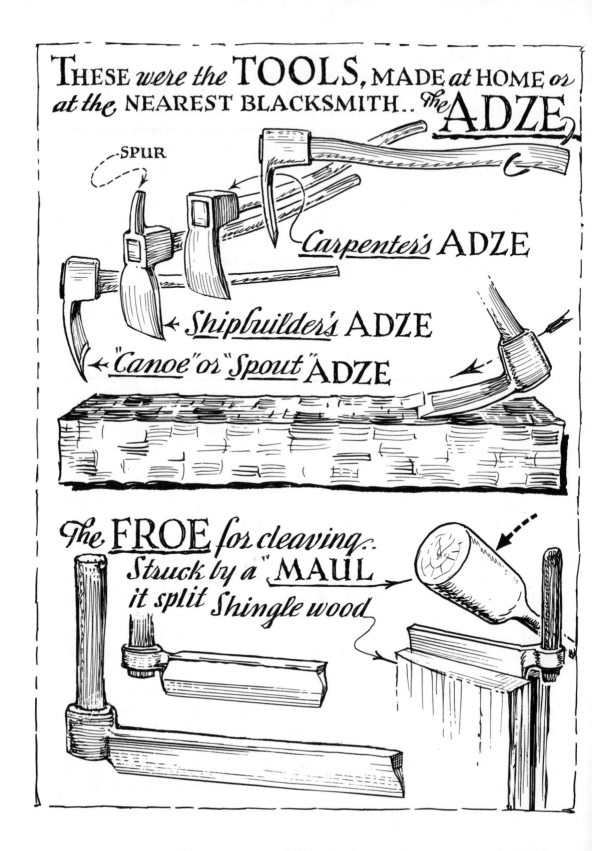

THESE *were the* TOOLS, MADE *at* HOME *or* *at the* NEAREST BLACKSMITH... *the* ADZE,

SPUR

Carpenter's ADZE

← *Shipbuilder's* ADZE

← "*Canoe*" *or* "*Spout*" ADZE

The FROE *for cleaving..* *Struck by a* "MAUL *it split* *Shingle wood*

The DRAWKNIFE
used with a shaving horse

Shingles usually needed a little trimming and smoothing, and that's where the shaving horse came in. Another sit-down job, the shingle was held in place by a "dumbhead" or clamp which was operated by the foot. A green branch to pull the clamp back when the foot was released, added to the automatic action of the shaving horse. Shaving was done with a nicely balanced blade, that was drawn toward the worker with two handles, called a drawknife. The drawknife was also used for peeling strips of wood such as the splint wood used in heavy baskets and as the hoops for barrels.

These five were the tools of the past that the barn-builder forged in his own forge. The ax, the broadax, the adze, the drawknife, and the froe were born ages ago, but the refinements given to them by the first settlers

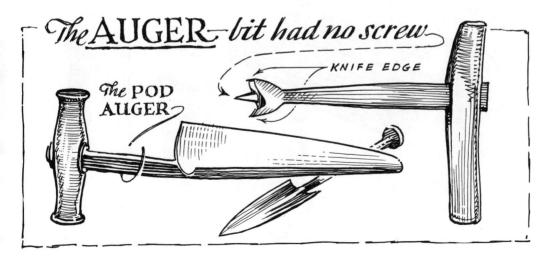

The AUGER *bit had no screw*

KNIFE EDGE

The POD AUGER

37

allow them to be described as American. The other tools of those days were very much like modern tools except for a fuller use of wood and some refinement of design. The auger looked like a giant corkscrew except for the absence of the pointed screw on the end; in its place was a sharp point and two cutting knives edged at an angle. The woodscrew was a late development, for until between 1840 and 1850, woodscrews had flat ends instead of sharp points.

A list of the old tools might sound little different from a modern list. In 1622, England gave some written advice for adventurers to the New World, telling them of the many cases where families had left the homeland poorly equipped, suffering privation and death as a result. "Those leaving for Virginia," this declaration read, "must provide themselves with the following tools for a family of six:

> 4 hoes, 3 shovels and 2 spades
> 2 broadaxes, 5 felling axes
> 2 steel hand-saws, 2 two-hand saws
> 1 whip-saw with file and set
> 2 augers, 6 chisels
> 2 pickaxes, one grindstone
> Nails of all sorts.

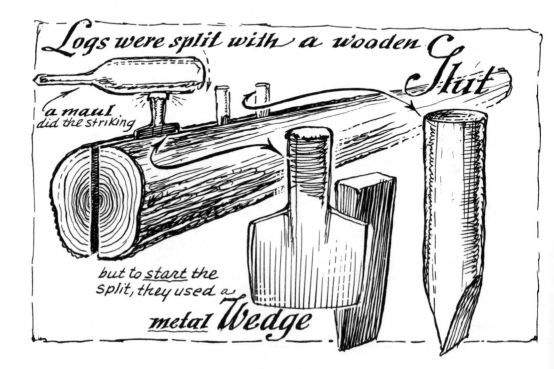

Logs were split with a wooden *Glut*

a maul did the striking

but to <u>start</u> the split, they used a metal *Wedge*

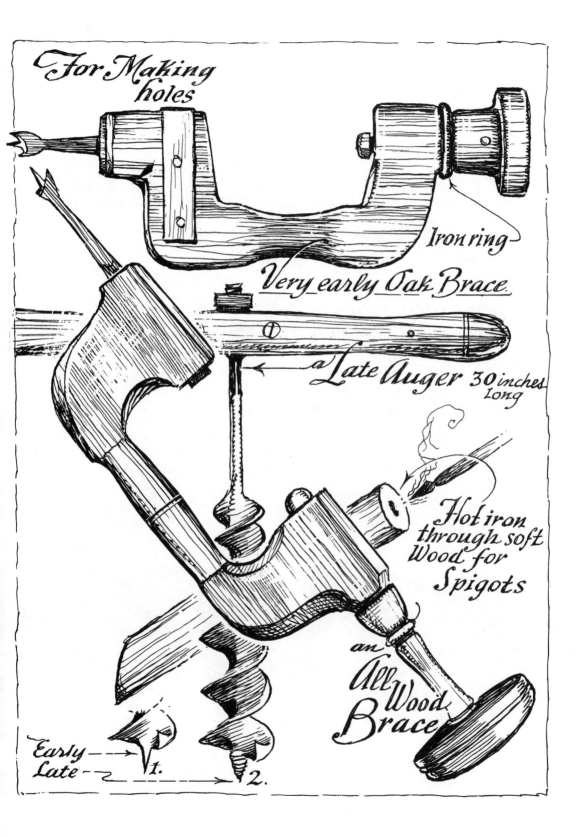

For Making holes

Iron ring

Very early Oak Brace.

a Late Auger 30 inches long

Hot iron through soft Wood for Spigots

an All Wood Brace

Early →
Late →
1.
2.

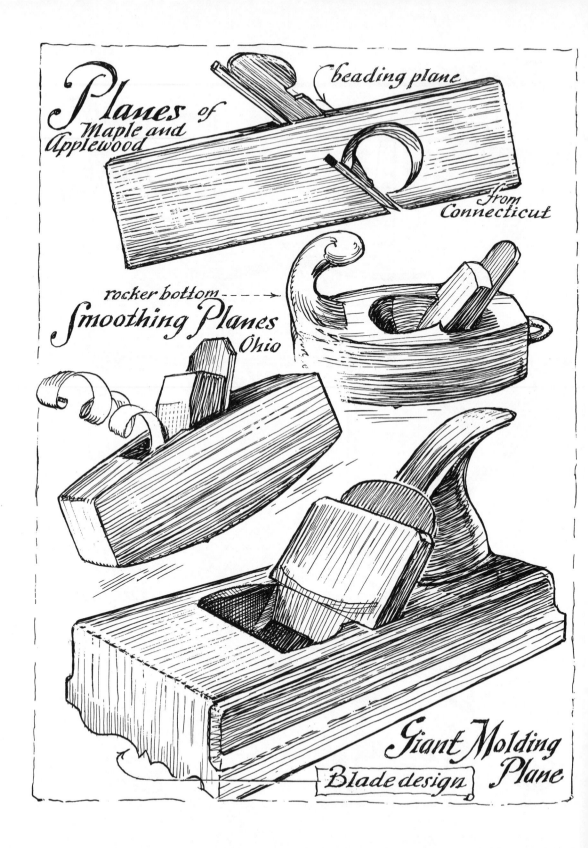

Planes of
Maple and
Applewood

beading plane

from
Connecticut

rocker bottom

Smoothing Planes
Ohio

Giant Molding
Plane

Blade design

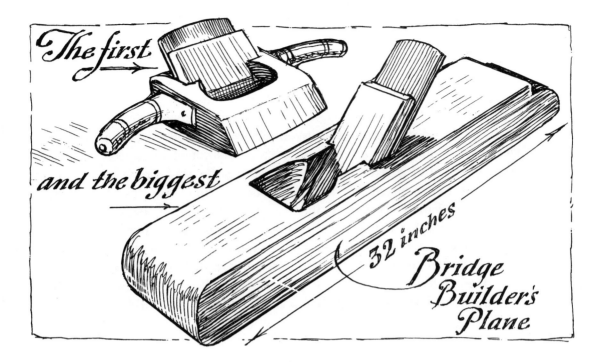

The first →

and the biggest →

32 inches

Bridge Builder's Plane

IRON BANDS

IRONWOOD HEAD

This is a

BEETLE

used for
DRIVING

41

If you happen to find a few flat-cut wooden wedges in your own old barn, perhaps they are gluts, which is just an unpleasant-sounding word that means wooden wedges for splitting logs. It seems incredible that plain wooden pegs can split a big log in two, but if you know your rail-splitting, that's the way to do it. The settlers had few steel wedges to spare and they found that just one steel wedge may be used to start a split and if followed up by plain wooden gluts, the job could be done as well as if all steel wedges were used. Gluts were about a foot long, fashioned of specially hard wood, while green and often hardened further by heating slowly over hot coals. Gluts were driven in by sledge-hammers called beetles—hammers with hardwood heads that were bound together with bands of iron. Beetles were generally used for driving stakes into the ground but often took the place of a maul. The maul and beetle were made of ironwood, black walnut, or oak, and both tools were used for driving trunnels into place.

The plane was a later development, first used like a drawknife that was pushed away instead of being pulled toward you in drawknife fashion.

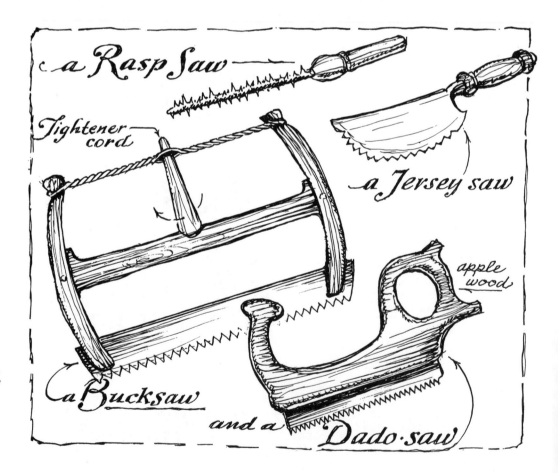

42

Some of the first planes were actually known as push-knives. The plane had an adjustable blade which was held in place by a hardwood wedge. Planes were used for beading, beveling, molding, and many other uses besides just smoothing a board, so each carpenter had a great assortment of planes on hand. He often had so many of them that they were kept piled in barrels. Early American tools have not found a popular market in the antique shops and many of the old wooden planes in their original barrels have found their way to the junk yard or have been burned for firewood although their cutting surface still does a perfect job. But the restored villages with their woodworking shops have revived interest in old tools and have already saved many a fine old wooden plane from the woodbox.

Some of the "bridge planes" were a yard long and were almost too heavy for the average person to manipulate. In fact, many of the old tools seem massive to the point of being unusable by the average carpenter of today, and it is assumed that the carpenter of yesteryear was a superman in size and strength. Some of them were just that, to be sure, for the times

The PITSAW

for sawing long beams

Iron handles

Wood handle

43

were rugged and every man's morning chores would be pretty stiff setting-up exercise for any man today. But the fact is that many tools like many carpenters were also small. Tools were made for the hand of the individual carpenter, some small, some large. Perhaps most of the smaller tools were destroyed while the larger ones survived. The proof of an apprentice's manhood, however, was said to be when he could plane a huge shaving up overhead and down behind his back and it was the custom in those days for the apprentice to print his name on this first gigantic planing with the word carpenter after it for all to see.

The first organized carpenters were the sawyers who specialized in sawing wood. When the two-man pit-saw business started, the sawyers rose up to let their annoyance be known, seeking protection for "members of the sawyer trade losing their just work in the community." But when the water-driven sawmill was established, the sawyers became violent and even banded together to burn the sawmills. This "union" of sawyers seems to be the first closely protected trade which went to many of the present-day labor-union extremes. The saw-sharpener, for example, kept his trade a secret and operated in a closed room with a bell handy. When the saw was sharpened, he rang the bell; before that, no one was entitled to watch him.

The pit-saw was a very long two-man saw designed to be used up and down instead of horizontally. Sometimes one man stood on a raised platform but the convenience of not lifting a log soon led to a pit with one man down below. The saw pit and the pit-saw became a necessary part of the barn building. As many barns were built into the side of a hill, the saw pit was ready-made and sawing went on within the barn foundation. Seeking an improvement on the pit-saw so as to keep its great length from "whipping," it was stretched taut in a frame or sash and this became the sash saw.

The sash saw went directly into the water-powered sawmill, with the sash and saw sliding up and down in a frame exactly like the mechanism of a present-day window; the whole contraption was operated by a water wheel and an actuating crank handle. Probably the first American sawmill was devised as early as 1630 for many have been mentioned as being in Delaware and New York State at around that time, but the earliest positive date concerns the one at Berwick, Maine, in 1632. A gang saw or series of saws set in one sash was devised a few years later in Virginia.

44 The sawmill was one of the busiest places in town. Where there was no town near a sawmill, houses and shops soon appeared, and many an American town owes its existence to an original sawmill. The wood that went to the sawmill was either bought outright by the sawmill operator or was left by a farmer who paid for the cutting. Payment in the old days

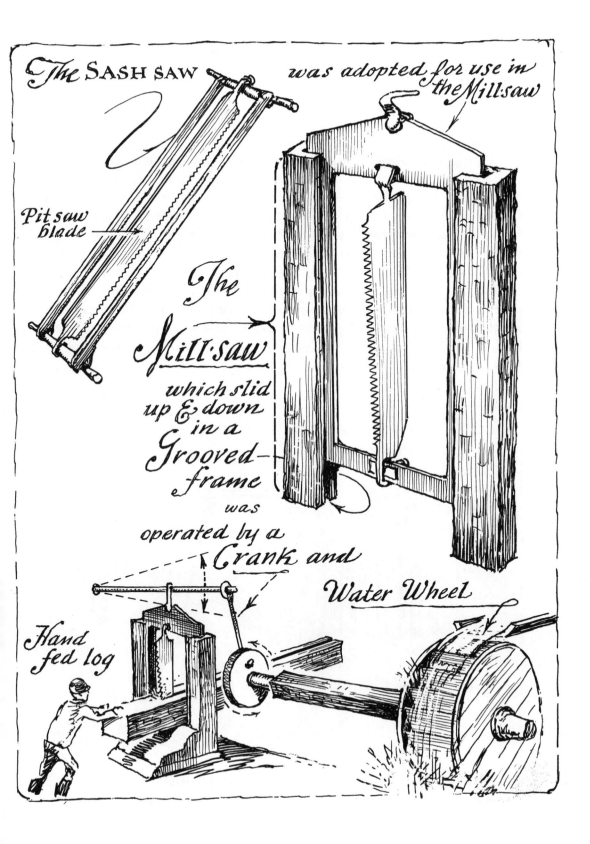

The SASH SAW was adopted for use in the Mill-saw

Pit saw blade

The Mill-saw

which slid up & down in a Grooved-frame was operated by a Crank and Water Wheel

Hand fed log

was never in cash but in wood (either standing or cut), butter, cheese, grain, or "what have you." So the sawmill operator often had to set up a shop to sell his barterings, and this established a trading base which expanded into warehouses, shops, and finally a trading community or village. There are so many towns named Millville, Millwood, Milford, Mills, Millington, Milltown, and so on, that the Post Office finds its biggest headache connected with the towns that grew up around these ancient mills.

Around the sawmill operator was an aura of importance that had many reasons for being. Because wood was often the only cash crop that the farmers could depend upon, the sawmill operator was often their town banker. When new roads were built and bridges erected, they always converged toward the mill to which the heavy loads of wood both cut and uncut traveled. The very river that actuated his saws was also the means of floating logs from distant places. Economically speaking, the sawmill operator of a hundred years ago was sitting pretty with America's first mass-production tool. The barn builder, the sawmill operator, and the bridge builder were closely allied. The simple trusses of the first bridges were tried out in barns and mills earlier, so, whereas the average carpenter

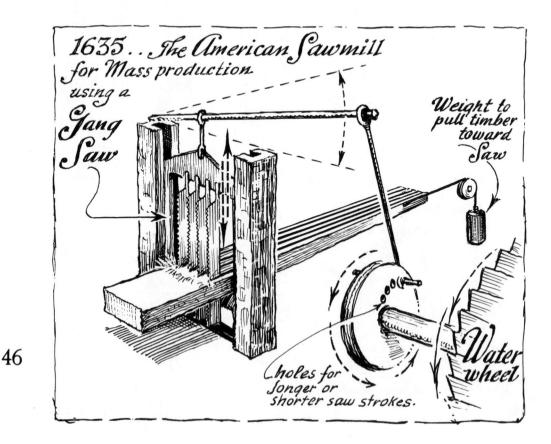

1635.. The American Sawmill for Mass production using a Gang Saw

Weight to pull timber toward Saw

Water wheel

holes for longer or shorter saw strokes.

46

"The Bridge builder built barns across rivers . . . ."

Kingpost truss in Mill and in Bridge

of today would not feel qualified to build a bridge, for the barn-builder it was simple. He just put out over water the same sort of structure he had been making on land.

In 1820 the circular saw was introduced by the Shakers who are reputed to have taken the idea from the ratchet wheel of a clock. Because the circular saw did its cutting continuously instead of by the slow up-and-down or intermittent method, the process of sawing was speeded up tremendously. Sawmills that used a sash saw and were cutting one hundred feet of lumber a day during the last part of the eighteenth century, replaced the sash saw with a circular saw that cut fifteen hundred feet a day.

Although one does not ordinarily think of the sled as a tool, to the barn builder and the bridge builder too, the sled was a necessary tool. Not the sleds that dashing horses pull in Currier and Ives prints, but the heavy timber sleds drawn by oxen or sometimes the sledges without runners that just slide their burden from one place to another. To lift a one-ton stone into a wagon would be impossible, but to roll it by leverage onto a flat sledge only a few inches high was all in a day's work. Even if it could be got onto a wagon, the wheels would sink into farmland soil and then even oxen couldn't move it. But with a sledge or a sled, heavy weights could be slid over hard ground and soft, through mud or snow, during all times of the year.

Most people might think that hauling heavy loads would be most difficult in winter, but in the olden times the winter was reserved for just that thing. Sled runners will compress soft snow into hard ice and runners

47

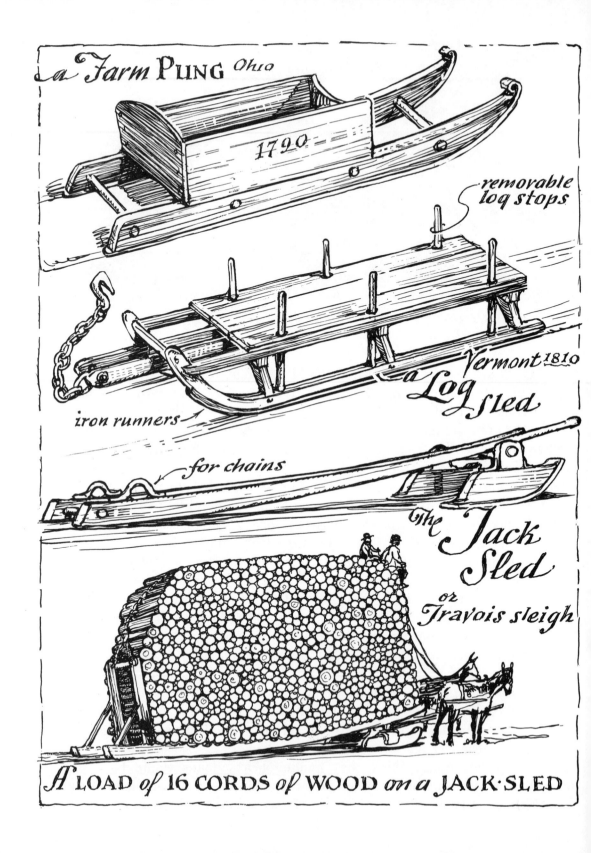

a Farm Pung *Ohio*

1790

removable log stops

iron runners

Vermont 1810

a Log Sled

for chains

The Jack Sled

or Travois sleigh

A LOAD of 16 CORDS of WOOD on a JACK·SLED

using a Pung..

1. Rock to be moved

2 Post and Pit

3 to Oxen

Pung

will slide easily over the ice with weights that oxen could not move by wheels on a dirt road. The greatest loads of wood have been pulled in this manner. The sixteen cords of wood shown in the drawing is no exaggeration and was traced from a photograph published in the *New York State Conservationist*. This is by no means a record, for a team of oxen can pull a heavier load.

Frequently one will see at the outer doorstep of a small farmhouse a flat stone as big as five feet by eight feet square, weighing over a ton, and wonder how it got there. The answer was leverage, oxen, the sliding action of ice during the winter, and a lot of hard work. But the sledge, or pung as it was called, was the tool used. Originally the word was tom-pung from which our toboggan was corrupted. It seemed to be the habit of calling each kind of sled by a nickname for there was the "Tom" pung, the "Jack" sled, and the "Bob" sled. One would move rocks with a Tom, carry wood with a Jack, and move light loads with a Bob.

Generally speaking, it is remarkable that with so few tools, the old barns were built as beautifully as they were. But when it is realized that log cabins were and still are being built with nothing but one tool, an ax, the necessity of many tools diminishes in comparison to the back-breaking labor that went into barn-building.

The Tool shed

49

☞ BARNS

It is pretty to behold our backsettlements where the barns are as large as palaces, while the owners live in log huts; a sign of thrifty farming.

—Lewis Evans, 1753

In the beginning, the American barn was without glass windows or metal hardware because of the very heavy tax imposed by the Crown. Doors swung on hickory hinges and the nails were made of oak pegs. The inner silk bark of white pine was used as paper to make windows and huge wooden treenails or "trunnels" were used to fasten the beams together. As more things were invented from the storehouse of the forest, the barn became more distinctive. The settler rose from the squalor of his temporary bark hut with the dignity of a gentleman adventurer and, with only utility as inspiration, his house and his barn—but particularly the barn—became something American.

In this day it is difficult for us to realize that the early barn-builder was a farmer who, as woodsman, could cut seasoned lumber from standing trees, and with tools forged by himself, build houses of true delicate architectural merit. A man rugged in build, firm of purpose, versatile, resourceful, and often a true scholar—who could quote from the Bible or from Greek classics—such, as often as not, was our early builder of barns and bridges.

If a farmer thought himself an inexperienced carpenter during the 1700's, he might send to Philadelphia for William Pain's *Carpenter's Pocket Manual With Compleat Directions for Building a Barn*. He would find this written in fine English and prefaced with these words: "Strength and convenience are the two most essential requisites in building; the due proportion and correspondence of parts constituting a beauty that always first attracts

50

the eye; and where that beauty is wanting, carving and decoration only excite disgust. In like manner, the affectation of gaudy dress in a man who has the misfortune to be deformed, answers to no other purpose than to invite ridicule." This suggests that the dignity of pioneer building was recognized and encouraged by the architects of that day. That a plain carpenter's manual should contain such beautifully worded wisdom is typical of early America.

The early American colonist settled in three widely separated areas. There were the Virginia colonists who came to Jamestown in 1607, the New England colonists who came to Plymouth in 1620, and the Pennsylvania Dutch who came to Philadelphia in 1683. The countryside where each pioneer settled was different, therefore the building materials used were also different, always according to what the landscape had to offer. The house of each farmer was also different, built to resemble that which he knew from over the sea. Yet all their barns had something in common and all looked as though they might have been designed by the same architect!

It might be said that the early barn is the best example of American colonial architecture. Each old barn was born of American soil and fitted to an American landscape for specific American needs. The early American home was varied in planning but generally European in design. While the Germans were building in Pennsylvania, the Dutch were farming in New York, the English were making white villages in Massachusetts and Virginia, the French were building cabins in the Maine woods. Swedes moved into Delaware and small bands of Poles, Italians, Slovaks, Finns, and Danes completed the picture of early American farmers. The barns in Europe were small, just big enough to house a few horses or cattle, but when they built an American barn, it became the symbol of a new life. From the beginning the American barn was big, like the hopes and plans for life in the New World. It was unlike anything built anywhere else. It was entirely American.

Old barns have a nostalgic attraction to American men, and although they are fast disappearing there are many who seek them out, even groups organized for their preservation. Not always knowing exactly why, we enjoy looking at hand-hewn beams with cuts as sharp as if they were done yesterday. Like looking at a family album, it gives a sense of continuity with the past. There are historic houses, mostly European in style, made into shrines for the patriotic American to see; certainly some of the early barns, which are so thoroughly American, should be made into shrines too.

We may be surprised to see articles in our newspapers about barns of the outlying countryside, and wonder why decaying and useless old buildings should command public interest. But one by one the old barn

51

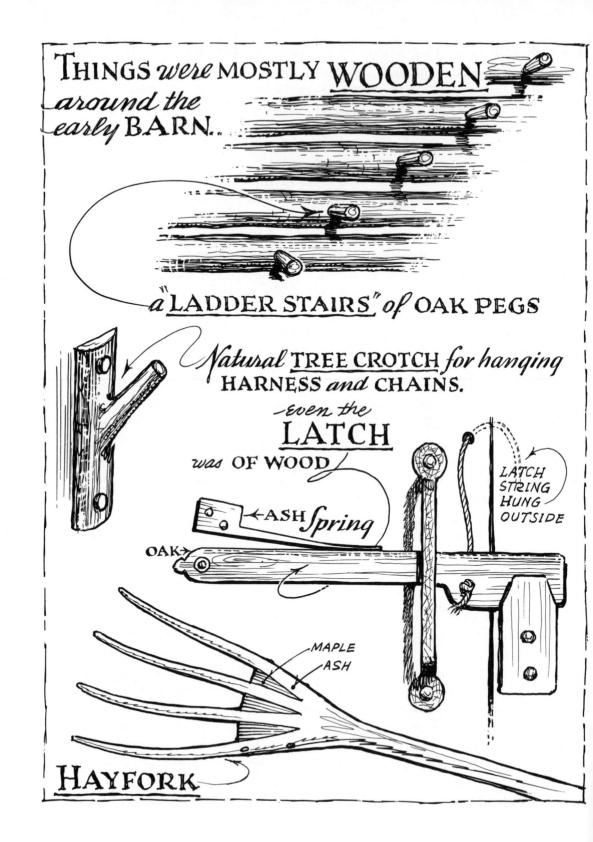

THINGS *were* MOSTLY WOODEN *around the* early BARN...

"a LADDER STAIRS" *of* OAK PEGS

Natural TREE CROTCH *for hanging* HARNESS *and* CHAINS.

even the LATCH *was* OF WOOD

←ASH *Spring*

OAK→

LATCH STRING HUNG OUTSIDE

MAPLE
ASH

HAYFORK

"collectors" are seeking out these remaining forgotten structures. Photographers find the old wood and the severe lines good for composition. Art classes gather around them with easels. Historians have found a new field. Even the family looks forward to a drive in the country with a weather eye out for old barns.

The barn is more easily spotted and is at its best during the winter months, when its severe mass complements the curves of snow-covered fields. If summer is the season of color and motion, winter is the time of stillness and form. Sun-drawn and bleached, the gray barn timbers become part of the winter landscape. The form of a barn assumes more comfortable irregularities as it settles a little each year on its weathered foundations. Whether you like it for its structural beauty or have just enough of the poet in you to see it as a symbol of pioneer man, an old farm building is the past as well as the present; vanished generations have built themselves into it. It may have outlived its usefulness as modern farming goes, but like an old apple tree that is too far gone to bear perfect fruit, its value as beauty and symbol remains.

The age of some old houses is uncertain but the history of a farmer's barn is a matter of business record, uncluttered by sentimental recollections. The date painted at the peak of a barn roof may be just an attractive touch to the antique lover, but it was put there in the same manner that a business house adds "established 1800" after its title. Barn records were kept in ledgers while the history of the old house is usually hearsay, full of romantic uncertainty. Whereas a house went up slowly, barns were usually laid out on the ground and raised with great ceremony in a day or two: the date of a barn raising was long remembered and duly recorded. There are two ancient barns near Setauket, Long Island, which the owner refers to as the "old barn" and the "new barn." The "new barn" was built in 1841 and the "old barn" was built only two years before, in 1839. It is interesting to note that although farmhouses changed with the trend of fashion from 1650 to 1850, the barn design varied little, sometimes not at all. It is as if the barn design were a standard symbol for the American Farmer: even when Victorian embellishments crept over the face of the farmer's house during the late 1850's and cluttered it with white scrollwork, the barn stubbornly remained outwardly stark, hand-hewn within.

Architecturally speaking, the pioneer builder showed his ignorance gracefully. His implements were a square, a compass, a straight-edge, and little else but good sound logic. What resulted was a severe and simple beauty without embellishment. The dynamic symmetry of barn shapes was no accident; it resulted from planning of the simplest sort, usually starting with a square or a series of squares. The sugar house shown in the

53

drawing is from an old "standard" barn design. Lines drawn outward from a square map out two hip roofs in complete harmony with the center section and even place the door in correct composition. Designs like this appealed to the settler's love of simplicity and the "square principle" made it a plan that was easy to copy. So this same barn design may be seen repeated in farmhouses, schoolhouses, and outbuildings. The drawing also shows a saltbox shape devised in the same manner, drawn from a square and the elements of that square. This planning scheme explains why so many very old New England barns have forty-five degree roofs, fitting harmoniously into the square pattern, and not merely to carry off the heavy snowfall as architects are quick to explain.

This method of drawing lines from one point to any other point within a square in order to obtain mathematical symmetry is not always obvious when one looks at the old barn shapes, but the harmony of line is there and the result is striking. The scheme is more obvious in the well-placed windows and doors seen in some of the old houses. Today we too often place windows with no thought of putting them in artistic relation with the whole form of the house; the result is as though the builder stood at a distance and threw windows at the house, leaving them wherever they fell. In some of the later houses it is even possible to trace stairways from the outside by the erratic placing of little staircase windows. Without knowing what they really mean, people perplex their architect with an order to design a house "with nice lines, like an oldtime barn." What they are actually referring to is the dynamic symmetry of early barn design.

The only part of the barn which was copied from the old country was its roof, but even that did not last for long. Many of the settlers were expert at roof-thatching, so it was natural that the first American barns wore a thatched roof; but the severe winters of New England quickly discouraged that. Furthermore, the danger of fire both by Indian attacks of flaming arrows or by fireplace sparks was of importance. Thomas Dudley of Salem reported to the Countess of Lincoln in England that, in 1631, "Wee have ordered that noe man shall build his chimney of woode nor cover his house with thatch." Thatched roofs remained late in Pennsylvania but those in New England were quickly replaced with clapboard and bark shingles. Bark shingles were made as large as a yard square, but their irregularity and inefficiency led to wood shingles. In about 1650, shingles were nailed fast to the bottom either with small wooden pegs or with hand-cut nails. Measuring as much as a yard long and made of cedar or cypress, they were fine weatherproofing by virtue of their soft-wood ability to breathe with atmospheric changes and to contract quickly with moisture. Even now, one might be able to see daylight in a thousand places on looking up

54

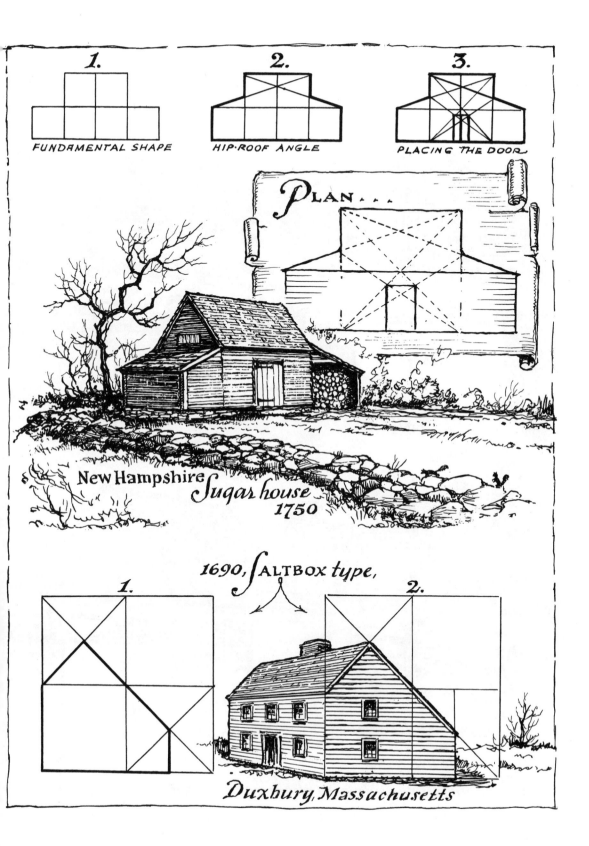

1. FUNDAMENTAL SHAPE

2. HIP·ROOF ANGLE

3. PLACING THE DOOR

PLAN . . .

New Hampshire *Sugar house* 1750

1690, *Saltbox type,*

1.

2.

Duxbury, Massachusetts

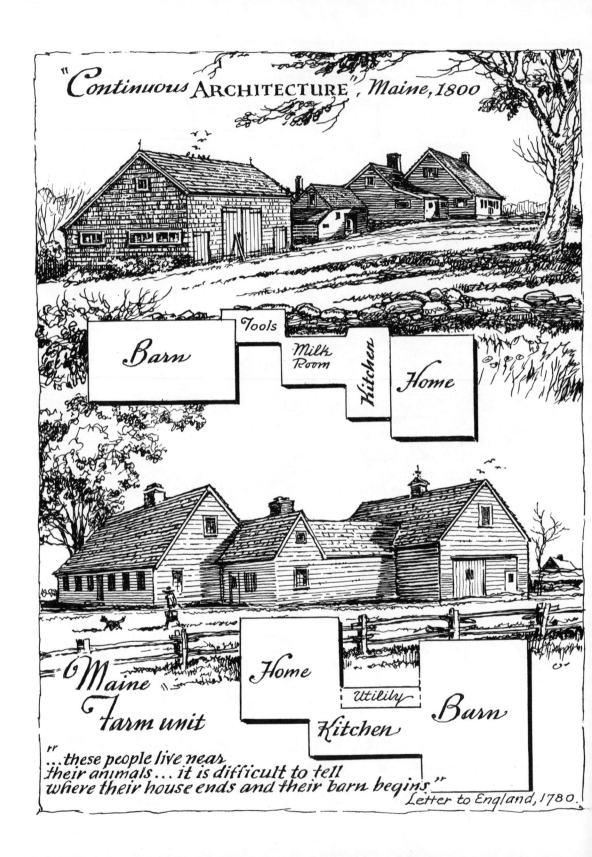

"Continuous ARCHITECTURE", Maine, 1800

Barn — Tools — Milk Room — Kitchen — Home

Maine Farm unit

Home — Utility — Kitchen — Barn

"...these people live near their animals... it is difficult to tell where their house ends and their barn begins"
Letter to England, 1780.

through the shingled roof of an old barn; yet not a drop of water will leak through, even during winter snows, because wetness draws the shingles together. Even prestorm humidity will draw shingles together. Notice also, in looking along the line of old shingle roofs, that all the nails have often come partly out, sticking up out of the smoothness of roof surface like porcupine quills. This phenomenon is caused by the years of swelling and contracting of shingles tending to "squeeze the nails out." A sped-up film of a roof during a summer shower would probably make it look as if the roof were alive and breathing.

Weather has always had a great deal to do with the planning of a barn, both for the health and comfort of the animals and for the protection of barn timbers and the stored grain. That explains why so many old barns can now be remodeled into cheerful livable houses while so few houses could be remodeled into barns. Long before the ax fell, the early barn-builder plotted out the routes of sunshine and wind, the slopes of drainage and decided just how the seasons might affect his barn site.

There seems to be no strict rule about placing the barn in reference to the farmhouse. The farmer tries to place his barn in a central manner so that in all weather the least amount of traveling is necessary. Where snows are heaviest, the idea of "continuous architecture" seems to prevail, such as seen on the early Maine farm. Here a farmer could operate his farm and take care of the animals without even leaving his roof; as one English traveler remarked in the year 1800, "The farms are like little attached villages . . . it is difficult to tell where the farmer's home ends and the stables begin."

In the Midwest where there are no hills to deflect the wind and the "snow falls horizontally," there is often a fence or even a rope stretched from the house to the barn so a farmer might not get lost on his way to the barn. This might sound ridiculous but there are many cases where a farmer missed the barn, walked in circles and finally froze to death within shouting distance of his own home. One interesting case tells of a farmer and his son, one heading toward the barn and the other leaving the barn, both with heads down struggling through a heavy snowfall. They met head-on as they turned the corner of the barn and were killed with fractured skulls. What material for a double tombstone and the quaint sort of epitaph our early tombstone carvers made!

JOHN MOODY, 1801.
Killed at noon on the fourth of November,
in raising his barn he was hit by a timber.
Be ye also ready for in such an hour
cometh the Son of Man.

Most Midwest barns are placed with their sides facing the cardinal points while many New England and Southern barns had their corners, instead, pointing to east, west, north, and south. Prevailing winds always ruled the position of buildings. Some people might insist that old barns and farmhouses were placed according to the direction of the highway without realizing that what is now a roadway was then probably only a cowpath. Old graves were usually planned so the "spirit could rise with his face to the east" but this of course was a religious practice and had nothing to do with weather.

A barn without a weathervane looks slightly naked, but, in the early days, weathervanes were used for telling wind direction and not as ornaments. The thousand and one designs of weathervanes known as Americana today are not as old as you may think. To begin with, recall that the first farmers did not believe in decoration; in fact it was part of their religion not to decorate anything—least of all, their barns. A farmer with an iron eagle or pair of spanking horses on his roof would be looked upon as showy and vulgar. The very first weathervane, believe it or not, was exactly like our aviation "windsock," a socklike piece of hanging cloth which waved in the wind. This true windsock was first used in Scotland during early golf games; it was devised to tell the velocity and direction of the wind, for at that time golf balls were called featherballs as they were filled with feathers. To play the game one had to be something of a meteorologist or have the ball carried away by the wind.

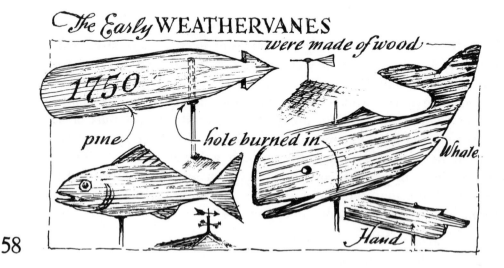

The Early WEATHERVANES were made of wood —

1750

pine

hole burned in

Whale

Hand

58

An early New England weathervane-maker was asked if he could design something to tell the velocity of the wind too. "What I use around these parts," said he, "is a length of chain. When the chain stands out straight, I know there's a gale a'blowin'." The joke became standard, and many of the early Yankee weathervanes contained chain motifs in them.

The early farmer kept weather records in his diary. He regarded his weather almanac highly and watched the skies frequently because his every move was either helped or hindered by weather. The weathervane on the barn was a more important instrument than a clock is on the farm today. The first weathervanes were light and sensitive, made of wood and were nothing but a simple arrow, a pointing hand, or where the barn was near the coast, a fish or whale. Most of the later weathervanes were so ponderous that only the strongest wind could move their weight. During the nineteenth century, encouraged by the Pennsylvania farmer's love of color and his ability to make things of iron, the ornate weathervane became a vogue, leading to such fancies as vanes where the wind made tiny men saw wood, ducks flap their wings, and farmers swing a scythe. But they became so complicated that few told accurately where the wind was coming from.

Living so close to nature, it is easy to understand why the settlers were weatherwise people. Today we speak of a house "nestling into a hill" or being "well located in a plot"; they spoke of a house or barn being placed "well into the weather." We speak of wood as being "weather-beaten," but they referred to it respectfully as being "weather-*cured*." Whereas we hide from weather, architecturally speaking, they were the first to utilize the movement of wind and weather. Records of early New England seem to describe colder weather than we have today; only a hundred years ago there were regular stagecoach routes over frozen lakes and rivers that now have not seen ice for years. There was a winter sled service from Staten Island to Manhattan in New York, and the Hudson River, as Currier and Ives will testify, was the rendezvous for ice-boating clubs. Water in the christening bowls of early Boston meeting houses was kept from freezing with hot coals and everyone brought his own foot-warmer. The standard New England place for keeping inks and other watery liquids was in the warm fireplace closet.

The settlers had a perfect right to be impressed with such coldness and they were quick to borrow devices from the Indians for keeping warm. One trick, that of using the insulating quality of snow as a "warming blanket" is still used in the back country of the west. On an old saltbox barn, the long slant of its roof will be facing the north or whatever direction the prevailing winter wind might be in that area. The lowest edge of the early saltbox barns reached to within a foot or two of the ground. When winter approached, it was the custom to bank this space with leaves, hay, or cornstalks mixed with sod, so that the snow could pile up over the roof from there and the wind would not reach the interior of the barn. "Slope your barn 'gainst northern blast." reads an old almanac, "and heat of day is made to last."

The simple gable was probably the first barn roof design, but the saltbox came quickly afterward. Many of the so-called saltboxes are really "lean-tos" because they were originally a simple gable with a later addition that makes one roof side longer than the other. The true saltbox was built around the great slant or "north roof" as it was often called. "Hips" are also found frequently to be later-year additions and "bevelly jogs" almost always were afterthoughts. "Gambrel" and "Snug Dutch" roofs were more complicated designs typical of the later 1700's; they were built by experienced builders who planned for no afterthoughts and seldom can there be seen an addition to either of these two designs.

Before the 1700's the barn, generally speaking, had no glass windows. There were merely wooden doors that swung open for light and air, or slatted louvers that were left open permanently. Sometimes there was a row of bottles "clayed" into a window recess for light to come through, but these were always changed over to glass when glass became available in America. This sounds crude to us now, but remember that the early castles of the European rich had no glass windows either, but just open slits called "wind eyes" from which the word window is derived. The louvered openings near the barn roof peaks were still called "wind eyes" before 1700. These openings are typical American devices which allow air

60

circulation to reach the underside of the roof for preventing rot; they also keep the loft cooler during summer.

Many of the old barns were ventilated by pigeon holes, which were scattered decoratively about the upper reaches of the sidewalls. Although we now think of pigeons as being city birds, many of the early farmers preferred to keep pigeons rather than chickens. When he wanted a heavier bird for eating, he'd choose a duck or a wild turkey; but the children were given pigeon as a regular diet and pigeon pie was for the whole family. In those times wild pigeons were plentiful, often blackening the sky when they flocked. The Indians killed pigeons just for their fat and kept huge barrels of it for community use. By soaking dried reeds in melted pigeon fat, "rush lights" were made and stored as we keep matches on hand. It is strange that birds which we now regard as a great delicacy were once killed solely for their fat.

Today when we build a roof, one of the first pieces put into place is the ridge pole or ridge rafter, which is the topmost line of the roof gable. The early barn and house did not usually have this "necessary" piece of wood; it simply crossed the rafter tips and was trunneled with a mortise joint. Later (and simply in order to hold the peaked rafters in place while the rest of the roof was being worked on) a very thin board was introduced between the rafters called a ridge piece. As years went on, the barn ridge piece became more important and larger in size so that the age of later barns can often be told by the presence of this ridge piece and the size of it.

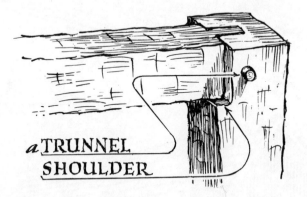

a TRUNNEL SHOULDER

When the barn roof did not have a steep pitch to spill snow off, the supporting struts within the loft had to be all the stronger. The two standard arrangements for supporting the long roof were the "post-and-collar" and the "great-strut." It was usually in the center of the middle collar that the date of the barn's raising was inscribed.

Often an aged pine is left standing close to a barn, and knowing how farmers cut trees away from their shingle roofs to avoid damp-rot, one

61

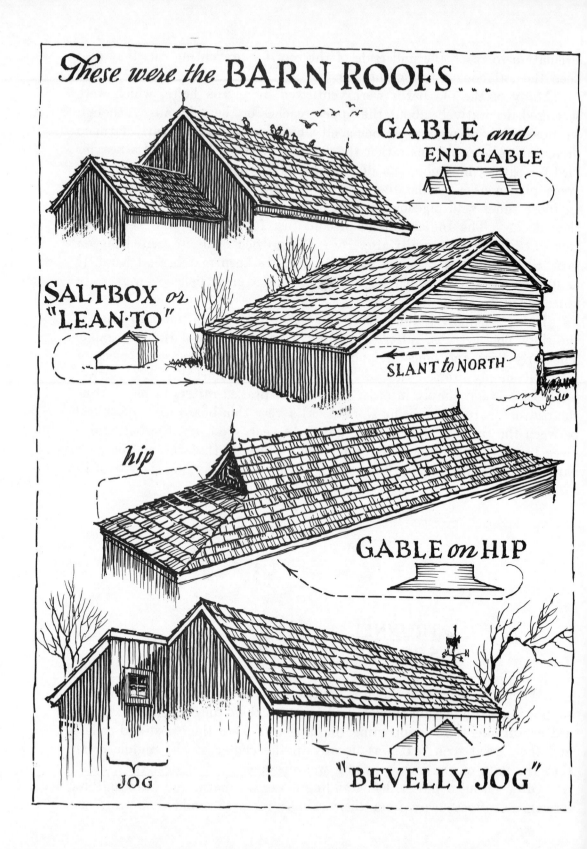

These were the BARN ROOFS...

GABLE and END GABLE

SALTBOX or "LEAN·TO"

SLANT to NORTH

hip

GABLE on HIP

JOG

"BEVELLY JOG"

"SNUG DUTCH" or snub-nosed

"DOCKING"

ENGLISH Gambrel

DUTCH Gambrel

BROKEN GABLE

DUTCH-KNUCKLE

might wonder why. But the old-timer knew that a pine will shower its needles on roofs of its own kind with no harm. An insulating matting of moss and pine needles was valued by many and the name given to it was "pine-moss roof." There was an early saying that shingles laid in the dark of the moon would never warm, and there are still "shinglin' nights" among the mountain folk of the South. Whether it is superstition or science is problematical, but some of the old pine-moss roofs laid in the dark of the moon are still flat and waterproof after a hundred years of weather.

Modern shingles are dipped in a preservative, but the oldest shingles were placed on raw. There are mentions of soaking, heating, and even smearing shingles with cow dung, but generally speaking the change from bark covering to shingle covering involved no preservative measures. The right wood in the right place will need no paint. The locust posts that have outlived several sets of wire, the ancient cypress sewer pipes of New York, and the shingles that are still serviceable although the holes still show where their nails have long since disintegrated, vouch for the soundness of wood. Not until the end of the eighteenth century did it seem necessary to paint wood. Even the earliest bridges went unpainted despite the continual splashing of water and the general dampness of river sites. Moss-covered and green with age, the remaining bridge timbers seem to have rotted only as much as iron would have rusted.

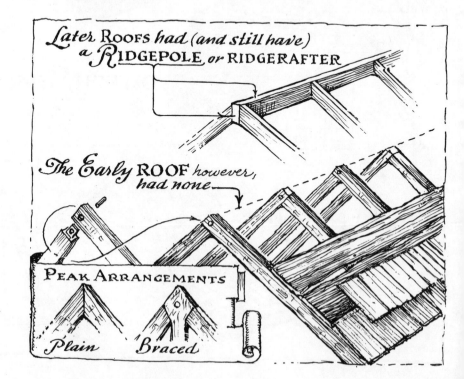

Later Roofs had (and still have) a RIDGEPOLE or RIDGERAFTER

The Early ROOF however, had none

PEAK ARRANGEMENTS

Plain   Braced

In the earliest settlements it would have been considered a useless extravagance to paint one's house and to paint the barn would be vulgar and showy. But toward the end of the eighteenth century the art of wood seasoning gave way to the art of artificial preservation and the farmer became paint-conscious. Ready-made paint was entirely unavailable and so, like everything else, it had to be made at the farm. The Virginia settlements began painting first and their paints had the quality of stains sinking into the wood as much as covering it over. Using lampblack consistently, they evolved a fine taste for grayish pastel shades. For outbuildings, the color red vied with ocher or "oaker" as the word was often spelled. Such announcements were seen as, "To be sold, two dwelling houses, kitchen, storehouse, dairy, and meat house, all painted in ochre [October 17, 1776]."

The northern farmer had not the Virginian's accessibility to the colors and oils; if he were to paint, he wanted something he could raise on the farm as well as mix at home. He found that red oxide of iron and skim milk with lime added made a plastic-like coating that hardened quickly and lasted for many years, giving birth to our famous American "barn red." The theory that barn red was taken from the Indians and that blood was used. though not true, is not without some foundation. As an idea taken from the Indians, farm-stock blood was used in the very beginning, mixed with milk and used for decorating cupboards and interior surfaces. But

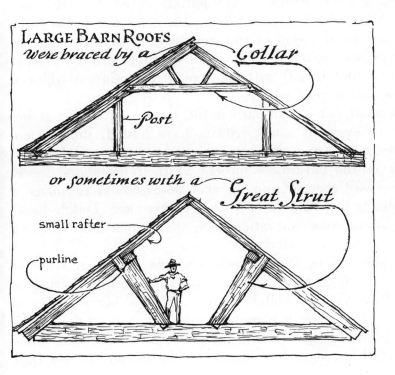

LARGE BARN ROOFS were braced by a *Collar*

Post

or sometimes with a *Great Strut*

small rafter

purline

65

limited quantities of blood and its lack of preserving qualities made the mixture useless for large surfaces and, of course, for outside painting. Another red that was taken from Indian lore, called both turkey red and Indian red, was made from clay mixed with the whites of wild turkey eggs. Turkey blood added to the mixture gave it a deeper mahogany shade.

Even as late as 1850, milk was being used to make paint. Here is a recipe taken from an 1835 Almanac:

TO MAKE FARM PAINT

skimmed milk	4 lbs. or half gallon
lime	6 ounces
linseed oil or neatsfoot (cow's hoof glue)	4 ounces
color	1 and a half pounds.

(for outside painting, add 2 ounces of slacked lime, oil, and turpentine.)

The milk-base paint hardened so well that it often caked off in sheets where it had failed to soak into soft wood. Linseed oil was found to have that needed soaking quality and when it was introduced as a paint base, a new farm crop appeared. Farmers pressed oil from their own flaxseed and soon no barn or toolshed was without a few barrels of the stuff. Red was now accepted as a standard color for the barn; the color was found to be warmer in winter because it absorbed the sun's rays. The red oxide was available and the mixture became six pounds of Venetian red (35 percent sesquioxide of iron ground in oil) with one pound of rosin and thinned with four gallons of raw linseed oil.

Thus the traditional red of the barn is the result of function rather than of decoration or even, as some writings have hinted, superstition. Because it was considered unnecessary to paint the "right wood in the right place," many of the old-timers sneered at their neighbors' newly painted barn and accused them of copying the "superstitious Germans of Pennsylvania." Actually copying from these German and Dutch barns was just an expression of color starvation from the somber New England colorings.

Red clay was plentiful in Pennsylvania and the European sense of color ran riot with red bricks, red cows, red geraniums, and red barns. Of course, when the Pennsylvania Dutch farmer added a big ornamental design and, for lack of a better explanation, said it was "just for luck," he was accused of having designed a hex sign to frighten away the devil. Actually these so-called hex signs have no more superstition in them than the same designs that appear in any farmwife's quilt. The designs for a patchwork quilt were made with a ruler and a compass; the farmer borrowed the same idea for his hex sign. To guard against lightning or fire or disease to the cattle? With tongue in cheek, perhaps yes, but in the same manner as we today pick up a four-leaf clover or hang a horseshoe over a door. At one time the farmer wore a red stocking or a piece of red in his hat for the same reason that a hunter wears a bright red hat—to distinguish him from game and to protect him from hunters. It was the custom for a farmwife to send her husband off to the fields with a red handkerchief or flag of some sort for him to wear or to hang nearby so that she could see him from a distance. From all this evolved the farmer's red bandanna which he wore around his neck as much for identification as for soaking up the sweat. For awhile the southern farmer accused the northern farmer of wearing the red bandanna for superstitious reasons, but today, of course, we never even hear of such nonsense.

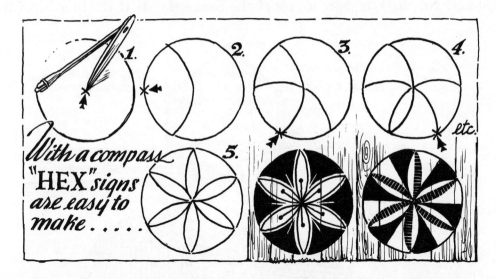

With a compass "HEX" signs are easy to make.....

Superstition had very little place on the early farmstead. Some of the European folklore reached our countryside, but the farming man's sense of humor always laughed down banshees, fairies, and luck charms. Our folklore began in a printing age so that the characters in them could not be illogical nor could the tales get taller with each repeating as with word-of-mouth folklore. Dull as it sounds, our folklore is mostly built up around real people like Casey Jones, John Henry, Johnny Appleseed, and Davey Crockett. Duller still in comparison with ogres and witches, our folklore sounds a note of mission and a sense of responsibility.

When England imposed a large tax on metal, the settlers saved every piece of scrap iron they could get their hands on. If a horse threw a shoe

67

it was as bad luck as if you had lost one of your own shoes, and finding it was, naturally, lucky. Yet the idea has grown up that anyone who now finds a horseshoe automatically acquires luck. Carpenters in the old days always tapped a finished piece of timber with their knuckles with a "well, that's that" attitude. From that small gesture Americans have coined a phrase and when they are through work and ready to go home they are said to "knock off." "Knocking on wood" also was revived in a similar way. Originally a Druid gesture of worship, knocking on wood at the barn door was a farming habit many years ago. When the stock had been taken care of and the team bedded down for the night, the farmer closed the barn with, we might imagine, a silent prayer that no harm would befall it. After closing the door, it was the habit to touch the wood of the doorframe with a rap for luck, and we have ever since been knocking on wood when we hope for the best.

Early American farm life has influenced many of our present-day customs. No one was more aware of the connection that the barn has with

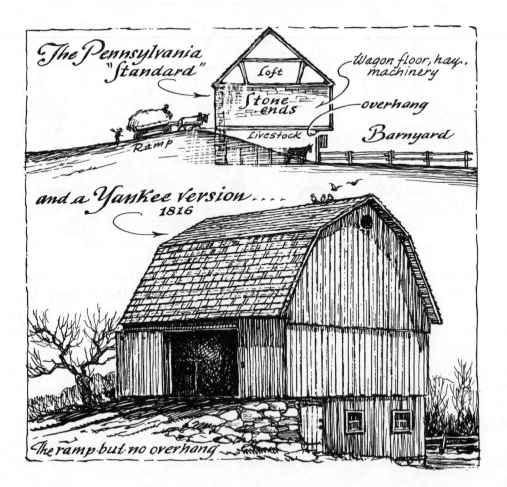

The Pennsylvania "Standard"

Loft

Wagon floor, hay, machinery

Stone ends

overhang

Ramp

Livestock

Barnyard

and a Yankee Version ....
1816

The ramp but no overhang

68

Christmas than the farmer. Christ, of course, was born in a barn. The children were told that on Christmas night the cattle spoke and kneeled in honor of the Saviour. Gifts were left in the barn for the children to find in the morning, and to keep them away from the barn while the presents were being prepared, the legend was that misfortune would befall anyone who listened to the cattle "speak" on Christmas Eve. Although we hang a Christmas wreath on the door of our house now, it was once hung on the barn door, and the cattle were dressed in garlands and fancy ribbons for Christmas day. All this, however, occurred after 1740 for up until that time Christmas was just another working day in America, particularly for the Puritan who had strict laws against any kind of Christmas celebration. In 1740, the Moravians founded Bethlehem in Pennsylvania and began the Christmas as we now know it, done up in a German manner with Saint Nicholas and all.

Hallowe'en was originally the eve of All Saints' Day, and it became confused with All Souls' Day which is the time that the living pray for the souls of the dead. But the unorthodox way that we now celebrate the "eve of All Saints' Day" with witches, the farm broom, pumpkins, apples, and cornstalks, leaves little doubt but that it all originated on the farm.

The very first barns were experiments. Without architectural merit, they were the temporary shelters that were thrown up when winter came, and were like the caves and mud shelters that the settlers themselves lived in before they had the time to erect a suitable house. Except to bring home the misery of those first months, there is little reason to discuss the construction of the first barns. What we are most concerned with are the barns beginning with the eighteenth century for with seventy-five years of New World agriculture behind them, the settler had really turned farmer and had evolved a rural American culture that was reflected in the things he built. Certain touches in design became typical of the countryside and one could soon pick out the Pennsylvania barn by its stonework and the way it nestled into a hill, the Maine barn by the way it was attached to the farmhouse, and the Western barn by its high peak and great roof sweep to the northwest.

The credit for a standard early American barn design stands between two camps—that of New England and that of Pennsylvania. Pennsylvania barns contain several "first" factors and they have indeed been copied, but they are too distinctive to be a standard or average. The barns of Pennsylvania used stone and red brick; they specialized in an overhang which they called an "overshoot," or an overshot loft. Their mixed architectural design often sported decorations. Such features as these are not at all standard in other early barns, but the following *have* been borrowed

69

throughout the country. The Pennsylvania barn was usually placed against a hill. It most often faced south and had a number of Dutch doors opening into the barnyard, its north side snuggled into the protection of the hill. Its second floor was usually accessible from the hilltop, and when there was no hill, a dirt ramp was constructed. In this manner, harvests could be taken directly to the loft and stored without hoisting. The ground floor housed the livestock and with one end of the barn snuggling into the warmth of the hill, the other end faced south where Dutch doors opened into the barnyard. This arrangement was a good one and replicas of it crossed the Alleghenies with very few changes. Both Yankee and Southerner copied the general lay-out, but the other Swiss and German features stayed right in Pennsylvania.

The Mennonites of 1700 built for permanency; they had little faith in any wood but oak and they used stone wherever possible. Asked why he'd built a barn wall five feet wide, a Mennonite gave the classic reply, "Why not?" Whereas most of the early barns of New England are gasping their last at the present time, many of the stone Pennsylvania barns are good for another two hundred years, even though they are agriculturally outmoded. The Western copies of the Pennsylvania barn seem only to have grasped the interior arrangement and the habit for making everything big. The fine carpentering became scarce, the wood seasoning was poor and bark was left on some of the timbers. But there was less attempt at permanency during the agricultural trek toward the West.

There is no record of any "first" Western barn. The farmer who first moved into the promising West must have been a perplexed person, for everything was vastly different. Wood was scarce on the plains, water could not be depended upon, and all the methods of preparing for winter that the farmer had learned in the East were useless on the flat stretches of open land. The first Western barns were cattle shelters made of nothing but poles and straw. A middle-nineteenth century book, *Barn Plans and Outbuildings*, says: "Farmers in the newer portions of the west do not have stables for their cattle or snug sheds for their sheep. Stock raisers are called upon to make the winter as comfortable as possible for their animals with the limited means at their command. Sheds of poles with roofs of straw are extensively used and with profit . . . they furnish at the same time, shelter from storms and feed for the protected animals. New hay is packed on after each storm. Those who have traveled over the cattle ranges of the west have been struck with the skill displayed in the construction of these shelters. The only trouble with them is that they are so satisfactory that the farmers are apt to forget that they are temporary and build nothing to replace them."

70

...in *Pennsylvania* the *Barns* are "banked a'hill, stone to *Weather*"

...and *Wood on the Southern side*

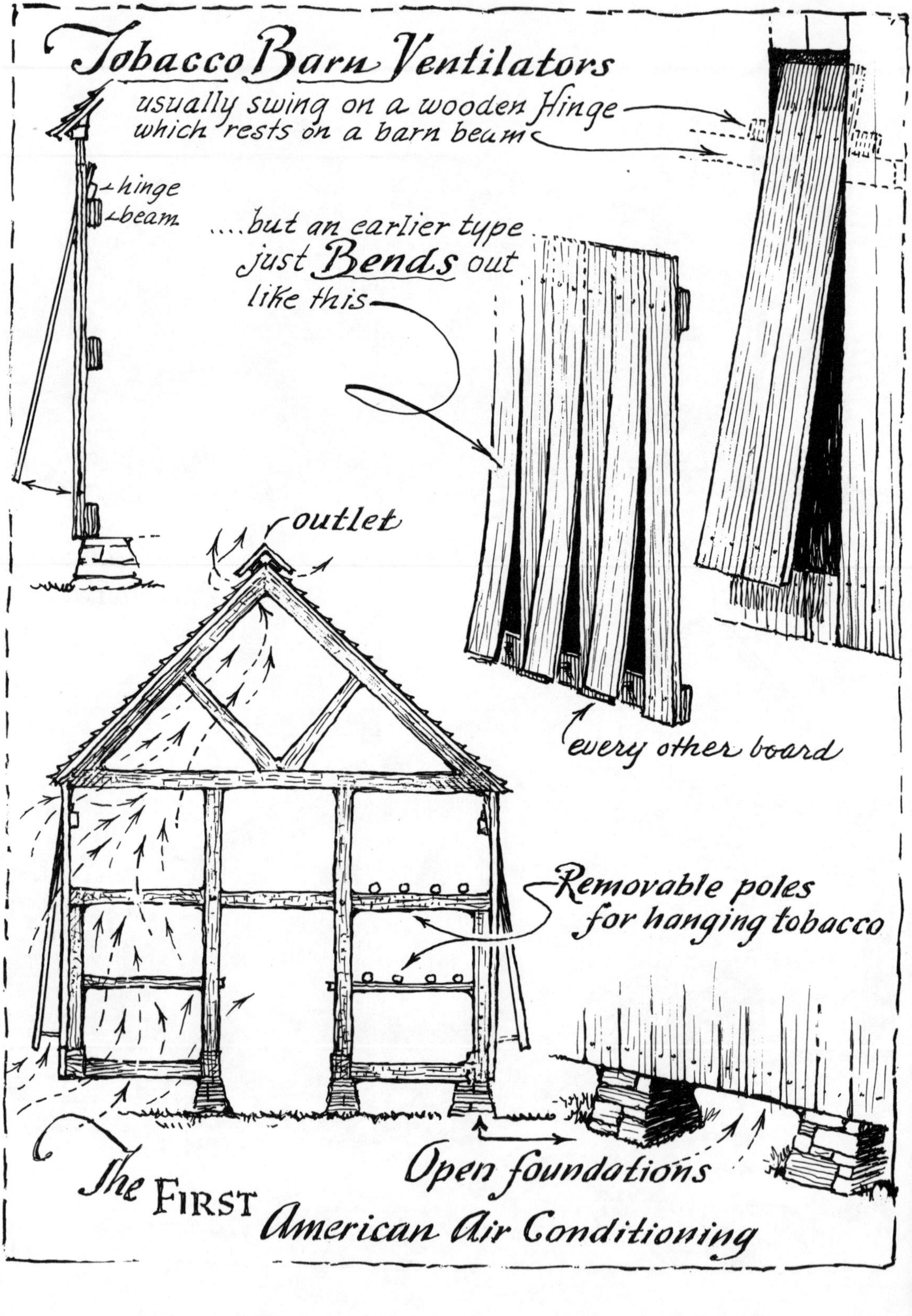

Tobacco Barn Ventilators

usually swing on a wooden Hinge
which rests on a barn beam

hinge
beam

....but an earlier type
just **Bends** out
like this

outlet

every other board

Removable poles
for hanging tobacco

The FIRST
American Air Conditioning

Open foundations

Early
Tobacco Barn Types

1859
New England

Open LOG BARN
1806
Virginia

Rain hood
Open vent

"Top hat" barn
North Carolina

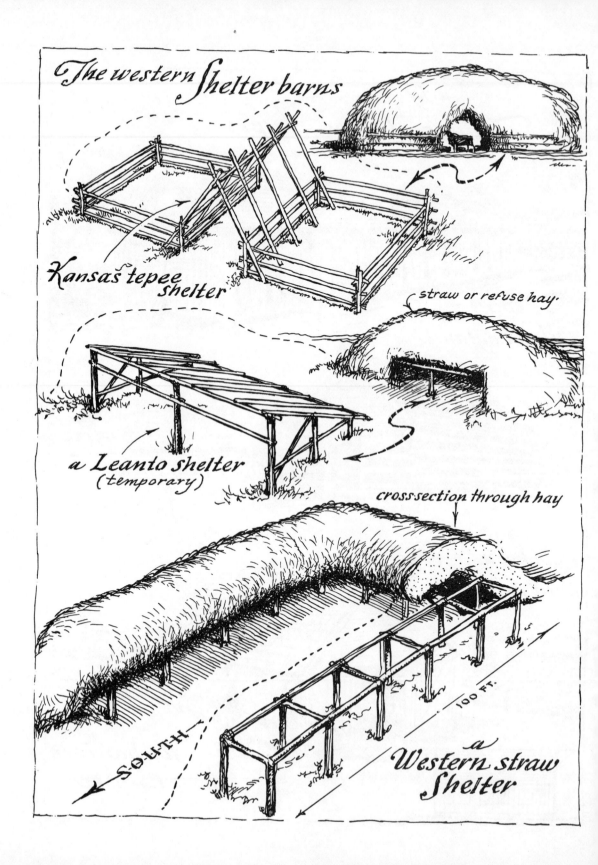

The western Shelter barns

Kansas tepee shelter

a Leanto shelter
(temporary)

straw or refuse hay.

cross section through hay

SOUTH

100 FT.

a Western straw Shelter

The field shelter of the West was really an adoption of the haystack or "field barn" as the built-up haystack was called. Farmers now call them "stack silos." The early farms had beautifully built stacks, often covered with conical shingled roofs that were raised for new hay to be added. A 1954 copy of *Farm Quarterly* reads: "Do we need any barns for beef cattle? The field barn that is built right where the hay is cut, and cattle feed through stanchions below it, makes an ideal wind shelter and automatic feeding station." Which shows that some of the old ideas of farming might still return.

Although we think of a silo as being something tall, the word "silo" is from the French and its meaning is "a pit." The trench silo has been with us longer than the stack idea; either on the surface or in a trench, the silage was packed in a pile running north and south. With no cover at all except ground limestone and sawdust, a correctly packed stack silo will have

no more spoilage than a few inches on top and about a foot on either side. They can be built right where the grass is cut, which saves labor for the farmer; for this reason you seldom saw an upright wooden silo on the earliest farms. Besides, there were not a great number of milch cows to be fed. Cows in those days were most important for use in breeding the oxen which were the tractors of their day.

The great dryness of the flat country made many of the rules of barn-building learned in the East useless. Trunnels came loose in the high-altitude air, and mortise joints creaked in the western winds. By the time that barns were being built in the West, iron bolts and screws were already being made, so the old wooden trunnels were not always used. One way of making wood trunnels hold better was a western custom of "nicking" the trunnel before hammering it in. This idea came from the habit of doing

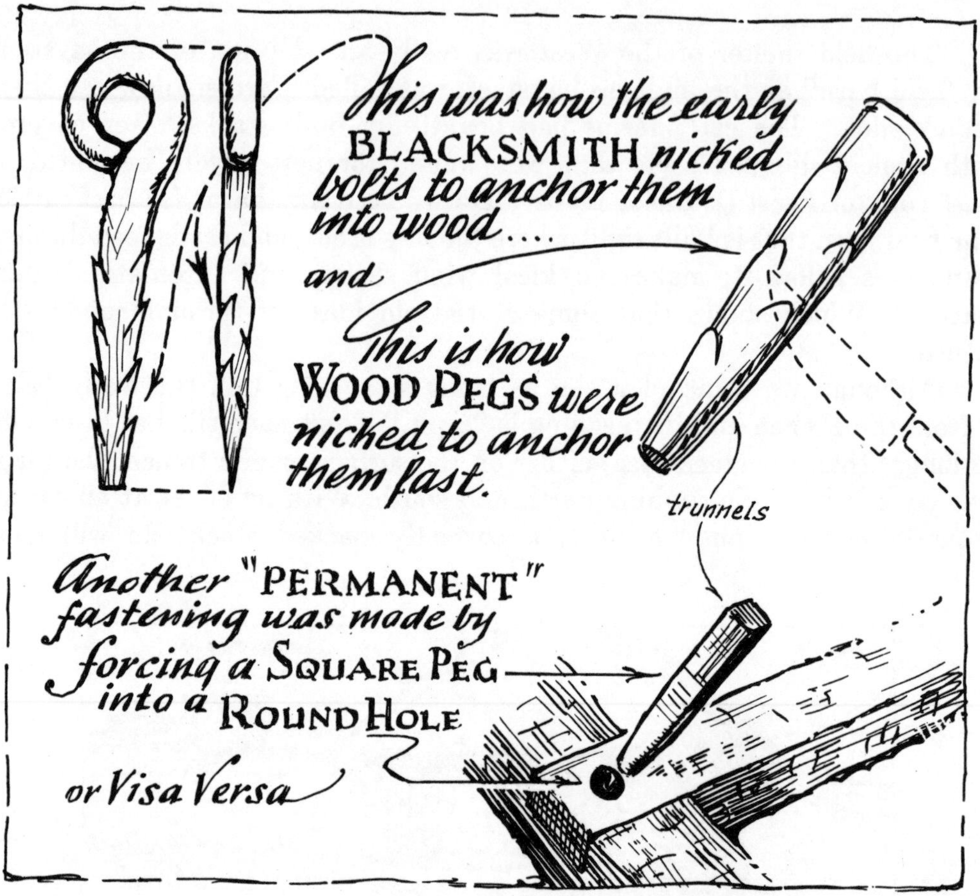

This was how the early BLACKSMITH nicked bolts to anchor them into wood....

and

This is how WOOD PEGS were nicked to anchor them fast.

trunnels

Another "PERMANENT" fastening was made by forcing a SQUARE PEG into a ROUND HOLE

or Visa Versa

the same thing to iron gate-post bolts to keep them from coming loose, as the drawing shows.

The barns of the West were not without the dignity and romance of American farm life, but the change from eastern farming was such that many of the arts of woodworking and seasoning were lost in the transition. But even changes and mistakes are sometimes healthy. In 1844, the Wales bull Chance broke out of his pen and on February 13, 1845, "Sir David 68 was born," who turned out to be the greatest show bull of all time. As one Hereford breeder said, "Thank God for those poorly seasoned and brittle boards."

What the barn lost by way of carpentry in its trip westward, it made up for in simplicity and size. As delightful as the eastern barn is by being a part of the landscape, the western barn is impressive by breaking away from the flatness. Sudden, massive, like a ship at sea, the western barn is distinctive. The flat country became a proving ground for many new ideas in barn-building. In the middle of the nineteenth century, the rich farmers of the East were inspired by the American's gift for invention;

76

the West was new so why not move westward, go whole hog, and try one's hand at new barn designing? One of the more radical ideas to come out of that age was the round barn which is still being tried out today. The famed octagon house of 1850 was preceded by the octagon and circular barn of 1830. Designed at a time when the farmer had risen his fastest in the national scene, many things were being done to modernize the farm and make farming easier. Planned on the theory that a circle encloses the maximum amount of floorspace with a minimum of wall, the idea was good but the proof was poor. Hay storage required complicated devices for loading, and the pie-shaped stalls would have been best only for pie-shaped animals. The expense of building these round-shaped barns and the risk of endangering the whole structure by one weak bit of engineering made of the round barns experiments that failed. The idea caught on, however, as a new way of building houses and around 1848, Orson S. Fowler presented the octagon house as a solution for all those who wanted to get away from the conventional rectangular form. It made a better house than it did a barn

Two western styles
...the 1800s...

77

because it gave more window space for each room and it provided a thousand pie-shaped closets and spaces for water tanks and gadgets. It lasted longer than the octagon barn, but only a few octagon houses were built and those still standing are looked upon as no more than American curiosities.

When the farmer builds his house he draws a rough sketch for the architect, but when he builds his barn you will find him sitting up nights planning and expressing himself in design. He knows that the welfare of his family depends upon the comfort of his cattle. No matter how things change on the farm, the biggest and most expensive thing there will always be the barn.

To the farmer of today, the early barn has become as useless as a pair of oxen or a kerosene lamp. The farm has become so changed that within the next few years not one of the old architectural features will have remained. But as long as man farms, which is as long as the world eats, there will still be the smell of hay and the sounds of farm life and with them a great respect for the farmer of the past who was poor equipment-wise but so rich in having lived the American life to its fullest. Ruskin said that one cannot love art better than to love what it reflects; while there are still farmers who find sentimental attraction in the early barns, you may be sure that the typical farmer still lives. And as long as there is an urge to preserve the personality of the people who created these things, the typical American still lives.

78

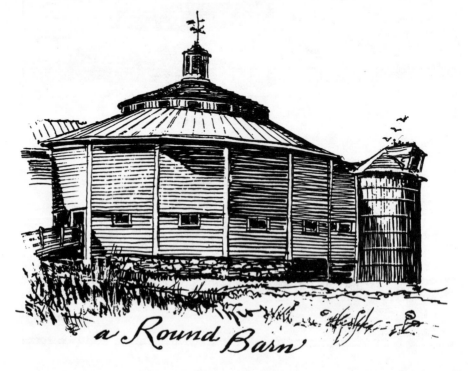

a Round Barn

Maryland Stone Silos

This chapter ends here, but in a more important way it will continue, because the reader will now notice many of the old barns where before he might have looked without seeing.

STOP *and pay* **TOLL**

1. EACH FOOT PASSENGER, 1 CENT
2. HORSE AND RIDER.......... 4 CENTS
3. 1 HORSE CARRIAGE...., 10 CENTS
4. 1 HORSE SLEIGH........ 5 CENTS
5. HORSE WITHOUT MAN.. 3 CENTS
6. NEAT CREATURES...... 2 CENTS
7. SWINE..................... 1 CENT

ℭℎℯ BRIDGES

We crossed the river by a wooden bridge, roofed and covered on all sides, and nearly a mile in length. It was profoundly dark; perplexed with great beams, crossing and recrossing it at every possible angle; and through the broad chinks and crevices in the floor, the rapid river gleamed, far down below, like a legion of eyes. We had no lamps; and as the horses stumbled and floundered through this place, toward the distant speck of dying light, it seemed interminable. I really could not at first persuade myself as we rumbled heavily on, filling the bridge with hollow noises, and I held down my head to save it from the rafters above, but that I was in a painful dream; for I had often dreamed of toiling through such places, and as often argued, even at the time, "This cannot be reality."

—CHARLES DICKENS, 1842

THE COVERED BRIDGES came much later than the first barns. In fact, covered bridges are not as old as most people think. The first American bridge patent was for a covered bridge and it was issued on January 21, 1797, to Charles W. Peale, the famed painter of George Washington. He became interested in bridges as a member of the Town Board of Philadelphia. Recognized as a great artist and designer, he was called upon to plan a bridge over the Schuylkill. Eight years later, a bridge was built by Timothy Palmer on the site suggested by Peale, but Peale's bridge never got beyond his paper plans. The *Railroad Gazette* for October 8, 1886, comments: "When the Market Street Bridge was finished in 1804 it was the intention that it should remain open, free to action of the sun and air, exposed as well to rain and storm. Judge Richard Peters, a prominent stockholder of the company which erected the bridge, was the author of the plan of covering it at the

80

sides and surmounting it with a roof. It was his opinion that if the timbers were left open and the roadway exposed to the alternate action of storms that would soon lead to decay and destruction. So the sides were boarded up, with the exception of spaces for windows. A long roof was placed over it, and the bridge was nothing more than a wooden tunnel, leading from one side of the river to the other." And so, as far as most experts agree, the American covered bridge was born.

As shown on the following page, the earliest of American bridges were "corduroy" in construction, just logs stretched across supporting timbers. Next came variations of arches and trusses, but the span was always no greater than could be negotiated with one single stick or long timber; in other words, there were always just two stringers side by side, arched or trussed for strength. In 1785, however, Enoch Hale put a bridge over the Connecticut River at Bellows Falls: it was three hundred and sixty-five feet long and it was the first American bridge with spans greater than the previous one "strengthened" stringer type. Variations of this new type called for the necessary joints to be boxed in for protection from weather. The timbers were pinned together with turned white oak dowels dipped in linseed oil and the complete trusses were boxed in with soft pine to "soak" the dampness away from the bridge itself. As shown in the drawings, the top plank or weatherplate was always slanted to take the rain away. The

1785 bridge by ENOCH HALE

Evolution of the Covered Bridge.....

First.... the CORDUROY bridge of LOGS..1650
Without bracing **1**

2 **3**
a TRUSS added, then
BOXED in from the WEATHER

1700

1790
Open bridge
West Dover, Vt.

4
Then PARTIALLY
ROOFED
(BRIDGE OVER the MOHAWK 1810)

Riverton, Connecticut, example slants its top sideways and away from the roadway while the West Dover, Vermont, example slants with the roadway in peaked roofs. It is easy to see how this boxing suggested a complete housing and an eventual covered bridge; most of these partly covered or boxed bridges were roofed over later and only the shorter spans like the West Dover and the Riverton bridges remained open. The Mohawk Bridge shown in the drawing was built in 1808, but was not covered with siding and roofing until some time between 1825 and 1830. Notice that the toll-house end is completely covered. Like many of the early bridges, it was anything but beautiful; their charm lay first in their eloquent expression as a symbol of the era in which they were built; secondly in their ability to become, as the barn did, part of the setting and rooted in the countryside. This effect gives rise to the saying that all covered bridges look alike, yet taken away from their setting, they would have appeared very different.

Disappearing at a rate of almost one a day, there are now about two thousand covered bridges, some still used, many hiding out their declining years just beyond sight of the new highway and the concrete bridge that has replaced it. And some there are that are not only hidden but forgotten as well, their ruins crumbling back into the landscape from which they came. There are covered bridges in thirty-three States, with Pennsylvania in the lead. Next comes Ohio, which surprises most people who think of the covered bridge as existing only in New England, and then, believe it or not, comes Indiana. Fourth on the list is Oregon and fifth (though most think it is first) is Vermont, so often called the "covered bridge state." Although the rate of destruction makes the count impermanent, the list probably carries on with Alabama, West Virginia, New Hampshire, Kentucky, New York, and California in that order.

BOXED BRIDGE
Riverton Connecticut.
with slanting top planks
1782

If the old American covered bridge is passing into oblivion, the floating bridge has already gone—except for one lone example, the Floating Bridge at Brookfield, Vermont. Built in 1936 by the State and the Town of Brookfield at a joint cost of twelve thousand dollars, this structure is the fifth of its kind to be floated over Colt's Pond since 1810. Three hundred eighty oak barrels, hot-dipped in tar and chained together, keep its 320 feet of framework afloat to the joy of the townspeople who steadfastly refuse the highway department's offer of a new bridge to replace it. Perhaps they feel it is a monument to the resourcefulness of Brookfield's early settlers and perhaps they are thinking back to the legend that gave their floating bridge its birth. The pond, it seems, was too wide for a single span and its mud bottom offered no possibilities of sinking piers for multiple spans. Despite the warnings of the selectmen, many townspeople continued to take advantage of the short cut over the frozen pond during winter until one man broke through and drowned. After a meeting it was decided to stretch a raftlike path of logs, chained together, right on top of the ice so that people could walk over it with some safety in case of weak ice during a thaw. When the ice finally did melt, the raft became a bridge, floating perfectly by means of its well-seasoned logs. In this manner, although only usable in ponds and still water, the New England floating bridge was born.

Although the first pioneers never saw one, the covered bridges are just old enough to be an important link in American history; they seem to mark the difference between the day of the horse and buggy and the automobile. Just as Washington was supposed to have slept in an unending number of houses, he was also reputed to have crossed many covered bridges which were built fifty years after his death. Even today, Connecticut people are bringing out written proof that Washington crossed their famous covered Bull's Bridge. Washington did cross an open bridge near that site, but the present bridge there was built by Jacob Bull in 1858.

The BROOKFIELD·FLOATING·BRIDGE

The experts seem to agree that the roof of the covered bridge was merely to protect it and nearly all of their accounts mention the farmer who explained that bridges were covered for the same reason that women wear petticoats—"to protect their underpinning." This is true to a great extent—witness the fact that many of the earlier bridges had no roofs although the trusses on both sides were boxed in with, of course, narrow roofs or top boards across each protective housing. But after collecting all the various reasons that the "ancient people" have given for covering their bridges and analyzing them, it might be that there is not one reason but many. Six sound reasons are as follows:

To keep water out of the joints, where it might freeze during winter or cause rotting during summer.

To keep the roadway dry, for the inner floor was often oiled and was slippery if it became wet from rain.

To strengthen the structure; the added weight more than made up its bulk by making the bridge more solid.

To give the bridge a barn appearance; farm animals did not relish crossing a rushing river and were more liable to run and not walk.

To keep the bridge from drying out; in very hot weather, the bridge would tend to dry out and loosen, causing it to creak and sag.

To keep the snow off; although this was the commonest reason given, it does not seem the best. It is true that during a heavy snowfall, although the highway could be cleared, an open bridge would keep the snow "encased." During most snowfalls, it was necessary for the toll-keeper to "snow-pave" the interior for everyone used sleds during winter in those days.

85

TOLL HOUSE at Gaylordsville

People ask why early American bridges were built of wood without remembering that almost everything a hundred years ago was made of wood. Expense had little to do with it. Although records of bridges costing a few hundred dollars will impress us today, we forget that a few hundred dollars then is equal to many thousands now. One public scandal involved eight hundred dollars for labor on the Trumansburg bridge in New York State, but a fairer price for the cost of the average covered bridge seems to be between one and three thousand dollars. In 1857, bridge carpenters were paid sixty to sixty-five cents a day, a salary which included, however, three meals.

Here is one of the earliest records of what it used to cost to build a bridge. The date was 1780, which was before the time of covered bridges so it is presumed to be for a simple open bridge.

BILL FOR BRIDGE BUILDING

114 days work chopping	22	6s
20 days work hewing	6	6
42½ days ox work	4	5
2900 feet of plank	4	7
1500 feet of boards	1	10
Pine timber	1	10

86

The committee met to vote on this bridge on October 20, 1780, and the bill was receipted on August 10, 1781. Not a bad record for speed particularly when the work was done through the snows of winter and the rains of spring.

Let's take a typical, average mid-century American covered bridge and thumb through some of the transaction papers to see what such a structure costs and how it was built. In 1832, little help could be expected from county, state, or town authorities, but the factories, grist mills, sawmills, and a cutlery works near Gaylordsville, Connecticut, needed a new bridge badly. Oak, chestnut, walnut, and pine grew tall in the nearby hills and the present bridge had seen its day. So a group of businessmen organized the Gaylordsville Toll Bridge Company and agreed to build a covered bridge and maintain it "for the convenience and safety of the travelling public." Shares sold for twenty-five dollars and fourteen hundred dollars was raised: eventually the bridge cost $1,500.14, including:

4000 feet of two-inch oak floor planks	$100.00
1800 feet of long string pieces	324.00
Mud sills of heavy chestnut timber	25.00
Boards to cover the bridge	60.00
Carpenter work complete	400.00

A full day's work of ten hours for a man and a pair of horses was worth two dollars and fifty cents, a man and his ox team charged two dollars. The wood came from the surrounding hills and ox teams hauled the logs to a nearby sawmill. The price of fifteen hundred dollars included leveling and grading the road approaches and hauling the stone for the abutments from a marble quarry a mile away. A bill was proposed to raise two cents on the dollar (payable in grain) for the repair of the bridge, if damage were caused by flood or freshet. The bridge was washed out completely in 1854. The second bridge was built in 1876 and the cost indicated a hundred percent increase in values, for that bridge cost three thousand dollars.

Sometimes a bridge such as the Gaylordsville bridge was named after the town it was near, but often, when buildings started being built around a secluded bridge, the community finally took on the name of the bridge. But a covered bridge seldom remained nameless. One Ohio bridge was named by children who were chased by its irritable old toll collector; it was known as Old Meaney's Bridge. Old Maid Parker Bridge in Rutland, Vermont, got its name from the caustic old maiden who owned the land on one side of the bridge. Another bridge in Indiana had fine broad sideboards that disappeared with annoying regularity. When it was found that the boards were being stolen and used for wall-papering boards, the bridge was from that time on known as Papering Board Bridge.

One bridge in southern Ohio received a coat of fine red paint by a patent medicine company for the privilege of advertising rights on its sides.

The sign which spelled out WIZARD OIL in ten foot letters had such publicity value that the bridge soon became known as the Wizard Oil Bridge. That old bridge is long gone but the modern highway bridge built recently at the same site is still called the Wizard Oil Bridge though few people passing over it know the reason why.

Traffic was held up in another bridge while attendants captured a panther that had escaped when a circus wagon struck one of the rafters and upset its cage. For years after, people hurried through it, for the legend was that the panther never was caught and it still lay in wait within the bridge. The bridge was referred to as the Panther Bridge and business decreased so, particularly after dark, that the bridge owner painted his own name on the portals and called it Old Johnson's Bridge. The romance of covered bridge names is rich in anecdote, much of which has been forgotten; you will find names such as Noah's Ark, Joy Bride Bridge, and Tweetsie Bridge. "Tweetsie" was an obvious nickname for the Tennessee and Western, North Carolina Railroad—T.W.N.C.—which ran a narrow-gage track over the bridge. Such names, when tracked down, unveil a history and a humor typical of the times past.

When a cigarette company recently put the picture of an imaginary covered bridge on its cigarette carton and followed it up with publicity and a song called "The Kissing Bridge," any inaccuracies in the picture, such as the absence of any truss at all, were more than made up for by creating new interest in covered bridges for the people of America. Actually there was only one bridge called The Kissing Bridge for they were all kissing bridges in the sense that one was supposed to be entitled to kiss his girl while going through the darkness there. They were also all known as "wishing bridges" because any wish made while going through one was supposed to come true. The one and only Kissing Bridge, which is long gone and forgotten, was over De Voor's Mill Stream in New York City, and it crossed at the point where Fifty-Second Street now intersects Second Avenue. Yet to this day, people who are not acquainted with the country's covered bridges and think they all look alike anyway, cannot refrain from remarking about any covered bridge, saying, "Look, there is the Kissing Bridge!"

The itinerant sign-painter who traveled by wagon seldom had to pay his way across a covered bridge; there was always a sign in need of repair or a change in tolls to be lettered, and a trade in those days was never passed up. One of the first metal signs in America printed in quantity was the familiar "Walk your horses or pay two dollars fine." Timid lady drivers often paid two dollars for the privilege of hurrying through a long bridge at night and the posted fine was frequently changed to ten dollars to discourage such goings on.

The evangelists and reformers who traveled the country with a sign brush and white paint were not always content with painting their biblical mottoes on large rocks; the old barns and bridges were always under attack during an unguarded moment for they would suddenly and miraculously display such wisdom as "Prepare to meet your God," "The Wages of sin is death." When an Ohio bridge caught fire, the scene was given a comic note by the sign on its side which read "Turn or burn." Another abandoned and ruined bridge in Indiana is without any floorboards and closed to traffic; a reformer's sign across the portal still reads, "Repent for the grave lies just ahead."

No rock, fence, tree, or bridge or barn was sacred to the old-time advertising man who set out with his wagonload of posters and signs. Even outhouses, if within seeing distance from the road, received their share. In those days, paper was good and ink was thick with varnish, so many of the old posters are as colorful today as they were a hundred years ago. Thirty thousand summer suns and winter snows have decayed most of the old advertisements but those that were tacked into the snug confines of a bridge canopy or a barn shed have just weathered along with the wood, still telling you not to miss the big circus next Saturday or to use Indian Corn Cure. Many a farmer's family will still mistake an old circus poster for this year's notice and set off to see a show that folded its tents over a century ago.

A circus parade that went through a covered bridge was always an event. Coming to an agreement as to the tolls on wild animals was an almost impossible task, for animals riding in wagons were charged a different toll than those that were led across. But with the help of a friendly conference and a few free passes for the toll-taker, the parade went through except, sometimes, the elephants. Some bridges had rulings that elephants must go singly across or even ford the river elsewhere. One circus giant named Long Tom Fawcett wore for effect a stovepipe hat that made his advertised eight and a half foot height so much higher that he had to stoop to pass through; he always put his signature on the portal face of every bridge he passed through, reaching almost to the roof to do it. In later years, when he left the show, Long Tom worked for a roofer and he could nail the lower shingles in place without getting on a ladder.

A favorite during the early part of the last century were the Negro minstrels who traveled by wagon from place to place. As with the circus, one man went ahead by horse and buggy to "put up paper," that is, to advertise the coming of the show, and he too, was known as the "paper man." Scarcely a barn or covered bridge hasn't at some time or other had a minstrel poster glued to its sides. The paper man arranged rates on bridge

They might all look alike ·· but ··

Irasburg Vermont

Salmon River California

Baraboo River Wisconsin

Camp Nelson Kentucky

North Wilkesboro North Carolina

Rushville Indiana

Esperance New York

How different every covered bridge!

Tygert's River W. Virginia

tolls, gave away free passes for favors and generally paved the way for a full house at the minstrel show. From all reports he was usually quite a fellow. When the town was large enough he'd often set up his stand near the covered bridge and, in blackface, with a banjo hung from his shoulders, sing and improvise his own musical announcements like the minstrels of old. It is interesting to note that Negroes have seldom, if ever, been known to play the banjo. That myth is contrived from the banjo-playing blackface minstrels who seem to have left the lasting impression with us that the early American Negro and the banjo went together.

No one liked a trade better than the Yankee peddlers; these men toured the countryside selling tinware, combs, clocks, locks, tools, and "Yankee notions." They were known never to pay cash to a bridge toll-taker but usually crossed the bridge richer than when they approached it. There was always a swap to be made in penny whistles, candy, pipes, or some sort of novelty. Many peddlers sold musical instruments and one supersalesman dressed himself in military regalia, selling applewood flutes that were made in Connecticut. Going from town to town on a white charger with saddlebags packed full of flutes, he often sold out flutes, saddlebags, horse and all, and trudged back on foot for a new supply. All the toll-bridgekeepers in Connecticut knew him, and the best advertisement for the flutes were the well-equipped toll-keepers who had all swapped flutes for bridge passages and who all seemed to be expert flute players.

In the very beginning, it was the custom to raise bridge money by lottery, which was legalized by special acts of law wherever the church frowned upon gambling. Ready money such as was collected in tolls frequently caused trouble and some town fathers actually found difficulty in keeping down the number of bridges. One resourceful and successful bridge owner built a tavern on the other side of the bridge which, of course, meant a two-way toll for each trip to the tavern. On the other hand, there were special rates for doctors, clergymen, and large families. When it was necessary to cross a bridge to attend church, the toll-taker often gave free access, even kept shoe cloths at both ends of the bridge so that church goers could emerge dust-free. Rates varied greatly, but the tolls averaged one cent for each foot passenger and four cents for horse-drawn vehicles. "Neat creatures" [cows] were charged one cent and sheep or swine went across two for a cent. Every bridge had its sign ordering drivers to walk their horses, followed by the toll rates; but sometimes a blackboard was used and rates would be changed at will. Farmers seldom carried money with them, so charge accounts were frequent and some of the old wagons still have seat boards scratched deeply where drivers kept their own account by making a mark each time they crossed the bridge. The tolls were changed so frequently

Windsor Bridge on the Connecticut

that the older signs have been redone or thrown away, but the earlier the toll sign, the more amusing is the quaint wording. One sign reads: "For each chaise, chair, sulky or other riding carriage drawn by one horse, ten cents. For each coach, chariot, phaeton or other four wheeled vehicle for passengers drawn by more than one horse, twenty cents. For each cart or other carriage of burden drawn by two beasts, ten cents and two cents for each additional oxen or pair of horses."

The toll-taker was usually a town character who could graciously take the abuse of criticism concerning the management of the bridge; others just became accustomed to it. He was always at hand for a game of checkers and he knew all the gossip and scandals of town. Many toll-takers were so often in bad favor that they spent their hours alone in knitting, a popular pastime among most bridgekeepers. The toll-taker usually kept record books, some of which are turning up to add to the romance of American history, with entries describing wolf-hunting parties, funeral processions, posses, and so on.

Despite the caution against sway and destructive vibration as might be caused by horses galloping over them, covered bridges were often used as drill halls for troops. One bridge in Alabama became a blockhouse for a troop of Union soldiers who, inside, successfully held off an enemy attack of Confederates in 1862. The large space and protection from weather made covered bridges perfect meeting places for town gatherings, particularly for meetings that the church would not accept. Lighted by candles and kerosene lamps for the secret meetings of vigilantes during peacetime and soldiers during war, covered bridges must have made rich and ghostly pictures of the time. Few of us think of covered bridges as having been lit by oil lamps, although many of them were. Wired now for electricity, the mystery of night within a covered bridge is completely blasted away with a flick of a switch. But those who look closely may see where the old lamp was hung by the countless scratchings of matches on the soft pine clapboards.

An interesting item on the record books of the bridge at Sheldon, Vermont, occurred in 1864. A group of Confederate raiders stole down across the border from Canada and robbed the bank at St. Albans, Vermont. Their plans for escape included the burning of the bridge at Sheldon, but before the bridge could be destroyed, a party of Federals caught up with the plans of the raiders and chased them through the bridge and back into Canada. Ironically, although the bridge lasted sixty-eight years more, it was destroyed by fire in 1932.

The last entry in the toll-book of Center Bridge which connected Stockton in New Jersey with the Pennsylvania shore, was on January 9, 1841. It related a hair-raising cruise by a deputy toll-collector named Fell. Down the river he sailed on a piece of his own bridge, which, along with five others, was washed away by the tremendous flood. There is no mention of why Mr. Fell was in the bridge at so precarious a moment, but the story of his trip is a thriller. After speeding for five miles in the churning water, with houses, cows, and the five other bridges to keep him company, he came to the stubbornly resisting Lambertville-New Hope bridge. His portion of bridge and private craft smashed through this, taking him merrily on toward Trenton. But at Yardley, just this side of Trenton, Mr. Fell's craft came to a halt where he disembarked, rested awhile, and took the stage the twenty miles back to his bridgeless toll-house. Here he was greeted with cheers and "a salute from a cannon."

TOLL GATE at WINSTED, Connecticut

93

Such are the tales that keep the story of covered bridges alive, but these are also the tales that limit public interest by classifying the bridges as no more than quaint curiosities of the past. The greatness of covered bridges was their part in the public enterprise of their time and their straightforward expression of functional structure. As the barn was an expression of America in the eighteenth century, the covered bridge took over that burden for the nineteenth century.

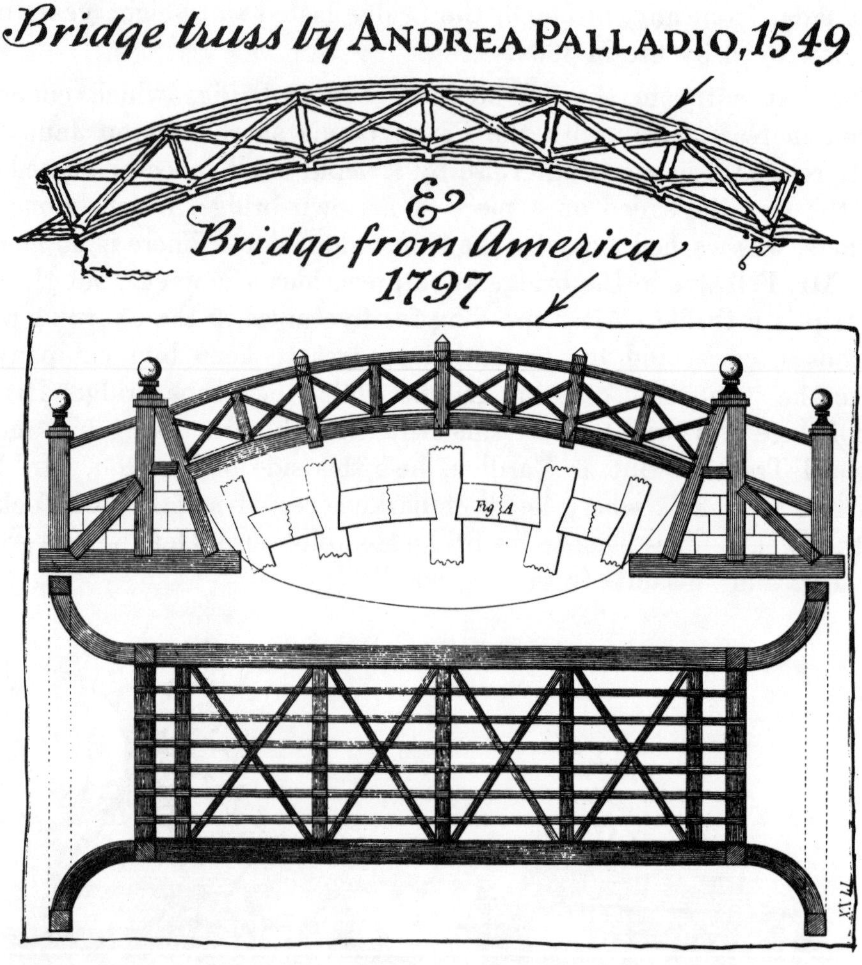

Bridge truss by ANDREA PALLADIO, 1549

& Bridge from America 1797

The workmanship on covered bridges was usually done by men who were little known outside of their own community and the results were more an exhibition of the small-town mastercraftsman than of the engineer. Yet the designs were those of the professional bridge-builders such as Palmer, Wernwag, Burr, Town, and others. At that time it was fashionable to try one's hand at bridge designing and many successful businessmen retired into the study of engineering with the goal of inventing a better bridge truss.

94

When a patented truss was used, the inventor received his royalty according to the length of the bridge that used his idea. Highways were becoming the lifeblood of the nation and the man who could build a better bridge was the hero of his day.

Just before the advent of the covered bridges, the American bridge-builders were trying to put architectural grace into their structures. The builders of churches were called in to design trusses and classic designs from the ancient bridges were being revived. The plan is from a 1797 handbook on building and it shows a bridge sixty feet long; the engineering is borrowed directly from Palladio. Just about this time Lewis Wernwag was beginning his career as an apprentice bridge-builder with a great urge to "put beauty back into the barnlike structures that Americans are throwing across their rivers." Using the Palladio principle, he later designed his bridge called "Colossus."

The cornerstone of the Colossus was laid in 1812 at Upper Ferry, later Fairmont, on Pennsylvania's Schuylkill River. Although its single span of three hundred and forty feet was not the longest of record, the Colossus was the most celebrated of all covered bridges until it burned down in 1838. Accounts of the Colossus conflagration describe it as "picturesque and at times, sublime": "the splendid sight," an account relates, "continued for some time, the gazers looking on in rapt silence . . . the bridge with a graceful curtsy, descended a few feet, hesitated and then with a gentle swanlike motion, sank like a dream down on the waters. But the moment the fabric touched the waves, a simmering, hissing sound was heard while ten thousand sparkles shot into the air. The moon which was just rising, appeared through the dense veil of smoke to add to the illusion." The end was in keeping with the drama of its erection and twenty-six years of fame.

The Colossus was not a typical American covered bridge at all, but its fame had kindled the spark that inspired builders throughout the country to try their hand at building the classic trusses into serviceable bridges for their own villages. There were several designs to choose from and

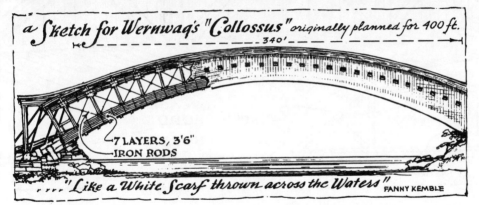

a Sketch for Wernwag's "Colossus" originally planned for 400 ft.
340'
7 LAYERS, 3'6"
IRON RODS
". . . . "Like a White Scarf thrown across the Waters" FANNY KEMBLE

95

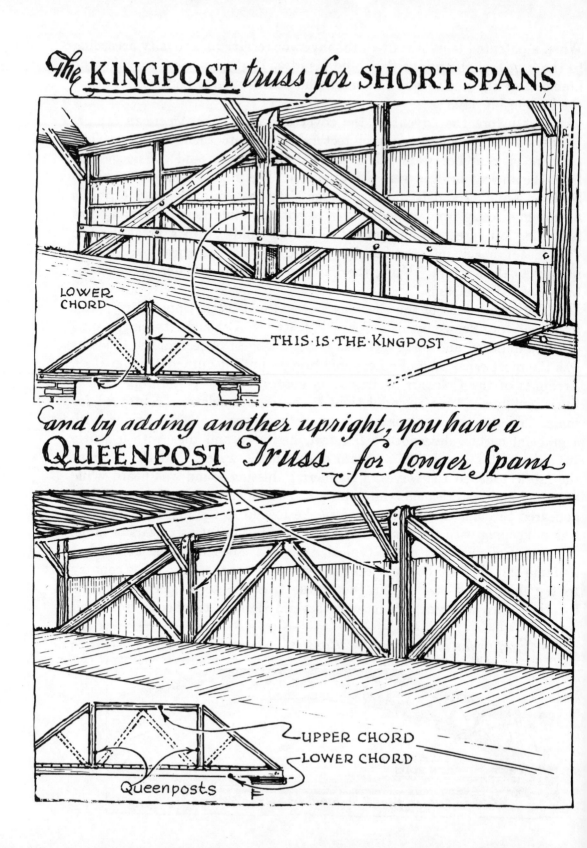

The KINGPOST truss for SHORT SPANS

LOWER CHORD

· THIS · IS · THE · KINGPOST

and by adding another upright, you have a
QUEENPOST Truss for Longer Spans

UPPER CHORD
LOWER CHORD

Queenposts

Strengthening a *Weak span* with a *Kingpost*

1.   2.

although each bore the name of an American designer or patent-holder, the ideas actually went back to ancient principles. The simplest and first truss tried in America was the kingpost truss. This consists of a center upright or kingpost in the middle of the span, with two compression pieces slanting downward and outward toward each shore. Many simple unbraced spans were later strengthened by the addition of a kingpost truss. But this arrangement was limited to small bridges because the compression pieces were limited in length. The kingpost truss shown in the bridge interior is that of Pine Brook Bridge in Waitsfield, Vermont. To make this principle adaptable to a longer bridge, two uprights are spaced across the span and the

a Boxed-in Kingpost

The Old Red bridge over Mill River, Kensington Conn.

result is a queenpost truss. The queenpost interior shown in the drawing is that of a bridge at Wolcott, Vermont. The kingpost and queenpost bridges have appeared both "bare" and boxed in from the weather, and many have been covered over with a roof during later years. By using a cross instead of an inverted V in the middle of a queenpost truss, a stronger design results and this is called a Warren truss. All these simple trusses were already used in barn structure, so the barn-builder was right at home constructing small bridges.

97

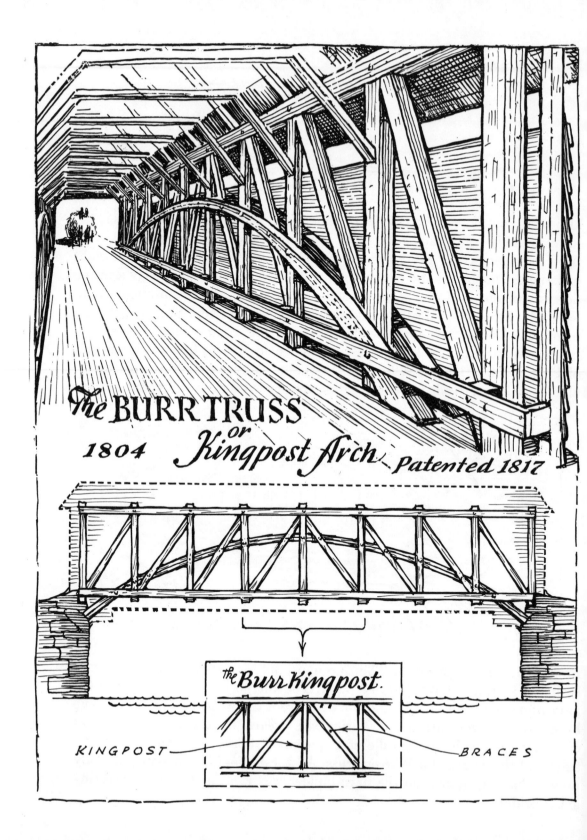

The BURR TRUSS
or
Kingpost Arch
1804
Patented 1817

the Burr Kingpost.

KINGPOST

BRACES

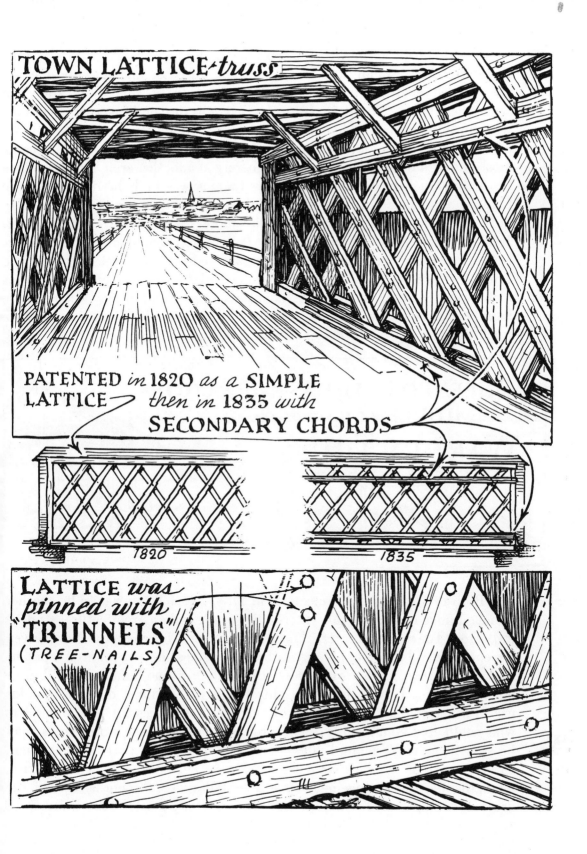

TOWN LATTICE-*truss*

PATENTED *in* 1820 *as a* SIMPLE LATTICE *then in* 1835 *with* SECONDARY CHORDS

1820

1835

LATTICE *was pinned with* "TRUNNELS" (TREE-NAILS)

The greatest problem of all bridge building was to make one long single arch that would still be strong. The kingpost and queenpost could not be just enlarged indefinitely. There had to be something added to strengthen them. Theodore Burr devised a series of kingposts combined with an arch. What he had in mind was to strengthen the series of kingposts with an arch but what really happened was that the arch became most important and the kingposts merely made the arch stronger. One of the first such bridges to make Burr famous was built in 1804 across the Hudson at Waterford, New York. This bridge was in prime condition up until the time it was destroyed by fire more than a hundred years later. Ironically the cause of the fire was faulty electrical connections. About thirteen years after designing it, Burr patented his Burr-arch truss. By the time Burr was forty-seven years old he had built forty-five bridges; his ideas were used or modified in countless others and many bridges were later strengthened by his arch. So many bridges are traced to Burr that he is called by many the father of American bridge building.

A QUEENPOST·TRUSS *with a* **CROSS** *in the* MIDDLE *is known as a* **WARREN TRUSS**

STOWE, VERMONT

Born in Thompson, Connecticut in 1784, Ithiel Town was to be another famous bridge-builder. A carpenter in his youth and an architectural student in Boston, Town built Center Church and Trinity Church on the New Haven Green while still a young man. As a bridge engineer he was granted a patent in January 1820 for his own truss. Using it in a one-hundred-foot bridge outside of New Haven, he sold rights to his patent for a dollar a foot for use in other bridges and became one of the first successful bridge-builders who could live comfortably on his royalty income. His lattice-truss may be seen in most Vermont bridges and in almost every part of the nation. In 1835 he took out a second patent for an improvement on the lattice, strengthening the arrangement with a secondary set of chords. One of the great advantages of Town's lattice-truss was that most of the bridgework

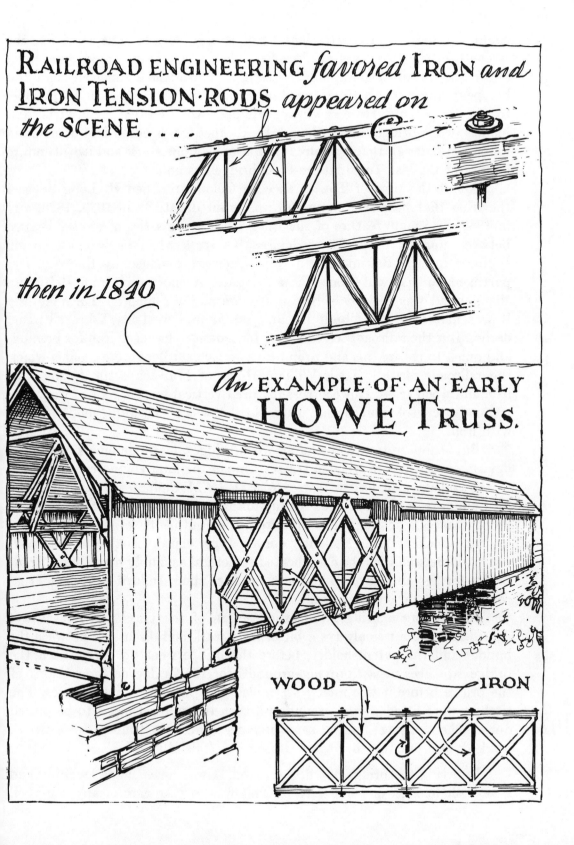

RAILROAD ENGINEERING *favored* IRON *and* IRON TENSION·RODS *appeared on* the SCENE . . . .

then in 1840

An EXAMPLE·OF·AN·EARLY HOWE TRUSS.

WOOD →

IRON ←

could be made from shorter lengths of timber, but as time went on, the strength of the truss was also proved. The lattice design could take much abuse and an abnormal amount of weight. Town was a supersalesman and he spent much of his time traveling about the country, even to Europe, to sell his patents. He was always equipped with posters, pamphlets, and models of his bridges and although his competitors accused him of claiming patent on a design that was already in use, his fame stuck and it will endure long after the last Town lattice-truss bridge has gone.

About the time of Town's success, Colonel Stephen H. Long devised the truss that bears his name and was granted patents in 1830, 1836, and in 1839. The main feature of the Long truss was a series of crossed beams, between upright posts. Long devised his truss when he was consulting engineer for the Baltimore and Ohio Railroad, assigned by the War Department to map out that railroad's route. A short way from Baltimore the railroad was crossed by the Baltimore and Washington Turnpike and it was here that Long built his first bridge and used his X-braced panel design. But the railroads were looking for a design that used iron for bracing, and quick to realize this and to improve on Colonel Long's cross panel which the railroads already liked, William Howe of Massachusetts designed an iron and wood truss. Howe's truss featured vertical tension rods of iron. The railroads were sold and so were many of the towns which were "modernizing" with iron.

But stubborn to the idea of all-wood bridges, many designers continued devising new kinds of wooden trusses. One of the later engineers who added to the collection of bridge trusses was D. C. McCallum who patented the McCallum truss in 1851. Used mainly for railroad bridges, this truss features arched braces reaching out fanlike from the abutments (often held in place by iron "buckets") and a slightly curved upper chord. Looking at the drawing it will be seen that the complicated structural assembly made it a difficult bridge for the amateur to build and the McCallum Inflexible Arched Truss reached an early obsolescence.

In building a bridge, the exact design of the truss was not always copied and there was always a bit of legal work and discussion between the builder and the patent-holder, before the bridge went up. Very often the bridge site became a "proving ground" for the bridge or for sections of the bridge before it was finally assembled and put out over the water. The timbers were fitted on the ground and then taken apart again to be placed during the "raising" in the same manner that barn timbers were fitted, marked, and put together again during the "raisin' day."

In laying the bridge out first on land, it was never made level but had a very slight arch or camber to it. This was to take care of any sag when

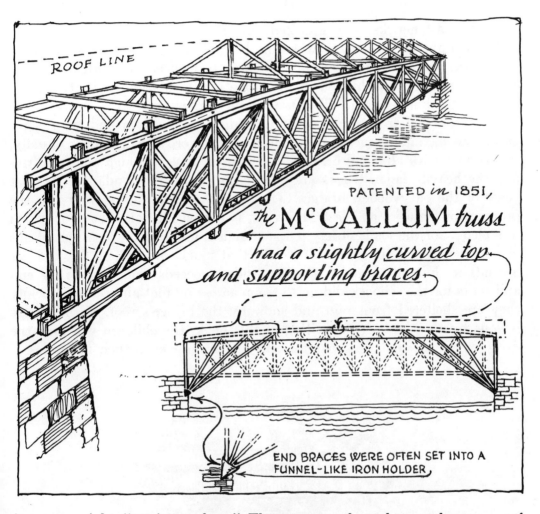

ROOF LINE

PATENTED *in* 1851,

The M^cCALLUM *truss*

had a slightly curved top
and supporting braces

END BRACES WERE OFTEN SET INTO A
FUNNEL-LIKE IRON HOLDER,

its own weight "set it to place." The amount of camber used was one of the builder's skills for only he could add together his own inaccuracies along with the softness or shrinkage of the wood used and estimate exactly how much differential there would be when the structure was on its own. Although the building was usually done by local men, a few builders rose to fame as bridge experts and were asked to do "outside jobs" of bridge building. One of these was Nicholas Powers. His first bridge was built at Pittsford Mills, Vermont in 1837; it was one hundred and thirty feet long and close to thirty feet wide. Nicholas was only twenty-one years old then, but his bridge still had life in it when it was torn down ninety-four years later. One of the most famous bridges that Powers built was the one at North Blenheim in New York. Put up in 1855, it has a single span of a hundred and twenty-eight feet. Powers said, "If the bridge goes down when we knock the trestle out from under it, I never want to see the sun rise again." And to prove it he sat in the middle with his legs dangling

103

when the last chocks were knocked out. It sagged only a fraction of an inch and right on the dot to where he had predicted. They say that when an ardent prohibitionist town official came to inspect the bridge building, a jug of whiskey was hidden in the stone abutments and it is still hiding there, as the builder said, "like an alcoholic cornerstone."

Most of the remaining covered bridges are well posted with signs giving the maximum amount of weight allowed to cross their spans. Actually, this is done with all small bridges, but in these days of rough and fast driving, the heavily laden trucks are one of the things that endanger the last years of the old wooden bridges. The last covered bridge standing in the province of Ontario, at West Montrose, is posted for only two tons which was plenty for the loads of hay it was designed for. But the local school bus now crosses it and the bus itself weighs that much. So, twice a day the bus unloads its human cargo on the near side, proceeds alone to the far end and waits for the school children to troop across by foot and reload. Luckily they are sheltered from rain and snow by the bridge's roof. If the bridge is gone by the time of the writing of this book, the children will miss the daily experience that their parents will cherish forever in their memories.

Greenfield Massachusetts

A small Gallery of Covered Bridge Types

TUNBRIDGE VERMONT

the FARTHER NORTH, the
steeper the roof

...from the Collector's
Sketch Book

bridge at
Clark's Ferry, Pa.
2088 ft. long

10 spans

Elizabethton Tenn.

a "smallest" at
Marshfield Vt.

a Ventilated bridge, Lake Sunapee region

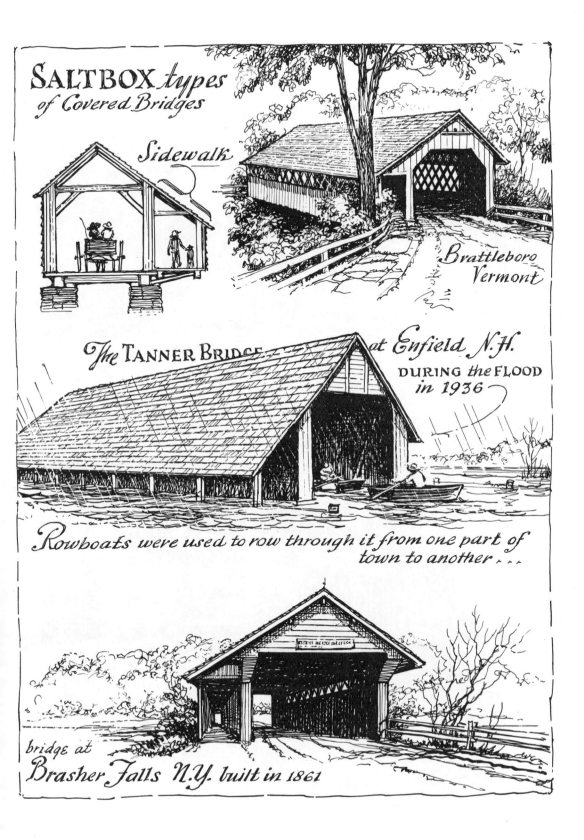

SALTBOX *types*
of Covered Bridges

Sidewalk

Brattleboro Vermont

The TANNER BRIDGE *at* Enfield, N.H.

DURING *the* FLOOD *in 1936*

Rowboats were used to row through it from one part of town to another...

bridge at Brasher Falls N.Y. built in 1861

Covered Bridge
PORTALS *are their*
Countenances

LYNDON *Vermont*
bridge

BRIDGE NEAR
XENIA, OHIO
built in 1830

a frequent
Pennsylvania portal

Earlville Pa. 1856

New Hampshire "barn" portal

Stewartstown N.H.

often designed in
this manner

Southern Portals
were usually Overhung & simple

Weston Virginia

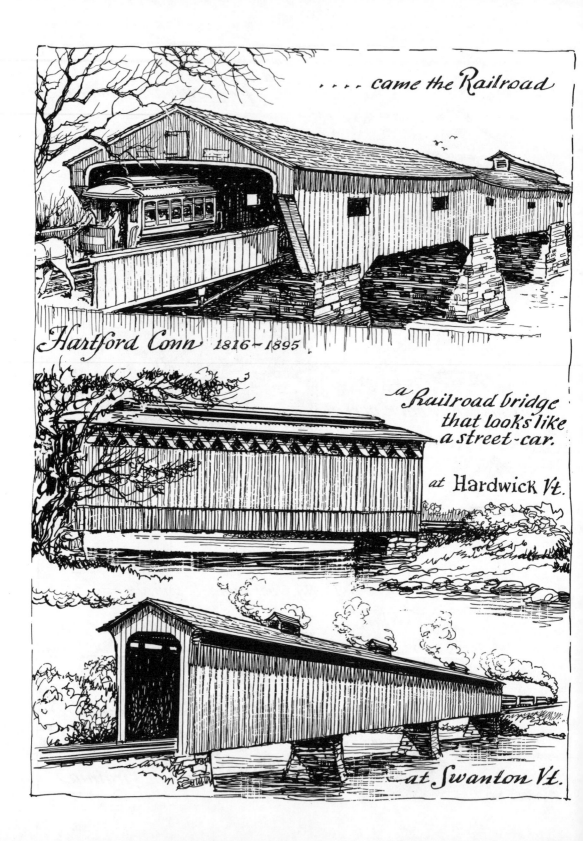

.... came the Railroad

Hartford Conn 1816-1895

a Railroad bridge that looks like a street-car.

at Hardwick Vt.

at Swanton Vt.

Some unusual designs . . .

boat-like Knox Bridge at Valley Forge Pa.

The "Ferryboat Bridge" Newtown Falls, Ohio

"Top hat" bridge North Wilkesboro N.C.

Over the marshes on stilts at Manoc Alabama

A CENSUS OF COVERED BRIDGES

EVERY DISCUSSION about covered bridges sooner or later comes around to the questions: "How many covered bridges still exist?" and "What State has the most of them?" These questions are virtually impossible of answer with any finality, for so many factors are involved. Some months may pass without the loss of a single bridge while, within a week, two or three might be destroyed by fire or by the march of state highway building. Also, many bridges are forgotten ruins—should they be counted, too?

The census below, made by Richard Sanders Allen of Round Lake, New York, is the result of many trips up and down the land, aided by much painstaking research into many local records and traditions. Figures for a few of the states are of necessity only approximate, but in most cases the list is definitive.

I am most grateful to Mr. Allen for permission to end my book with his—

Census of Covered Bridges in the United States during the summer of 1954

State	Count	State	Count
Alabama	60	New Hampshire	54
California	16	New Jersey	1
Connecticut	3	New York	33
Delaware	4	North Carolina	3
Georgia	50	Ohio	349
Illinois	10	Oregon	149
Indiana	174	Pennsylvania	390
Iowa	13	South Carolina	5
Kansas	1	Tennessee	5
Kentucky	35	Vermont	121
Louisiana	1	Virginia	8
Maine	11	Washington	7
Maryland	8	West Virginia	52
Massachusetts	12	Wisconsin	1
Michigan	6		
Mississippi	1	Railroads	26
Missouri	8		
		TOTAL	1617

112

OUR VANISHING LANDSCAPE

Our Vanishing Landscape

by

Eric Sloane

Author's Note

THE PATTERN of our early landscape was capacious and orderly. Its texture, which were the people and their farms, had the mellowness and dignity of well-seasoned wood. Close at hand there were lanes with vaulting canopies of trees and among them were houses with personalities like human beings. At a distance it was all like a patchwork quilt of farm plots sewn together with a rough black stitching of stone fences.

But the advance of "improvements" has done blatant and rude things to much of this inherited landscape. It began with billboards and roadside stands, soon to be followed by bungalows to match. We thought these things were forgivable indications of a growing countryside and that, so far from becoming typical American scenery, they would soon rot and disappear. But this pattern of organized confusion quickly led to sewers and paved streets. Supermarkets and shopping centers appeared, flanked by homes that looked like more supermarkets and shopping centers. The few remaining scenes with vaulting canopies of trees and houses with personalities like human beings, soon looked uncomfortable and apologetic.

In America there are still a few quiet white villages and people who feel protected by their town's inherent taste and its persistence to stay as it was. There are still those who motor out to the villages with the belief that these landmarks will always remain. But they are both wrong; the growing changes rung on the landscape of today are the Americana of tomorrow.

119

There have been admirable volumes of photographic reverence for early American landscape, but they are usually accompanied by a nostalgic evoking of the past which indicates that to accept any taste of yesteryear would be masquerading in Colonial costume. Restorations, too, often put the brand of "curious and obsolete" on early design. Some people can pass by an enchanting architectural relic without even noticing it. Paint 1792 over the front door and it at once becomes a notable landmark to them.

One "restored Early American village" in New England displays treasures of primitive design, but the exhibit also includes a building with the bones of a prehistoric mastodon. It is like the modern parent who says, "In the old days, children were extremely polite"; so the child is led to believe that good manners are something of an obsolete past.

The general trend of architectural thought today is that a new structure must not look like an old one, else we have not progressed. "Progress," however, must sometimes mark time to let good taste catch up with it whenever the two have not moved in step. In our hunger for improvement, we have unnecessarily changed many things. The concrete superhighway is indicative of rapid progress; equally so is the sad disappearance of the adjacent landscape.

This book which is the sort of thing referred to as a "mirror of the past," will have done its job well only if it first reflects the present, as a mirror really does. When a man has lost sight of his past, he loses his ability to look forward intelligently. With this thought in mind, I hope that my sketches in word and drawing will amount to more than drippy nostalgia.

120

1857

ASKED to name some physical symbol of America, the first thing coming to mind might be the skyscraper. But the tree which once imaged the New World, still symbolizes it more than anything else. Our entire wealth came from the forest, even up until the beginning of the present century. The Iron Age was necessarily a Wood Age too, for our forests were stripped to make charcoal, then the only smelting fuel.

When the romantic era was cluttering parks with statuary, New York was planning a Central Park monument to the American Pioneer. In searching for a subject, Bryant, who was descended from Mayflower Puritans, was consulted. He recalled that the forest was really the backbone of the New World and that "the groves were God's first temples." "Why not plant a tree?" he said. "You could find no more suitable symbol."

You might wonder why modern lumber does not last the way it did in the olden times. What did trees have then that they don't have now? Much has been attributed to "proper seasoning" by "men who knew wood" and who "had all the time in the world." But the old-timers who really had less time than we have now with our time-savers, knew the answer. They were using first-growth timber, something you seldom hear of today. This was wood grown from untouched earth with the humus and peat and natural rot of age-old forests. Its grain was strong and destined to harden with the years rather than to decay. So-called "rotten" first-growth chestnut-siding has been replaced from two-hundred-year-old barns, only to show that, beneath the weathered surface, the wood was still good. In fact it was so hard that the saw-blade burned hot under its flintlike texture. Trees grown from farm-cleared fields are of second or third growth and they have neither the same strength nor longevity.

The oldest farmhouses were usually graced with one big first-growth tree. Often the farm homesite itself was chosen by the location of such a tree. Into that tree went the memories of all the forests of great trees that had disappeared around it. The farmer might have said he left it for shade or to please

121

his wife's decorative sense; more truly it was a deep-felt emblem that tied his efforts to the past, so that he might never forget the time when all pioneer man's needs came from the forest.

As you motor into the American countryside, you will frequently see, along the silhouette of ridges, such a tall tree rising above the rest. Old-timers recognize them as "forest trees" or "first-growth trees"; surveying records call them "markers." They are monuments to the days when the entire forest in that area was cleared away. All farmed land was once barren of trees except for these markers and the few farmhouse giants that remained. "As I stand on the hilltop" reads an account of 1810, "the farms are mosaiced up to the river bank and even through the deepest wrinkles in the anatomy of land. As for the trees, as far as my eye can reach, I can count them on my two hands."

Forests in America were first looked upon as enemies to agriculture. The ax was a weapon instead of a tool. Very few first trees remain but when one is beheld and you can visualize the original countryside covered with such giant growth the effect is almost overwhelming. It was indeed a world beyond present-day comprehension.

In 1850 James Fenimore Cooper wrote, "It is feared that few among the younger generation of trees now springing up will ever attain the dignity of the old-forest trees. Very large portions of these woods are already of a second growth and original forest trees are becoming every year more rare. It is often said as an excuse for leaving none standing, that these trees of old forest growth would not live after their companions have been felled; they miss the protection which one gives to another, and exposed to the winds, would soon fall to the ground. As a general rule, this may be true; but the experiment of leaving a few, might have proved successful."

These lines were written when only a few "forest trees" remained in New England; the impact of their great size and the tragedy of their loss was material for poet and artist. We look in doubt at "exaggerated" trees painted by the artists of the Hudson River School, yet we might well ponder on how true a picture they may have painted.

It is difficult to believe that trees comparing to some of California's Redwoods, existed in the east; but records substantiate this fact. Here is an account from Forestville, New York, written in 1841: "Walnut creek in this town has its name from a black walnut tree, which formerly stood a mile above its mouth, and was 36 feet in circumference at its base, gradually and gracefully tapering 80 feet to the first limb. Its entire height was nearly 200 feet, and it was estimated to contain 150 cords of wood, or 50,-000 feet of inch boards. The bark was a foot thick. The tree was entirely sound when blown down in 1822. The butt, 9 feet in length, was transported to Buffalo, having been excavated, and was there occupied as a grocery store. It was subsequently carried by canal to the Atlantic cities, and, splendidly adorned, was exhibited for money to thousands of admirers."—*Gordon's Gazette.*

Today, a black walnut tree half that size would be considered a giant.

Not long ago there were many celebrated trees in America known almost as well as the persons or events making them famous. Perhaps the best known tree in New York and indeed the oldest fruit tree in America was the Stuyvesant Pear Tree which stood at the northeast corner of Third Avenue and 13th Street in Manhattan. Peter Stuyvesant planted it with his own hands in 1647 and for more than two centuries it lived and bore fruit. It was praised by journalists both here and abroad and poets found it popular material. In his "Address to the Stuyvesant Pear Tree," Henry Webb Dunshee said:

> Fam'd Relic of the Ancient Time, as on thy form I gaze,
> My mind reverts to former scenes, to spirit-stirring days;
> Guarding their sacred memories, as ashes in an urn,
> I muse upon those good old times; and sigh for their return.

123

In 1867, two wagons collided and broke the trunk of the Stuyvesant Pear Tree, bringing to an end its fruitful life of two hundred and twenty years.

Although we all know Ohio as the Buckeye State, few people know the buckeye tree after which it was named. Yet early European accounts tell of New World adventures in the "Buckeye country." Maine was known as the Pine Tree State before it was Maine, named by England whose scouts claimed the straightest pines for navy masts. Almost any schoolboy of a hundred years ago could reel off the names of trees that each state was famed for.

Missing more than any other tree of the old American landscape, is the native chestnut. Even today, when the only available chestnut is that from long dead trees or from old cut lumber, we accept "wormy chestnut" as a particular prize among woods, wormholes and all. From the beginning, it was a favored wood for barn-building and house-siding. It was a prime producer of tannin, and a bearer of food for man and beast. Thomas Jefferson grafted European varieties of chestnut trees in 1775 and about fifty years later Irenée du Pont de Nemours of Wilmington, Delaware, set out chestnut orchards that resulted in a rich distribution over Delaware, Pennsylvania, and New Jersey.

In 1904, the chestnut blight broke out in New York's Brooklyn Botanical Garden with an importation of some oriental plants and the disease spread concentrically for twenty years, killing surely and completely. The hulks of dead chestnut trees, some of which still stand, are almost frightening in size when you happen upon them among today's second-growth trees.

There are still dead first-growth tree giants standing, some nearby abandoned farmhouses or at intersections where they were originally left as sur-

124

veyors' markings. Their ability to withstand rot for fifty or more years, even after death, is remarkable to those who realize that the same wood today, even with paint, would show decay in five years. These hulks, mostly elm and an occasional chestnut, are things you will not find in the rural landscape of fifty years hence unless you search in deep forests. But today's artists and photographers have had their satisfaction in portrayals of the symphony of age, wherever an ancient farmhouse and first-growth tree could be found as subjects. Little did they know they were recording things of a vanishing landscape.

FARMS

IN THIS AGE, art and the farm might seem far apart. Yet words like "functional," "basic," and "traditional," that define modern art, also describe America's farms.

Whether it is a skyscraper or an old covered bridge, an oil station or an ancient grist-mill, these patterns of everyday life always reflect American culture. But the philosophy of farming has left the more lasting and profound mark on our national landscape and it has made an enduring cradle for the things we now accept as Americana. There are those modernists who receive the changing landscape as a healthy development, who even find character and functional beauty in gravel-pits and factories and billboards, saying this, too, is art. It is presumptuous for a layman to define art, but we might listen to Ruskin who in one of his Oxford lectures said, "There is nothing I tell you with more earnest desire that you should believe than this; that you will never love art well till you love what she mirrors better." America will always cherish the arts of farm life as mirrored symbols of an inherited philosophy.

In the beginning all civilized America was farms and all Americans were farmers who believed that farmers were the founders of civilization. The lessons that a farm teaches are, after all, not reserved for rural life. The evidences of farm living are more than just calluses. The strong individuality of our forefathers was largely a result of an independence that evolved from their isolated farm existences. Everything in those days came the hard way; work was never finished and the word "holiday" was unknown. In fact the only rest periods were Sundays or "Holy Days," from which comes our present word.

125

Farm life offers the complete satisfaction of knowing that each day's work has been truly productive, a joy scarce in present times. Yet strangely enough, the early American farmer's greatest satisfaction came not from his daily chores, but in his ability to make provisions for the future and in an awareness of his part in fashioning the nation to come. He equipped his home with far heavier foundations than were necessary. He built his barn to last for centuries and he laid a rail fence to survive ten generations. He built stone walls that have lasted so long that they are now a permanent part of the landscape. None of these things are done now, nor do we often consider doing them.

In 1798, Isaac Weld of Dublin reported of the American farmers, "these people are so certain of their future that they spend a lifetime building barns for future generations." Perhaps one of the great changes in American building and farming philosophy has been the abandonment of the enthusiasm for permanence.

A hundred or more years ago, whether you were a blacksmith, a butcher, a carpenter, a politician, or a banker, you were also a farmer. If you were retired, you were a "gentleman farmer." Even the earliest silk-hatted and powdered-wigged American had gnarled hands that knew the plow and the tricks of building a good stone wall. Before setting out for the day, there were chores to be done that often took as much time as a complete day's work for the average man of today. Taken from the word "chare," chore is an early New England expression that has since become an American word. James Russell Lowell's "Biglow Papers" written in 1848 in Yankee dialect, says:

> I love to start out after night's begun,
> And all the chores about the farm are done.

In England, *chares* were servants' work but *chores* were part of every American's life in the New World.

Early America might have been united by the feeling for independence that our schoolbooks emphasize, but we were also held together by the common bonds of farm life. Nowadays the average man in the street would be at a loss chatting with a statesman: a bootblack would wonder what to talk about with a banker. But a while back, we all would have been farmers, with a great many interests in common. Washington and every member of his first Congress farmed with their own hands. He observed that all America was farms and that all Americans were farmers, "a brotherhood of husbandry which knew neither politics nor class." Benjamin Franklin who was one of our first "city men," whose public affairs necessarily kept him away from

126

agriculture, still felt that farming was a necessary part of common education. He always referred to it as a way of life and a complete philosophy for existence. Even he finally succumbed to "that kind of life which is most agreeable" and bought a farm of three hundred acres. "I think it in duty to my children," he wrote, "to manage that the profits of my farm may balance the loss my income will suffer by my retreat into it." Like all early American farmers, he dedicated his life to the future.

Thumbing through old books and looking at the rustic past, we have good reason to be amazed at the way our forefathers lived, and to be affectionately amused at their crude efforts in comfort and convenience. Ox-yokes, butter-churns, foot-warmers, and such musty paraphernalia of yesterday are too often brought out in reverence by lovers of the past and cooed over by fashionable antiquarians.

On the whole, exhuming dead things is an unwholesome business and modern thought has little room for attic material. Unfortunately, the only recognized relics of yesterday's farmers are obsolete curiosities when the greatest relic, their philosophy of living, is seldom considered. We may decorate our homes with Americana to capture the early farm spirit yet completely ignore the way of life it reflected.

Although we are in a healthy era of attic-cleaning, even the most modern-minded must agree that some of the old things are worth saving. Deep thoughts and sacred memories can sometimes be preserved through symbols which at the moment appear insignificant or out of date. Every half century or so, an industry will undergo a hardy change when even its letterheads and trade marks are modernized, yet an old established business may lose recognition by discarding familiar symbols. One industrialist was urged to re-design the name and trade design of his business. "There isn't any design" the advertising man told him, "that can't be benefited by a periodic stream-lining and change." "I wonder then," the industrialist commented, "why they don't modernize the American flag."

There are still many ancient farms in America but the informal grouping of barns and outbuildings which once made each farmstead look like a tiny community, is missing because obsolete structures have been destroyed. The remaining buildings look stark and alone because they were once one of a rambling group. Even a well-restored farmstead could not wisely keep all the sheds and outbuildings of yesteryear's farm. After the house and the big barn, there was always a smaller barn, a spring house, icehouse, milk house, woodshed, and blacksmith shop. These, with the carriage shed and privy and chicken houses, all made up of a composition of geometric shapes that delighted the eye with its ability to blend with the contours of rolling land. All the old farms "scattered" or "rambled" in this fashion except the

Maine and New Hampshire farms which were "jined" or joined into a continuous group of buildings. This "joined architecture" enabled the farmer to do his complete chores during a bad snow, without ever leaving the shelter of his buildings.

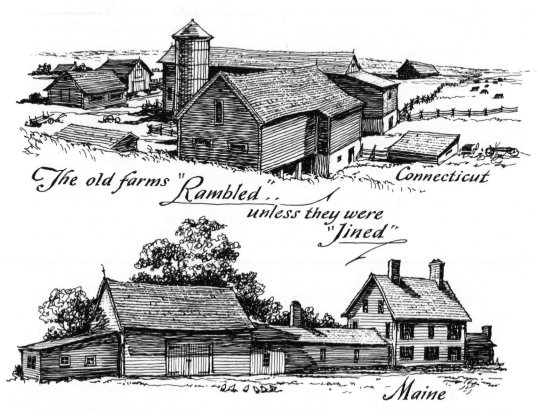

The old farms "Rambled".. unless they were "Jined"

Connecticut

Maine

There are those who will deny any disappearance of farm life, reminding us that America's modern farms which now "feed the world," are greater by far than they were a hundred years ago. This is quite true but it is the small "personal" farm that has disappeared from the over-all scene, while the big commercial farms have grown. Imagine yourself as the average business man of 1856. There were no automobiles then, so you necessarily had a horse. Perhaps you had two or three. Therefore you had a barn, and pasture, and a hay field. With that much, you probably had a few chickens and some live-stock too. Even the smallest house was incomplete without a barn and out-buildings behind it. When the family horse left the scene, farm life for the average person was on its way out. Soon the family car took over the old barn, the pasture was sold for real estate development, and home life lost its rural flavor so much that the American landscape reflected the change.

The modern interpretation of the early American farmhouse has strayed far from the truth. Such ornamentation as imitation split shingles, old-style hardware and decorative shutters will satisfy the average person, but the breathtaking beauty of the original design is usually missing. The secret, it seems, is not in decoration but in the body and outline of old farmhouses. At dusk, when only shapes can be seen, you can best spot the original farmhouses by their silhouettes. The effect of their proportions and lines is vastly different from what is being designed today, yet the differences are often subtle.

A great overhanging roof lends character to a Dutch type house, yet to make it so, might be "too costly." This means that the addition of proper character to the building is not worth that added cost. The few who insist on their house being after the old style, will learn that proper material is no longer available or the price would be too high and it would take too long to build such a house. How strange it is that with our modern time-savers we now have less time; and being the richest nation, we cannot afford homes exactly like those our pioneer farmers built.

Today's "ranch house" often lends itself best to modern air-conditioned living, but except for being Spanish colonial one-floored adobe farmhouses,

The old houses were distinguished in Form and Line rather than decoration

New York

Rhode Island

Massachusetts

Connecticut

129

There were Outhouses on the Farms . . . . .

The Blacksmith Shop 1800

The Outdoor Oven 1820 Pa.

Butchering Shed

The Wagon shed

Ohio 1815 Pennsylvania

Spring house 1850

Wash·house 1840

130

Well house

Dove Cote

Virginia 1801

The old barn . . . our first Garage

real ranch houses never were a true architectural style. What we are building might more accurately be called "split-level chicken houses" because the farmer's hen house always had these exact same functional lines.

The arrangement of rooms in the farmhouse was left to the wife, but to the farmer went the task of putting outbuildings in their proper places. The prevailing wind, rain-drainage, the contour of the land and proximity to the farmhouse, decided where the ground cellar, the smoke house, the summer kitchen, the butchering shed, the woodshed, the spring house and the wash house went.

The greatest slant of their roofs always facing the north and their entrances toward the south, outbuildings or "farm-outhousen" were part of a vanished American architecture that has been overlooked. Built with the same architectural care as the home, these buildings were actually as much part of the household, as any room in the farmhouse.

a Classic Privy, Evergreen plantation, Louisiana 1850

131

Wall-papered and curtained, discreetly embowered at a considerable distance from the back of the house, was the privy. It was not regarded with the petty humor that surrounds it today, but was taken as seriously as the design of a bathroom is today. The familiar crescent cut into these doors originally designated the building as being one reserved for ladies, for the moon was always regarded as being female. The sun being regarded as male, it was once used as the design on the doors for gentlemen.

It stretches the modern imagination to think of a privy being architecturally exquisite, yet those built on the southern plantations were delicately designed, often surrounded by statuary, and always in strict keeping with the style of the main house. It is a far cry from the back-house shed that New England country boys overturned as Hallowe'en sport, to the Greek Revival privies of the early south. In many cases where the plantation house was large and rambling, the builder found his fullest expression concentrated in this one small outbuilding, and the privy became a better piece of architecture than the home itself.

There is no evidence that the earliest settlers harvested ice, but they were aware of the low and uniform degrees of underground temperatures. Although most obsolete ground cellars have since caved in or have been covered up, the old farms depended on them for preservation of most food, protecting it against the heat of summer and the freezing of winter. The sketch of the Pennsylvanian ground cellar shows a popular and ingenious arrangement of placing the cellar against the cool walls of the well. Both the well and ground cellar are available to the outside kitchen just above. Some of the old ground cellars are still in use as "root cellars" for storing vegetables, others are supposed to have been used as hiding places for slaves or for protection

132

against the Indians; but vanishing from the farmstead scene, they are really yesterday's kitchen refrigerators.

A few years ago, air-conditioning experts utilized the coolness of cellars to force cooler air up and throughout the house wherever forced hot air is used for heating during the winter. Recently built atomic-bomb shelters have been reported to be the coolest places in the summer; some of them have been used for storage of fruits, being better than refrigerators for that purpose. We now think of a cellar as being the necessary thing to put under a house, but the first farmhouses used them for exactly what the word meant. It comes from the French meaning "pantry" or "store-place for food."

The fact that the earliest farmhouses had dirt floors is a reminder that there was no "foundation-room" or cellar (in the modern sense of the word) beneath. Often the whole farmhouse rested on the ground while the cellar (for food storage) was a short distance away.

If you own an old farmhouse, you might have wondered why your cellar walls have occasional protruding stones. These were put there to support shelves for fruit, and all the jars and crocks of preserves that were kept "cellarwise," at the right temperatures in summer and winter. Only when central heating became part of the house picture, were pantry stores moved upstairs to make room for the furnace and fuel.

The outside cellar door which became so dear to all childhood memories, was originally slanted to take the entrance of garden vegetables in a wheelbar-

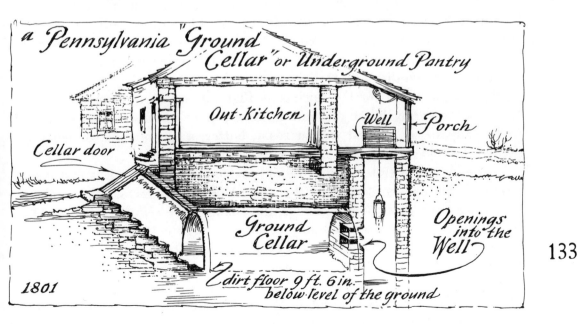

"a Pennsylvania "Ground Cellar" or Underground Pantry

Out-Kitchen

Well

Porch

Cellar door

Ground Cellar

Openings into the Well

dirt floor 9 ft. 6 in. below level of the ground

1801

133

row. It is a pity that modern house design so often forgets a good cellar door, built just for sliding. There are still children who would rather have one than to own their own television.

During the 1800's, farmers learned how to harvest ice and to preserve it in hay. By the late half of the century, the storage and sale of natural ice had become one of the nation's major industries. Railroads were always built to the icehouses which were the biggest single structures of that time. Their vastness can only be imagined by observing the foundations which are still evident along the shores of many northern lakes; some single ice-storage rooms were over five hundred feet long.

The first ice commercially transported was cut from Canal Street in New York City and sent by ship to Charleston, South Carolina, in 1799. From then on it was sent, packed in hay on canal-boats and sailing vessels built just for the purpose, to whichever parts could afford the luxury. In 1805, one hundred and thirty tons of ice were sent by Frederick Tudor on the brig "Favorite" from Boston to the West Indies. There is no record of what the ice weighed at its destination. By 1833, he had begun making shipments of ice to Madras, Bombay, and Calcutta, India.

Ice-making machinery (and finally the electric refrigerator) ended an empire of which there are almost no remaining records. Although they are still being manufactured, ice tongs are already found in antique shops and the old-fashioned wooden iceboxes, scraped down and waxed, are selling well as antique record-player cabinets.

Seventy five years ago, iceboxes were still city equipment. The farmer used his spring house or the well for his refrigerator. The spring house was less hazardous and more accepted for cooling. It was most elaborate wherever the farm kept cows for milk, which of course needed proper cooling. Cows were not as common on the early farm as you might think, for they were kept primarily for meat and for the raising of that famous farm-machine, the ox. Even with a spring house for milk however, there was also a big pail at the well, ready to be lowered with a roast, butter, a can of milk, or whatever needed the cold moistness of underground depths.

It is easy to understand why the old-fashioned shallow well is fast disappearing from the farm scene, being open and dangerous, less sanitary and outmoded by mechanical pumps. Frogs and snakes were regular inhabitants of the water one drank, accepted only because they kept the water clean from the insect world. Yet the water always seemed to taste clearer and better than that from today's house tap. It is interesting to note that the remaining shallow wells go dry much more often than they did a hundred years ago. Many of them have completely exhausted their water supply even without use. This may partly be attributed to milder winters and the less precipitation that this

134

century has had, but mostly it is the result of lands being drained off. Yesterday's forests and swamps and farms gave the land a natural spongelike quality for the storing of water. Today's drained and cleared land accepts rainfall like the wrong side of a blotter. Despite milder weather, floods are now more widespread because water flows over city streets, denuded forests, and "developed" or drained valleys, without soaking deeply into the earth as it used to. The wet decomposed vegetable matter that once composed forest peat and cultivated the virgin timber of yesteryear, has in many places become extinct. The effect upon the landscape is slow and unfortunately unnoticeable within our lifetime.

The brook

If you were to hear that "brooks are disappearing," the idea might seem fantastic. Yet a hundred years ago you could hardly go from here to there without confronting any number of fresh brooks. In the back country you will still find every valley fingered with running streams, but wherever the city has encroached and highways have come within earshot, the earth will have been sufficiently cleared and drained so that there is no rainwater reserve, and the old brooks, you will find, have disappeared.

Yesterday almost any community would have had many swimming holes, but useless mill ponds have been drained and the creeks have dried up. The old swimming hole is indeed a thing of the past for the average youngster.

Mark Twain once said that a farm consists of a creek for swimming, a hayloft for sleeping, outbuildings for exploring and an assortment of haystacks to relax in. You might think that haystacks are the only thing left of the old-time farm scene, but no. Even the smallest farm can now finance the ownership of an automatic baler that packs hay into modernistic boxlike shapes and

135

deposits them across the field with the artistic precision of Picasso. The old hay-wagon that used to wallow down the road with its wheels hidden beneath a mountain of sweet-smelling grass, is now resting out its last years in the sun, behind the barn, and the new-fangled square bales are whisked away in fast trucks, saving much time for something or other. The livestock might not notice the difference, but for the countryman whose youth was filled with the smell and feel of new hay, or the city person who always made a secret wish at the fine sight of a load of hay going past, something cherished has vanished from the farm scene.

The southern plantation is not the sort of thing the average person visualizes when thinking of a farmhouse, yet it also belongs to the historical architecture of rural America. No more valuable examples of buildings have ever been allowed to disappear from a cultural landscape. Symbolic of the many priceless plantations that have vanished from the south, was the famous Uncle Sam Plantation built in 1843. Made of gigantic cypress beams and handmade brick, the main house was the last example of Louisiana Classic. In 1940, the Director of the National Park Service sent a telegram to New Orleans, saying "Have learned of the impending demolition of the Uncle Sam Plantation near Convent, Louisiana. Can demolition be deferred short time pending investigation by National Park Service to determine possibilities for status as a national monument or historic site?" Unfortunately, the telegram arrived after the demolition was almost complete and the waters of the Mississippi had taken back the sand and stones that had once molded an irreplaceable monument of the plantation country.

It is ironic that in many cases, the log-cabin culture of the slave has outlasted the mansion elegance of the old South. The church in the cornfields, the cabin in the woods, and plantation roads worn by farm-wagon wheels and feet of many Negro field workers, have lasted long, and without the help of restoration. Yet there are many-roomed mansions rotting away like symbols of an obsolete past, tombs of the southern landscape.

There are still many log wagon-sheds, log corncribs, and log barns throughout the south, but time has nearly run out on the American log cabin. Built before fences and roads, they were already Americana to the people of the eighteenth century. Their mythological significance was used so much in Presidential campaigns that anyone without a log-cabin background was not considered a homespun American.

136

The log-cabin culture of the pioneer provided him with his home, his church, and his school. His fences were split logs and his fort was a pointed log barricade. But generally speaking, and contrary to belief, the log-cabin home is more southern than northern. Perhaps because they were built more

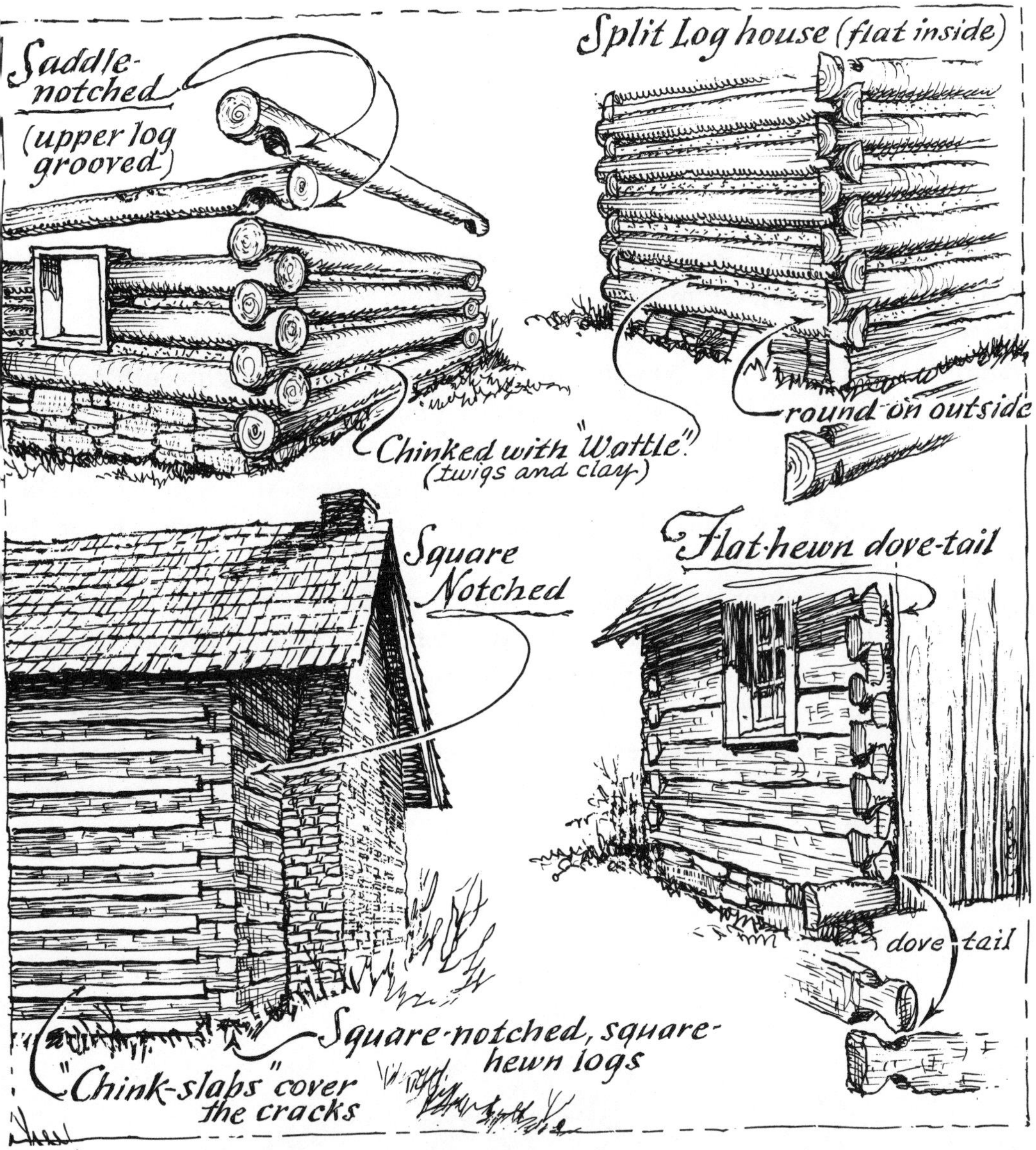

Saddle-notched
(upper log grooved)

Split Log house (flat inside)

round on outside

Chinked with "Wattle"
(twigs and clay)

Square Notched

Flat-hewn dove-tail

dove-tail

"Chink-slabs" cover
the cracks

Square-notched, square-
hewn logs

Hooded Log cabin Roofs

once covered Mud-and-
sticks Chimneys

137

recently in the south, you will find more examples there, intact against weather and snow rot. There are still nearly ten thousand log buildings left in Georgia, but the decrease from a survey in 1934 when over ten thousand were reported, indicates their complete extinction by the end of this century. Log churches had already disappeared there, and only one log schoolhouse was reported.

The log cabin was introduced to America in Delaware Bay where immigrants from forested Germany and Sweden first settled. In the earliest times there were no log cabins to be found in any of the colonial settlements of the English and Dutch. The New England log cabins of the eighteenth century were of the square-log type, more recent than the round-log cabins of the Swedes in Delaware. Where winter was severe, cabins were dovetail-notched at the joints and "chinked" or filled in at the open spaces with a plaster of clay and twigs called "wattle." A more recent weatherproofing was made by nailing narrow boards over the interstices.

Southern log cabins were generally saddle-notched or made by setting one log astride the other; the upper log was notched to "saddle" the one beneath. There was always a sizable space left between the logs of a southern cabin, which tended to increase as the timber dried and shrunk. "Through the cracks, as you pass along the road," wrote a traveler, "you may see all that is going on within the cabin and at night the light of the fire shines brightly out on all sides."

1850.

1950

138

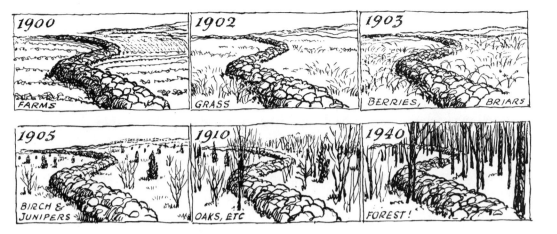

FENCES AND WALLS

THE THING that might impress you most about New England is its stone "walls." When they were built, anything forming an enclosure was called a fence. Whether it was made of roots or wood or stone, they were never referred to as walls; they are more properly called stone fences. Furthermore, they were usually topped with one or two rails of wood which have since disappeared into fireplaces as fuel, or rotted away with the years. So fences they really were.

You might wonder why anyone would have gone to such great labor building stone fences through thick forests; they wind over steep wooded mountains and into the deepest glens. But the truth is that when they were built, no forest was there. In fact there were no trees there at all, for the stone fences are no more than neatly piled rocks, gathered during the farm clearings of the eighteenth century. You would hardly think that towering trees could be of second or third growth, grown out of the cleared pasture and cornfields of less than a century ago. But the forest is untiring in its effort to take back its own, and from farmland to woodland is possible in one lifetime. Here is how it happens:

Imagine a farm abandoned as late as 1900. The summer after cultivation ceases, the plowed fields will have become overgrown with weeds. The next year you will find grass and berry seedlings that have blown in with the autumn winds. At the end of five years the fields will be a complete tangle of briars with occasional clumps of birch and juniper from seeds brought in by bird

139

droppings. In ten years these trees will be head high above the briars and in their shade will be hundreds of tiny oak and maple seedlings. In forty years the frail birches will have been crowded out by these stronger trees and with the stone farm fences still winding through them, the fields will look like woodlands that had never seen a plow. Fire or insects and disease may decimate this second-growth forest, or winds may blow it down, but it will miraculously build itself back again into third-growth timber in another fifty years.

The full-page drawing shows typical cleared lands of 1800, when only the marker trees were left standing along with a few farm trees. The result is a pleasant scattering of farmsteads, a main road running parallel with the river. It is interesting to notice that the 1900 highway civilization appears to have been pushed toward the road by the encroaching second-growth forest. Of course the next step could show the late 1900's where the highway civilization will have pushed back the forest again, uncovering the original stone fences of two centuries ago. Today's population will probably double itself in seventy five years, as a second (and the final) forest clearing should have occurred by then.

Our oversea neighbors of two hundred years ago could not believe our fences were anything but rude property divisions or barricades. "A mania for enclosures," they called it, and a typical criticism appeared in a 1780 London paper, saying, "The stripping of forests to build fortifications around personal property is a perfect example of the way those people in the New World live and think."

Our own views of that time appear in a diary of the early 1800's called "Rural Hours." It describes New York State at that time:

"Looking over the country from a height, now that the leaves have fallen, we found the fences attracting our attention. They are chiefly of wood in our neighborhood; zig-zag enclosures of rails, or worm-fences as they are called. We have but few stone fences here; stump fences are often of chestnut, which is considered the best wood for the purpose. Foreigners from the Continent of Europe usually quarrel with our fences, and perhaps they are right; they look upon this custom as a great waste of wood. They say they are ugly in themselves and that an open country, well cultivated, but free from these lines, portrays the idea of a much higher state of civilization, than lands where every half dozen acres are guarded by enclosures. General Lagrange, in the midst of his fine farms of Brie, says that he cannot like our fences. He thinks we should yet learn to do without them; he believes the cost of the wood, and the trouble of putting them up and keeping them in order, might be disposed of to greater advantage in other ways. Hedges, it is feared, will never suit our climate in this State, at least, unless it be our own evergreen shrubs. The

140

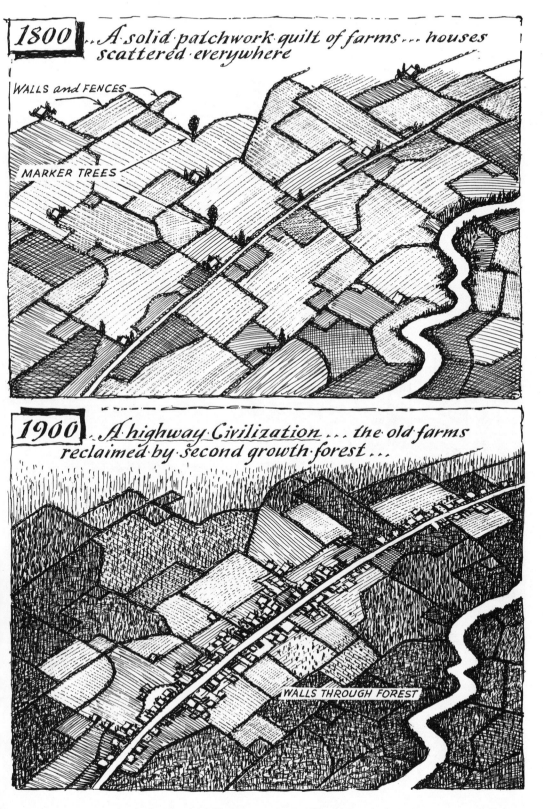

1800 ...A solid patchwork quilt of farms... houses scattered everywhere

WALLS and FENCES

MARKER TREES

1900 A highway Civilization... the old farms reclaimed by second growth forest...

WALLS THROUGH FOREST

141

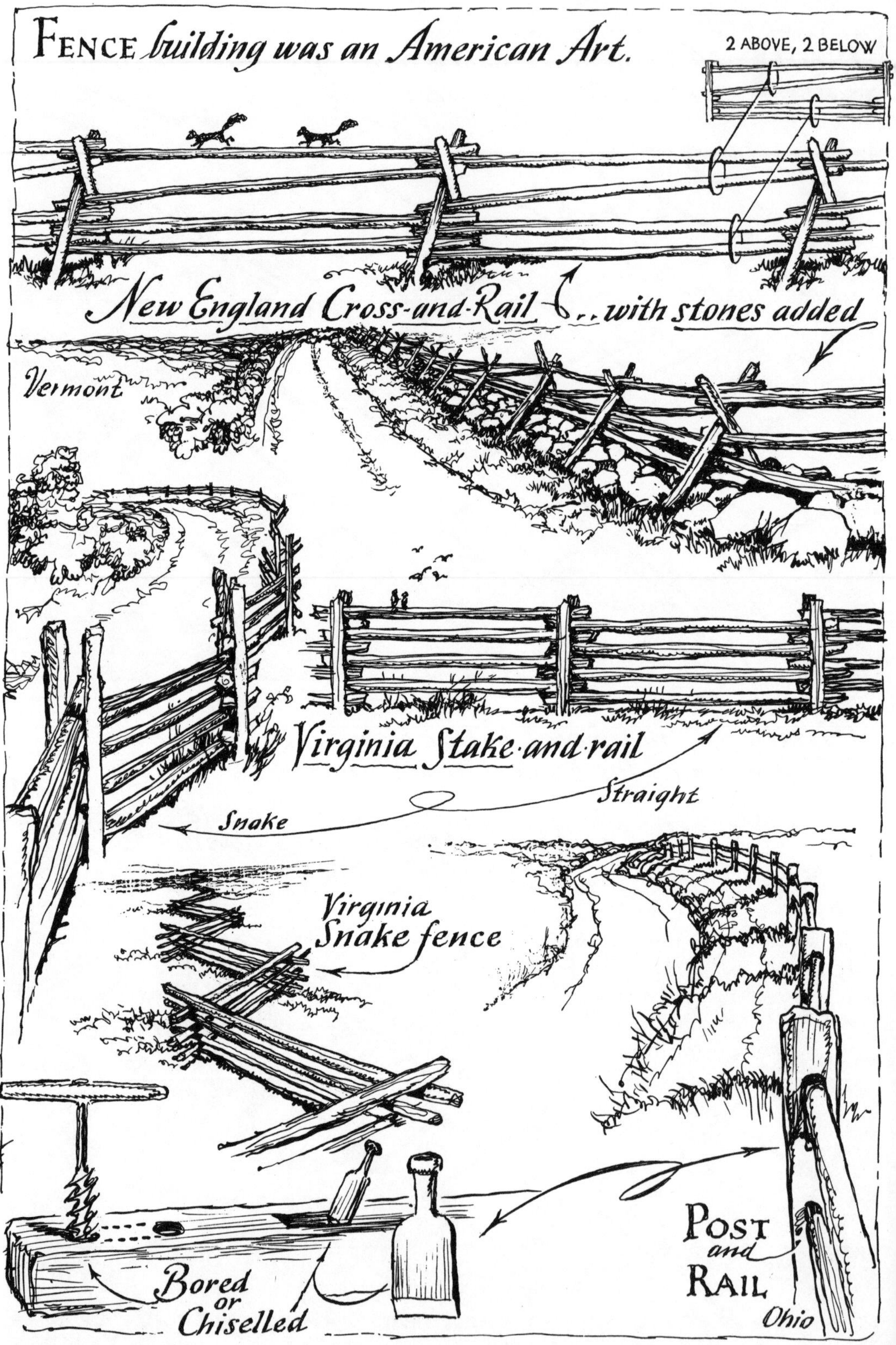

FENCE *building was an American Art.*

2 ABOVE, 2 BELOW

New England Cross-and-Rail ...*with stones added*

Vermont

Virginia Stake-and-rail

Straight

Snake

Virginia Snake fence

142

Bored or Chiselled

POST *and* RAIL

Ohio

hemlock is now coming into use for this purpose, in some neighborhoods. As regards appearances, hedges, close at hand are very pleasing; but at a little distance, they are scarcely an improvement upon the fence: they are still dark, stiff lines, crossing the country with a network of enclosures. Probably we might at least do with much less fencing in this country; it often strikes one that fields are unnecessarily cut up in this way."

What another nation thinks about our fence or whether we have a fence or not might at the moment seem of little importance. But at one time this was a great American issue. Our European critics, we must remember, used fences only for military reasons. Their farms joined into a pattern of landscape with divisions only of hedges or ditches. Their cattle roamed or were watched by shepherds. You have never heard of an early American shepherd because there were too many other things for the pioneer man to do. Fences did the chore just as well, and there were plenty of stones and timber to build them with. The Englishman, with his hedgerows and ditches, chose to regard the American fence in terms of its original derivation from the word "defence." He insisted we were trying to keep people out rather than to keep cattle in.

$ 2,000,000,000
worth of timber
1883

We had our fence problems at home too. In 1883, the Iowa Agricultural Report stated that the United States had six million miles of wood fence at a most conservative cost of three hundred and twenty-five dollars a mile. The dollar in those days was amazingly valuable, so when you realize that this figure amounts to nearly two billion dollars (the same as the national debt for that year) you will begin to realize the importance of the simple fence in the early American picture.

The rail fence not only lavished from four to six rails per section, but was also insatiable in its demand for good wood. As second-growth soft wood lasts only four years or so, the farmer who chose to build for the future used only virgin timber for his fences. A complete acre of first forest growth went into the fences of each ten acres of farmland. A moderate two-hundred-acre

143

farm would thereby require twenty acres of top-grade locust or cedar to enclose it. It has actually been shown in many cases that the western migration of southern farmers was not entirely due to the reported exhaustion of the soil as most history books claim, but also because of an exhaustion of fence material. In this age of wire fencing such a statement seems absurd. But if you depended on rail fence to surround your property at today's cost of sixty dollars a hundred feet, your fifty-acre farm fence would cost close to nine thousand dollars. In 1875 it would have cost about one thousand dollars or more than the worth of the farm.

Not long ago an important job in every American town was that of the fence-viewer. There is nothing for fence-viewers to do today, yet many towns still elect them and pay them for their office. Whether it is done with a Yankee sense of humor or not, the election of fence-viewers in Vermont is still a celebrated custom.

Fence-viewers decided the necessity and the sufficiency of all the fences in their neighborhood. They settled disputes between landowners, and they were liable (by fine) for the neglect of fences within their jurisdiction. Nowadays this strange office is usually bestowed on deserving citizens as a practical joke, but not so long ago, the plug hat and frock coat of the New England fence-viewer was a very official uniform.

The fence-viewer also had his deputies and assistants, two of which carried a Gunter's Chain for measuring acreage and fence mileage. A Gunter's Chain is a linked measuring-device sixty-six feet long, including handles on both ends. It was invented in 1620 by Edmund Gunter, an English mathematician: all road and land measurements since his day were shown on maps in "chains" or divisions of the chain.

To this day, the number sixty-six or denotations of that number occur frequently in historical research or in real estate records. It may be the measurement of a city block (usually three chains to a block, and one to a street), the distance between telegraph poles (one and two chains apart), the width of a canal-way (one chain), or the width of a highway grant (one chain, with the roadbed in the middle). The early "Broad Ways" were of such dimensions as the Duke of Gloucester Street in Williamsburg, Virginia, laid out in 1699 as a "great noble street of six poles" or one and a half chains.

The standard length of a rail or a section of rail fence was eleven feet, so that a fence-viewer could walk along a fence and by apportioning six rails to the chain, he could tell at a glance the size of any field. If he wanted to measure out exact chain-lengths, he could use any eleven foot rail as his measuring-stick.

Shorter distances were measured in rods, also known as "poles" or "perches." Why a rod should be sixteen and a half feet has mystified most students. But sixteen and a half feet happens to be just one fourth of a chain and the rod was once known as a "quarter-chain." Few know why a mile should be 5,280 feet long; but if you multiply a chain by eighty, you will soon find out $(80 \times 66 = 5280)$. Even the mystic 43,560 square feet of an acre is found to be the sum of ten square chains $(66 \times 66 \times 10 = 43,560)$. And it soon becomes obvious that most of our present-day measurements hark back to Gunter and his almost obsolete chain.

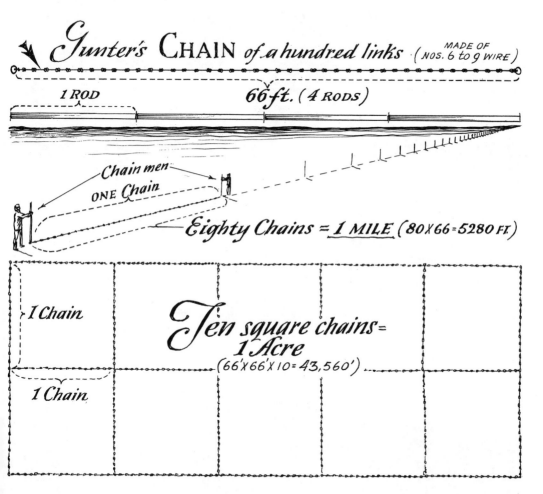

Gunter's CHAIN *of a hundred links* (MADE OF NOS. 6 to 9 WIRE)

1 ROD

66 ft. (4 RODS)

Chain men
ONE Chain

Eighty Chains = 1 MILE (80 X 66 = 5280 FT.)

1 Chain

Ten square chains = 1 Acre
(66' X 66' X 10 = 43,560')

1 Chain

One of the minor mysteries of old fences is the zigzag stone fence. Why would anyone place stones in such a fashion? The answer is simple: the stones were thrown there during a clearing, piled against an existing snake-rail fence. The rails rotted and disappeared, but the stones remained, winding across the land in the same crazy manner. Another small mystery has been old fence-posts that appear to have been charred by fire. Many people presume they survived a grass fire and that the cross-rails which are uncharred, had been

145

Wooden Farm Gates are now Americana

High-post Gate

Stone Gate-posts

New England slide-rail Gate

horse shoes

adjustable Tie-Slat Gate for varying sags

Weight

Stone box Gate

Louisiana Plantation

Bricks

Suspended Gate

Delaware 1860

146

added later. The truth is that most early fence posts were burned from the bottom and left charred, as a preventative against decay and insect damage. Farmers still use this method, whenever there is no creosote to dip the posts in.

Where the early stone fences came to an opening, there was often a square stone gate-post. The few of these that remain are usually mistaken for monuments or old hitching-posts. Very often the gate and the wall itself have been removed but the stone gate-posts were left because they had been so deeply implanted in the ground. Little has been done about recording early American farm gates: their ingeniousness, if not their historical value, warrants some architectural acknowledgement.

an Ohio fence ax

MILLS

No MATTER where you go in America, you will find millstones. Scattered about the countryside, sunk in the ground as monuments, placed side by side to make walls or for decorating inns and country gardens, people often wonder where so many millstones could have come from, since there are so few old mills to be seen.

The truth is that while most wooden mills have long since disappeared, their indestructible grinding stones have remained behind. "Dressed" with cut grooves, they turned one upon the other, crushing the grain and at the same time pushing it outward to spill off the ends of the stones. Because of a resemblance to plowed farmland, the grooves in millstones were called "furrows" and the plain surface of the stone was called "the land." The interesting patterns that resulted from the different millstone dresses are now almost lost records, yet many a Pennsylvania barn hex sign or farmer's patchwork quilt was inspired by his own preference in millstone design.

147

The many types of mills and their amazing number were a part of the American picture that is much overlooked today. The smallest village had more water-powered mills than the average person may now see in a lifetime of searching. And all this a mere hundred years ago. Time has run out on the American windmill, but there are still many water-wheeled mills hidden away in the mountain countryside, and people who will travel long distances to buy corn meal from them. Few are aware that they are buying more than quaintness however, for the meal that has absorbed dampness of the millsite, and has been ground under the slow turning of old stones, produces exceptional corn

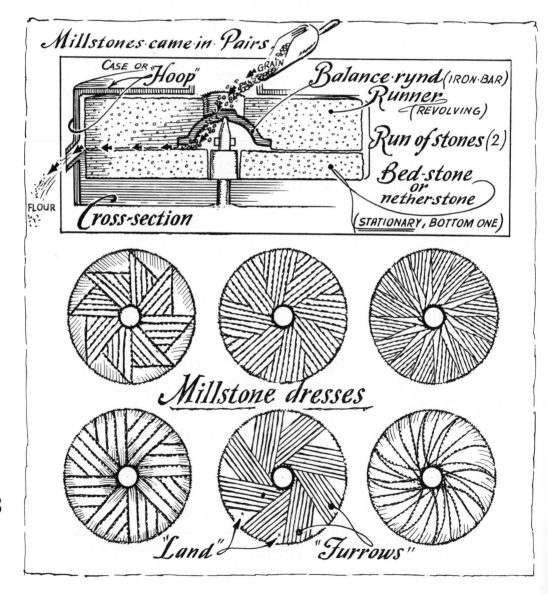

Millstones came in Pairs

CASE OR "Hoop" GRAIN Balance·rynd (IRON·BAR)
Runner (REVOLVING)
Run of stones (2)
Bed-stone or nether-stone
(STATIONARY, BOTTOM ONE)

FLOUR Cross-section

Millstone dresses

"Land" "Furrows"

148

bread. Yellow Bread, Shortening Bread, Spoon Bread, Hush Puppies, and Corn Meal Dumplings are all-American recipes that were designed for burrstone-ground cornmeal, warm from the mill. "When meal comes to you that way, like the heated underside of a settin' hen," as the old timers put it, "it bakes bread that makes city white bread taste like cardboard."

Because a few restored water-mills are still grinding flour, we might forget that the old time mills did many other jobs. Any chore that could be made lighter by water or wind power became work for the miller. A century ago in a small country community, where you would today find a total of ten shops

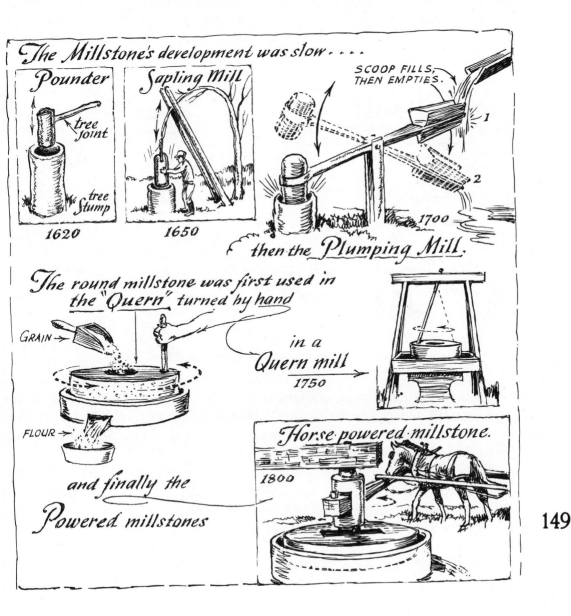

The Millstone's development was slow....

Pounder — tree joint — tree stump — 1620

Sapling Mill — 1650

SCOOP FILLS, THEN EMPTIES. — 1 — 2 — 1700

then the Plumping Mill.

The round millstone was first used in the "Quern" turned by hand

GRAIN →

FLOUR →

in a Quern mill 1750

and finally the Powered millstones

Horse powered millstone. 1800

149

and a few gasoline stations, you might have found water-powered mill wheels making axes, salt, barrel-staves, hats, pottery, bone-meal, doing calico-printing, and hundreds of other jobs.

The first type of mill in America strangely enough, is still found in the back-mountain country of the south. It is the water-powered pestle which has no wheel or complicated machinery. Used for grinding corn and mashing nuts, these devices called "plumping mills," "beating mills," or "sweep-and-mortar mills," worked by letting a stream of water fill a box on the end of a beam, until the box was so heavy it tipped itself. The stone on the other end of the beam lifted and fell unceasingly into a hollowed stump mortar. It is said that in the still of dawn, the sound of distant plumping-mills drifted across the early countryside and was often mistaken by travelers for Indian drums.

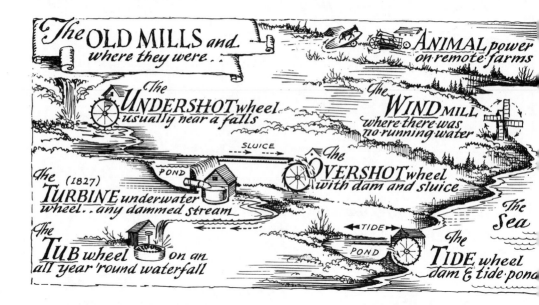

There were few more important cogs in the mechanics of American business than the millers and their mills. Whether there was timber to be cut, salt to be made, flour to be ground or meal to be milled, the village mill was always the link between farmer and industry.

The miller became a price-setter, counselor, buyer, and seller. Often he was banker and always he was the busiest man in town. Among the city fathers he was entitled to be called "master" along with the pastor. His advice on business and banking matters was sought and frequently paid for as would be the services of a lawyer. But mostly, he was host to the entire countryside, an early American politician and the New World's first captain of industry.

His earnings were primarily tolls collected for milling, but the bartering farmer of a hundred years ago seldom used cash. So the miller exacted a portion of the grain that he milled, as payment for his services. The first toll for grinding corn at Plymouth was set at four quarts out of each bushel ground. An act of 1824 in the Statutes of Connecticut allowed the miller to take three quarts of grain for milling each bushel; one quart for each bushel of malt, and only one pint for each bushel of meal. "A miller who took a greater fee," it further stated, "shall pay a fine of two dollars; one dollar going to the owner, the other dollar going to the treasury of the town where the offence was committed."

Because there were few connecting trails and no highways at all, each early village was dependent upon itself for every necessity. Often the smallest community had its own mills for flour, linseed oil, cider, salt, lumber, flax, plaster, tobacco, paint, grain, resin, and so on "down river" to where various smaller mills had set up shop.

In listing subjects of our old-time landscape, you might wonder why mills have been mentioned before roads. The reason for this is that mills were usually built on streams without any regard to land access. The roads came later, beaten as paths to the mills. There are still thousands of "old mill roads," leading only to nearby streams and mill-sites. Many towns and their original roads were built around this arrangement of mills, which explains why most inland towns are located on rivers and streams. The drawing shows the old mills and where each type was located. It explains how the local power of wind or slow-moving water or tide-water or swift streams, designated what type mill should be built there. In the remote backwoods where there was neither sufficient water or wind to operate a mill, animal-power was used.

There is too much controversy over when and where the first American mills were built to make an issue of it here. The first sawmill in Massachusetts is said to have been built in 1633 which was several years before they were introduced in England. In that year the first wind-powered sawmill in Manhattan was erected by the Dutch and the idea spread quickly to Long Island where windmills soon dotted the barren shoreline. Most Long Island windmills pumped sea-water into large shallow evaporating vats for the manufacture of salt. Others made flour and a few sawed wood.

The great seal of New York is built around a windmill design and, though few recognize the fact, the windmill was basic for the beginning of this richest city's industrial career. Very much like the present-day experience of approaching New York's skyline, is an account of nearing Manhattan in 1710: ". . . as we sailed into the harbor the horizon was pierced by scores of windmills, taller than any we have seen elsewhere."

151

Although we all know what a windmill looks like outside, few are familiar with the inner workings. The drawing shows a "whip" or "spar" with simple sailbars set through it, to be covered with canvas or sailcloth, making the propeller or "sail" that actuated the mill. Notice that the bars close to the hub are set at a steeper angle (20 degrees). This is done because the velocity of the sail increases with the distance from the axle and the sail tips must therefore slice the air at a much greater speed. Sails were usually from thirty to forty feet long which delivered a power of about 65,000 foot-pounds per minute. As wind power was first the problem of the sailor, boat builders became the experts at windmill design. Sailmakers made the canvas vane-covers, and even to the usual captain's hat of the owner, there was a completely nautical air about all windmills.

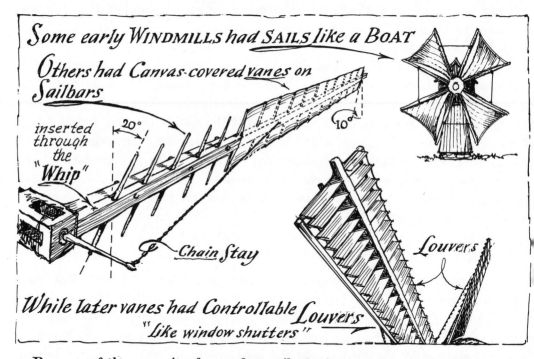

Some early WINDMILLS had SAILS like a BOAT

Others had Canvas-covered vanes on Sailbars

inserted through the "Whip"

20°

10°

Chain Stay

Louvers

While later vanes had Controllable Louvers
"like window shutters"

Because of the necessity for reefing sails during strong winds and the dangers of sudden gusts which sometimes turned mills into monstrous machines of uncontrolled power, a careless miller's life was always a short one. What with being whacked in the head by a spar, thrown aloft from a whirling sail, or being caught in the wheels and ground up in the gears, "killed at his mill" was a frequent miller's epitaph. Millstones used when a fatal accident occurred were henceforth considered unlucky. They were sometimes used as gravestones to mark the last resting place of the unfortunate miller.

One of the advantages that a windmill has over the watermill is that it does not freeze. During the very cold winters of pioneer days, water-wheels were sometimes frozen solidly under tons of ice for the entire winter, while coastal windmills still churned the snow-filled air.

There were some stationary windmills which faced a prevailing ocean breeze, but most windmills had to be turned to face each changing wind direction. There were several devices for turning them into the wind, but most adjustable mills were of the "post" and "smock" type. The post-mill was a mill-house balanced and pivoted on one central post: the whole mill turned (by hand or by horse) until the sails faced properly into the wind. The works of a smock-mill, however, were in a rotating hood raised high above the stationary mill-house below. The smock-mill was later equipped with "flyer-fan" wind-wheels which went into action only when the main sails were aimed wrong; this gadget moved gears which did the mill-turning job automatically. Small smock-mills were of the tower-and-tailpole type, using a long log with a wagon wheel on the end, to turn the tower-head and aim its sails into the wind. Two men could manage this when they were only revolving a

Anatomy of a
SMOCK MILL .
whose white dome resembles a *Smock*

the "*Flyer*"
only turned if facing wind ....
then it actuates this gear and turns Dome back into the Wind.

Elevator lifts Grain into
Hopper
which falls into
Millstones

153

"smock" or tower-head. But to revolve the big post-mills, where the complete mill-house turned on a pivot, horses or oxen were necessary.

The windmill men were America's first weather experts. A sudden squall, a predicted calm or a shift in the wind might have meant little to a farmer but weather was the wind-miller's stock in trade. When the wind stopped, so did his business; but when the miller got "caught with his sails up" in a squall, the damage could be great. An uncontrolled windmill turning wildly in a storm wind until its sails ripped off must have been an awesome sight.

Sailors in the bay often used windmills as weathercocks and set their sails according to the direction of the mill-sails. Long Island ferries advertised their services as "operating daily, except when the windmills on the opposite shore have taken down their sails."

The builders of the first mills were the millers themselves, but during the nineteenth century, some carpenters and joiners specialized as "millwrights." A typical millwright's advertisement of 1800 read:

> JONATHON ELDREDGE,
> Hartford, Connecticut.
> Builder and joiner of sawmills, barley-mills, snuff-mills, corn-mills, tobacco-mills, mustard-mills, all made to be operated either by water or by horse.

Revolving head.

Stationary tower

Tail-pole

154

1813 Mill at Watermill L.I.

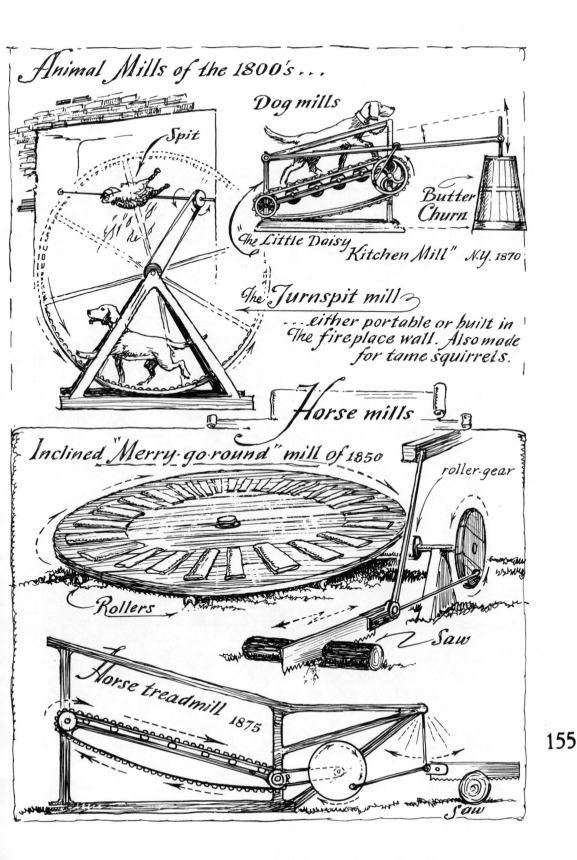

Animal Mills of the 1800's...

Dog mills

Spit

Butter Churn

The Little Daisy Kitchen Mill" N.Y. 1870

The Turnspit mill

...either portable or built in the fireplace wall. Also made for tame squirrels.

Horse mills

Inclined "Merry-go-round" mill of 1850

roller-gear

Rollers

Saw

Horse treadmill 1875

Saw

155

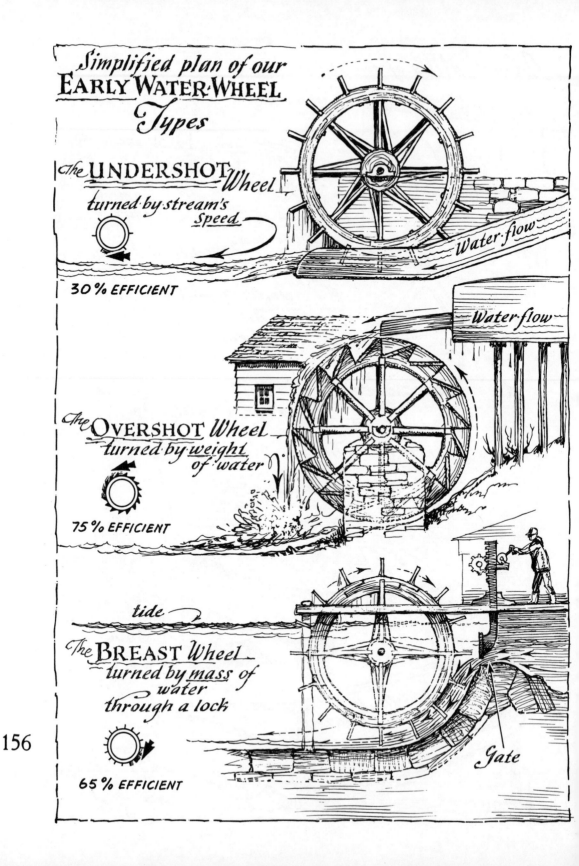

Simplified plan of our
EARLY WATER-WHEEL
Types

The **UNDERSHOT** *Wheel*
turned by stream's speed

30% EFFICIENT

Water flow

The **OVERSHOT** *Wheel*
turned by weight of water

75% EFFICIENT

Water flow

tide

The **BREAST** *Wheel*
turned by mass of water through a lock

65% EFFICIENT

Gate

Small horse-power mills were built for private work; they did innumerable jobs around the farm, from sawing wood to threshing grain. The drawing shows popular types as they operated when attached to a wood saw, but horse mills did many other kinds of milling. Although it sounds impractical, such mills designed for small farm animals and dogs were being manufactured and sold less than a hundred years ago. They did much of the necessary milling for farms that were a distance from town. Dogs churned butter, ground snuff, made linseed oil for barn paint and did other light milling. Large farms even employed "turnspit dogs" that ran inside circular treadmills in the kitchen and turned roasting jacks within the fireplace. Records tell of considerable competition as to which dog would take his place in the spit-mill and get his reward in bones when the meat was finally roasted.

The town mill was always a center where people came with their produce, so roads and bridges were soon built to the mills, and towns finally grew up around them. The first reason that the early villages settled near water was because there was no other way for transporting heavy loads. But they ultimately grew and prospered because of their water-powered mills. The Milfords, Milltowns, Millvilles, Millwoods and thousands of American places named after their original water-powered mills, are lasting testimony to the importance of the water-wheeled mill in the early American scene.

The three most popular water-wheel designs, the undershot, overshot, and breast water-wheels were built in a thousand sizes and variations but they were used according to location and the type of waterflow. The undershot wheel was seen mostly in fast-running streams or close to a waterfall, while the overshot wheel was found downstream in slower waterways, usually utilizing a dam, with a raised wooden sluiceway to carry water to the mill, the stream spilled over the top of the overshot water-wheel which was sometimes forty feet high, making it the most powerful type of water-wheel. The breast wheel took its power from its middle or "breast" section. A "high-breast-wheel" received power from above the height of the axle while a "low-breast-wheel" was fed from below axle-height.

The bucket wheel, which was not used for power, was copied from the Far East, where for centuries it had lifted water from river-level and irrigated farmland ten to thirty feet above. Water-wheels have since been used to open canal-locks, to lift canal boats, and to do hundreds of strange jobs of the past. Patents have been taken out to equip canals with automatic water-powered pulling-ropes to eliminate horses. Water-wheels have operated in farmhouses for butter-churning and other household chores, even with an attachment for rocking the baby's cradle and operating spinning wheels and looms.

The metal turbine which is a housed underwater wheel, replaced the wood water-wheel because, operating under the level of winter's ice, it was less

157

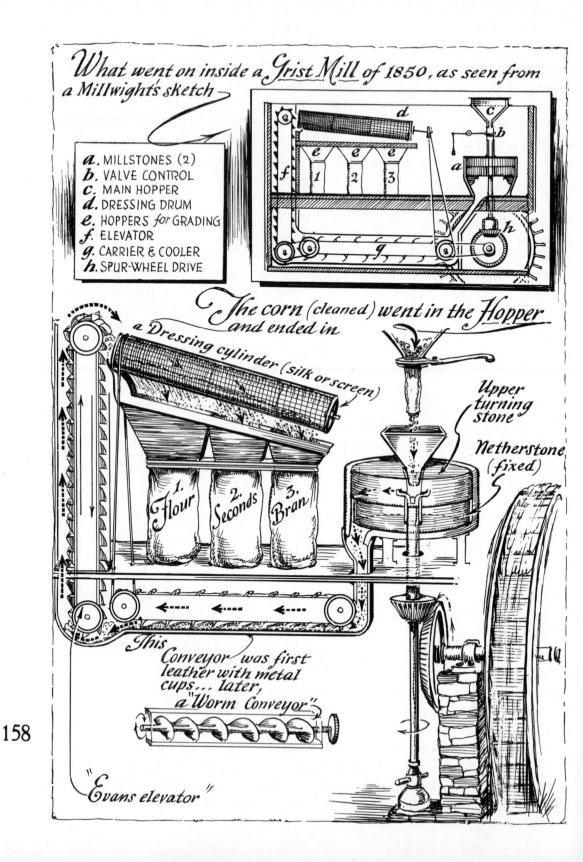

What went on inside a *Grist Mill* of 1850, as seen from a Millwight's sketch

a. MILLSTONES (2)
b. VALVE CONTROL
c. MAIN HOPPER
d. DRESSING DRUM
e. HOPPERS *for* GRADING
f. ELEVATOR
g. CARRIER & COOLER
h. SPUR-WHEEL DRIVE

The corn (cleaned) *went in the Hopper and ended in*

a Dressing cylinder (silk or screen)

1. Flour
2. Seconds
3. Bran

Upper turning stone

Netherstone (fixed)

This Conveyor was first leather with metal cups... later, a "Worm Conveyor"

"*Evans elevator*"

subject to freezing. Many of the early mills are now operating with modern turbines, turning the same ancient machinery, grinding corn and sawing wood as they did before wooden water-wheels began disappearing.

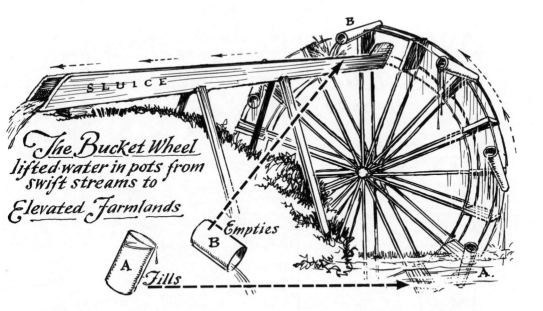

The Bucket Wheel lifted water in pots from swift streams to Elevated Farmlands

Most people accept the water-wheel as a means of turning machinery, but we might wonder what goes on inside the mill. The full-page drawing shows the working of an average grist mill, how the water-wheel turns an upper millstone on top of a lower one, grinding between them the meal which is fed from a middle "hopper." Differently cut millstones made various consistencies of flour, or they ground different kinds of products. Farmers often waited for the mill to change to certain favorite millstone dresses and millers had special days for milling produce in season. The mill-wheel sometimes took the place of a giant arm, turning a pestle in a mortar for grinding snuff or extracting oils from crushed seeds. The snuff-mill shown in the drawing is located below a room in North Kingston, Rhode Island, in a house where Gilbert Stuart was born. This was the type of equipment many farmhouses employed, almost as we might use a mix-master in our kitchen.

159

a SNUFF *Mill of 1750*

Gear

Pestle

Mortar

a Portable Wind-Sawmill L.I. 1790

Cog

Saw

160

Not all Windmills were Beauties

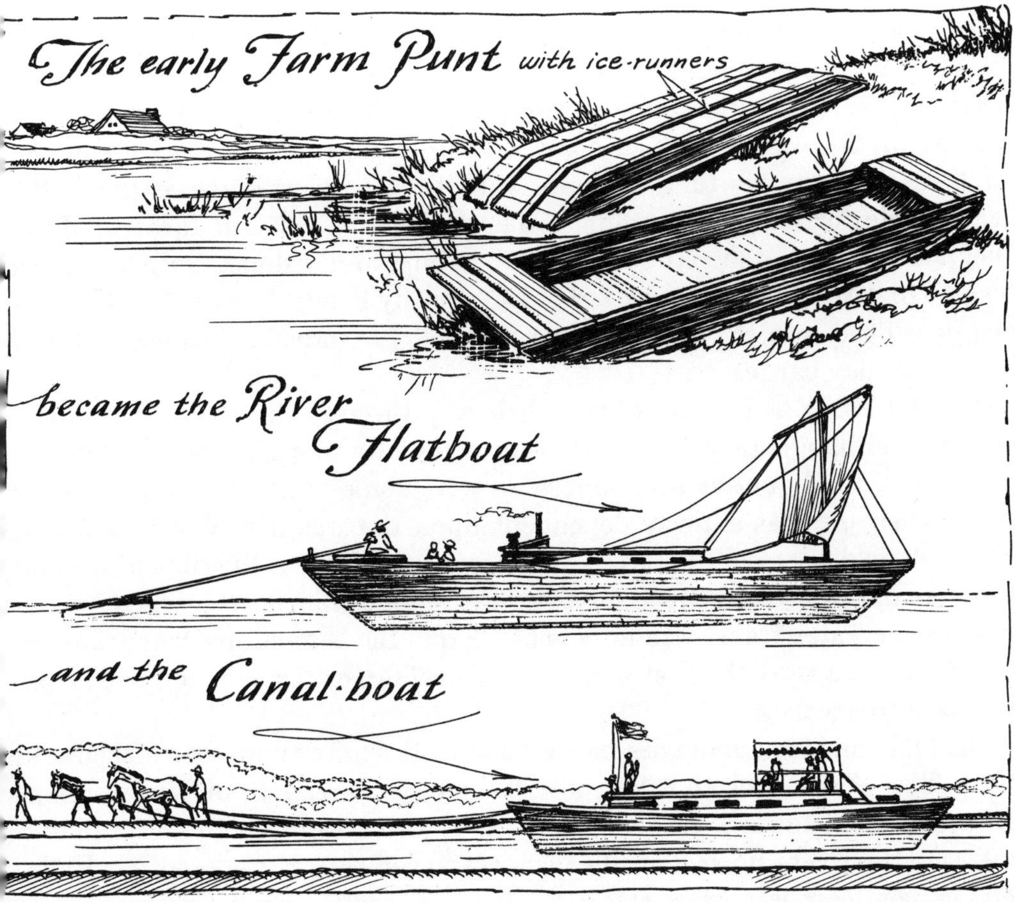

The early Farm Punt with ice-runners

became the River Flatboat

and the Canal-boat

THE SLUICEWAY that led water from the millpond to the mill was usually a boxlike wooden canal. Often it stretched over a thousand feet; when it was longer, a channel was dug in the ground and the American canal was born. For the idea set inventive minds to work, and by 1750 farmers had tried their hand at irrigation canals; canals were dug for floating logs across-country; where the sluiceway was big enough to hold a small flatboat, heavy loads of grain could be floated to the mill. Perhaps the idea grew from watching chil-

161

dren sail toy boats along the sluiceway stream, but the biggest promise for transportation in America was the canal. Wherever there was water, a roadway of water could be built.

Few farms were without one or two punts on their ponds. They were used as sleds in the winter and as boats during summer. When the ice in the pond was dangerously thin, the punt with its ice-runners underneath was the ideal vehicle for hauling anything from stones to wood and farm produce. They are best remembered as boats for eeling and fishing, without much thought to design and put together hastily by any handy farmer. Yet the pattern developed into the famous river flatboat, the industrial canal-boat and the present-day barge.

By 1800, roads had begun to web their way through the American wilderness. But although they were well represented on maps of the countryside, they were actually not as pronounced as were some of the buffalo and deer paths. Their use was entirely dependent upon the weather. When rain fell, the rough fields or even the forest was more passable than the ribbons of mud that were our first roads. Such passageways were confined to emergency trips or wherever water travel was impossible. From the beginning, Americans accepted waterways as the best method of traveling, or for moving goods from one place to another.

The Ohio and its tributaries offered a smooth highway of over a thousand miles. The Mississippi and Missouri waterways spread from New Orleans upward and out toward the Great Plains. If there were goods to be moved wherever the rivers flowed, roadways were never even considered. In Philadelphia, coal cost less when shipped from Newcastle, England than it did when hauled over the road from nearby Richmond, Virginia. The scale of prices in 1800 showed that one ton of merchandise transported from overseas cost about the same as it would if hauled over the roads in America for thirty

Specifications of a Canal (Farmington)

36'

Towpath 10'

4'

Berm bank 2' over water

20'

miles. This, plus the uncertainty of weather, made the sloop and flatboat the freight-car and motor truck of yesterday. The cross-country "road map" was more often a map of the rivers and streams with trails to portage from one waterway to another.

The Farmington Canal 1840

Northampton

Mass.

Southwick

Salmon Village

Simsbury

Northington

Farmington

Plainville

Southington

Beachport

CONN. RIVER

Mt. Carmel

Connecticut

New Haven

Long Island Sound

163

It took a month and a half to drift by flatboat from Pittsburgh to New Orleans and during the early 1800's about twenty thousand craft went downstream. The trip with the current was a one-way affair, so when one's final destination was reached, the boat was usually broken up and the timbers were used as house lumber. Many of the southern homes were built of ship's timber that came from a thousand miles away, which often explains northern-grown woods in their panels and staircases.

River flatboat design became more and more advanced and the idea of smooth water-travel proved to be sure, economical, and safe. A network of canals such as had already solved the transportation problem overseas, seemed to be necessary for the growth of the country. Every man with an engineering background—and some with no more than a political yearning—made his own inventive contribution to the world of canal design. Southern planters dug ditches and floated their tobacco to the river wharf instead of hauling it by horse. The whole country had become canal-minded.

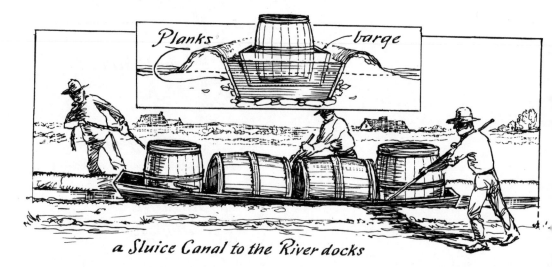

a Sluice Canal to the River docks

A first canal was built around the falls of the Connecticut River at South Hadley Falls, Massachusetts, in 1793. There were no locks, but boats were sailed into movable caissons and hauled to higher levels by water-powered cable-pulls. The first through-way canal was the Santee Canal in South Carolina, started in 1794 and finished in 1800. The first great canal was Clinton's "Big Ditch," the Erie Canal, and hundreds of connecting canals were immediately proposed. The wonder of it all was that there were no American engineers at the time, and neither was there any excavating machinery. With no more than the ingenuity of local surveyors and such simple tools as shovels and wheelbarrows, these man-made rivers were cut through the most difficult countryside. Using only timbers cut from the forest by hand and oxen to haul

164

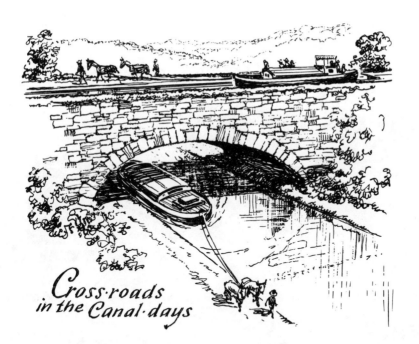

Cross·roads in the Canal·days

stones, canals were bridged and made to cross one over the other, into a lace-work of inland waterways.

Today you will find modern railroads using ancient canal-beds for their own trackbed. Sometimes you will motor through a high-walled section of farm-land that was first a canal-way before it became the highway. You might have thought that ditch running parallel to a railroad was for drainage. Actually it was once a canal; the present railway tracks are built on what was once the towpath. Or you might come upon some lofty bridge piers across a river where there is no roadway: you would hardly suspect that they once held a wooden aqueduct and canal-way, carrying it and the canal traffic high across the roar-ing river below.

Even to touch upon the rich story of American canals would necessitate a complete book. But to give a good example of their flourishing life and quick disappearance from our landscape, let us look at the Farmington Canal of New England, which was over eighty miles long. It opened three years after the completion of the Erie Canal (1828) and it operated until a little over a hundred years ago. Today few people know of this big ditch, dug by hand through the rocky New England hills, with locks that lifted boats as high as three hundred and ten feet. Few New Englanders have even heard of it.

165

Until the Farmington Canal failed because of the coming of railroad trans-portation and various difficulties with unfriendly landowners, its career was filled with a wealth of romance and historical interest. Much of its right-of-way was obtained through condemnation without proper payment, so angry

The Farmington Canal through Connecticut, typical of America's many Vanished and Forgotten Waterways

Now just a deep Lane through Milldale

Great Salmon arch at Granby

Part of the 7-piered Aqueduct over the Farmington River
(these 3 piers remained)

remains of Canal with Railroad on the towpath.
(One mile south of Cheshire, Conn.)
1920

Canal Passage through New Haven, used as a railroad bed

landowners either blocked off tributary streams used as the canal's water supply or dug away the embankments and let the water out.

Some farmers complained that their farms were cut in two. The canal company was forced to build suitable bridges across, but there was always a hay-wagon tipped into the canal, a bridge burned, or other trouble to contend with. Some farmers sued because the canal had taken away their water supply and others because the canal leaked onto their lands and flooded the crops. One farmer settled his grudge against a neighbor by breaking the canal embankment and flooding his enemy's farm; of course, the damage to the canal was much more than that to the flooded farm. The canal's lifetime was marked by floods, by ice during the winters and by a drought in 1843 which closed the canal for the entire summer. But the venture was far from being an entire loss. There were splendidly equipped packet-boats carrying passengers and freight from New Haven to Northampton in two days.

There were several stops along the way to change horses and for meals: people went to church by canal, shopped in nearby villages and enjoyed dancing and entertainment on the way. At Farmington there was a three-story brick hotel (later part of the Porter School) built to accommodate canal travelers. There are now communities in Connecticut that rose from back-country farmland because of the inland waterway, yet the present-day inhabitants could never believe that their village was the result of a canal that carried ships past its inland mountainsides.

On the Fourth of July in 1825, when Governor Oliver Wolcott turned the first spade of earth to commemorate the beginning of the Farmington Canal, his spade broke. It was said to be an evil omen and that the company would not last. However, it was the only part of a great network of canals proposed to supply New England that was ever finished. Although the project was dug with no more than spades, and by the sweat of farmers and common laborers, an airplane pilot could now trace its path across the entire State of Connecticut. Towns have sprung up along its web, railroads and highways have adopted its bed, and the countryside of New England is richer for its having been.

In 1848 the Farmington Canal boats docked for the last time. The taverns along the way became dwelling houses. At New Haven the canal's end became the site of a railway roundhouse. Farmers dammed up portions of the canal for their own duck-ponds. Farm boys found the lowering water filled with pickerel and cattails and the joys of a swimming hole. The Farmington, like thousands of other canals in America, was disappearing back into the landscape.

Significant of what canals meant to American business is an account of the opening of the Erie Canal from the New York State Historical Collection of 1841.

"The celebration procession," it reads, "moved in the following order:

"The Journeymen Tailors. The Butchers with Butcherboys, mounted and wearing aprons. The Tanners and Tannerboys in floats with men at work. The Skinners. The Cordivainers with six men at work making shoes. The Hatter's Society had a car with eight men at the kettle and others in different operations of hat-making. The Bakers with white hats. The Journeymen Masons. The Coopers in a car with men making barrels. The Chairmakers. The Potters and then the Saddlers. The Shipwrights had a model of a line battle-ship on wheels, drawn by ten horses. The Comb-makers, the Printers, the Bookbinders and Tinplate Workers came next, followed by the Societies and Associations of New York Industries. Many of these people will, through the canal, ply their business in distant places and stimulate trade that the horse and wagon might never reach."

What the canal meant to peddlers involves many an amusing tale. There were Yankee Peddlers who seldom left the canals, living at the inns along the way, buying and selling household equipment heavier than their wagons could have carried. Some of the first pianos were carried across country by canal, played as they went and ending wherever a purchaser was found. People often met the weekly boat from the big town which usually had one or two actor-peddlers aboard. In costume, perched atop the barge, singing and playing a flute or a banjo, his performance was ended by a brisk sale of Kickapoo Remedy or tin-plate kitchenware. The sale was always worth a repeat performance at the inn if the boat captain was agreeable, then on to the next town.

The Circus comes to town by Canal Boat

Circuses sometimes traveled by canal. Their entrance into town with a band playing on the upper deck and acrobats cavorting from the towpath to the canal-boat, like as not, with one of the elephants pulling the craft, was a sight to delight our great grandparents.

For a fee, handbills were handed out by the captain, and advertisements were displayed on the sides of the boat. Anything from a banner to a ten-foot billboard proclaimed the merits of Dr. Girard's Ginger Beer, Indian Worm-cure or the arrival of a minstrel show.

Excursions were advertised, particularly on holidays. For fifty cents you could have a round-trip day of it, with music and entertainment. Many of the boats specialized in carrying ice from the mountain lakes. The Morris Canal in New Jersey offered "cool summer rides, accompanied by a shipment of ice", just the way to relax while going to town. Long after the Morris Canal closed, New York canoe clubs used the route to paddle to Lake Hopatcong. Dozens of canoes might reach the end of the line at one time, filled with canoe-ists bronzed by the sun of fifty miles along the canal.

ROADS

EVEN TODAY, when you send anything across country you refer to it as "ship-ping." Express companies still have "shipping charges" and "shipments" ar-rive whether they come by freight car or by motor van. This stems from the time not long ago when freight sent across-country went only by ship or canal boat. Dirt roads were just not designed for freight and even the six-foot-high wheels of a prairie schooner bogged in rain or snow, when laden down.

The canals had taken even some of the tourist business, for the comfort of living-room steadiness and the pleasure of seeing the countryside float gently by without the discomfort of corduroy log-roads and jouncing "thank-you-ma'ams," made up for slowness. Charles Dickens remarked that no person should ever go by road in America who couldn't get there by boat. In describ-ing a coach trip on our roads he wrote, "A great portion of the way was over what is called a corduroy road which is made by throwing trunks of trees into a marsh, and leaving them to settle there. The very slightest of the jolts with which the ponderous carriage fell from log to log, was enough, it seemed, to have dislocated all the bones in the human body. . . . Never, never once that day, was the coach in any position, attitude or kind of motion to which we are accustomed!"

169

Even as late as 1870 many roads in New England were only clearings through forest, with few level stretches and often with stumps left in the middle of the road. In that year the Governor of Connecticut wrote, "What we complain of under the present condition of affairs is that all four wheels of our wagons are often running on different grades. This kind of road will throw a child out of its mother's arms. We let our road-makers shake us enough to the mile to furnish assault and battery cases for a thousand police cases."

Despite the hardships of coach travel, many remarkable stagecoach trips were accomplished which seem impossible today. For example, a trip from New York City to Philadelphia in this age can take up the good part of our day: even by airplane, which necessitates about an hour's road traffic to and from the airports at both ends, it is regarded as a good journey. Yet read an account of the same trip at the beginning of the century:

"Mr. Hyde's coach left the Holland House in New York at 5:55 A.M. and drew up at the Belvedere Hotel in Philadelphia at 3:20 P.M. The return trip was undertaken six minutes later and ended in front of the Holland House once more at 3:36 A.M. the next morning. The round trip of nineteen hours and thirty five minutes required seventy eight horses which were distributed along the route. Only one driver was needed however, and he was as fresh as a daisy when he stepped from the box." The coach was without shock-absorbers and its compartment was only thinly cushioned, with two thirty-six-inch seats facing each other. One movable seat contained a chamber pot, which must have added to the many rattles.

The use of seventy-eight horses might astound those who are not aware of how stagecoaches operated and that they were vehicles designed to pick up fresh horses at different "stages" along the way. But even with fresh horses, the average stagecoach journey was sometimes such an ordeal that riders made out their will before starting.

as Protection against Wash-outs
and Resting-places for Oxen
and horses on their way uphill,

(rain drains)

"Thank-you-ma'ums"
were not poor road design.

The ride from New York to Boston first took six days and each lap covered eighteen hours of road travel. The day started at two or three o'clock in the morning, when the traveler (who usually slept in his clothes) was routed from his lodging at the stagecoach inn for the next lap. The New York-Boston trip, however, was first planned as a pleasure ride and made to appear attractive in its first advertisement in the New York *Journal* for June 25, 1772:

THE STAGE COACH
between
NEW YORK AND BOSTON

Which for the first time sets out this day from Mr. Fowler's Tavern (formerly kept by Mr. Stout) at Fresh Water in New York will continue to go the course between Boston and New York, so as to be at each of those places once a fortnight coming in on Saturday evening and setting out to return by way of Hartford on Monday morning. The price to passengers will be 4d. New York, or 3d. lawful Money per Mile and Baggage at a reasonable price. Gentlemen and Ladies who choose to encourage this useful new and expensive Undertaking, may depend upon good Usage, and that the Coach will always put up at Houses on the Road where the best Entertainment is provided. If on Trial, the Subscribers find Encouragement they will perform the Stage once a week, only altering the Day of setting out from New York and Boston to Thursday instead of Monday Morning.

The Post Riders who carried the mail along the Boston Post Road ran on a twice-a-week schedule. Two men started out at the same time, one from New York City and the other from Boston. Speeding toward each other, they met half-way in Connecticut to exchange saddlebags and then set out in opposite directions. This half-way switch was accepted as a clever time-saver until it was realized that both riders traveled the same distance and no time was actually saved at all. The only convenience was that the riders were able to sleep in their own beds more often. At least the important two-hundred-and-fifty-mile link between Boston and New York had a day-and-night mail service, and by 1765 Benjamin Franklin boasted that a letter mailed in Philadelphia was sure to reach Boston by three weeks.

The early post office was first responsible for the erection of milestones, because postal rates were set rigidly, according to mileage. Benjamin Franklin devoted a great deal of his time as Postmaster General to the placing of milestones, and many of the stones standing in Pennsylvania and New England are said to have been set in place by Franklin himself. A more logical story is that he made special trips to inspect them, after they had been placed. He did

171

make such a New England journey by chaise while his daughter accompanied him most of the way on horseback.

Some of the earliest milestones were set on the road between Philadelphia and Trenton. They were paid for in fines by the Philadelphia Contributionship for the Insurance of Houses from Loss by Fire. Thomas Wharton and Jacob Lewis were contracted to make and place these stones, "the distance of a mile, one from the other, with the number of miles from Philadelphia to be cut solidly in each stone." Starting from Front and Market Streets on May 15, 1764, the Surveyor General of the Province set them all in place, possibly the first American milestones. He used a "clacker" set on the wheel of a wagon that measured out each mile, but the New England milestones were set by surveyors who laid out eighty Gunter's chains to the mile "because no two wheels turned the same number of times on a Yankee road."

Putting in the Milestones...
CIRCUMFERENCE MULTIPLIED·BY REVOLUTIONS = MILEAGE — a "clacker" counted the revolutions of a wheel for one mile

Before 1800, postal rates were often scaled to individual miles but the nineteenth century saw rates regulated and scaled to five- and ten-mile proportions. The *Farmer's Almanac* of 1813, for example, gives rates "of every single letter by land" as follows: "Every letter composed of a single sheet of paper not conveyed above thirty miles six cents. From thirty to eighty miles, ten cents. From eighty to one hundred and fifty miles, twelve and a half cents. From one hundred and fifty to four hundred miles, eighteen and three fourth cents. Over four hundred miles, twenty five cents." For each extra sheet of paper used, you were charged an additional postal rate. This is a reason why the early magazines and newspapers were printed on one sheet and folded over.

Envelopes were unknown before the early part of the 1800's and not until 1847 did stamps become necessary. *Historic Oyster Bay* tells of some children who went to postmaster James Caldwell's house to post a letter. "Mr. Caldwell did not take their money in the usual manner on this day, but handed them back a tiny picture of Benjamin Franklin which they were told to glue to the corner of the letter. It was the first postage stamp, of which there were two kinds, five and ten cents with portraits of Franklin and Washington." Because of a shortage of five-cent stamps, you were allowed to cut Washington (a ten cent stamp) in half and use it that way.

17 Miles to Litchfield. A Connecticut marker from about 1763

19 Miles from Philadelphia Placed on May 15, 1764

At first, letters were entrusted to the stage driver or even to friends traveling in the right direction. Deliveries were something special, usually left in a pigeonhole of the nearest tavern desk, but sometimes left by the stage driver in some secret crevice of a tree. When a farm was located far from town, the farmer was often clever enough to place a watering trough for stagecoach horses on the road, with a mailbox nearby. This afforded a pardonable stop for the coach, and time enough for the driver to put mail in the box.

The FIRST American Mail box →

173

Boots were made entirely by hand in those days, often fashioned by the wearer himself; therefore there was something especially personal about each man's boot. So it was the custom to put one's boot out for the collection of any personal message, and some of the first "mailboxes" of rural delivery were no more than farm boots nailed to a post.

The "deerpath" roads of yesterday shock most of us in this age of wide highways, yet the real wonder was that without road-building equipment, roads were possible at all. It is almost beyond conception that roads a thousand miles long, and canals through mountainous countryside, could be dug with no more than shovels and wheelbarrows. Without blasting or dredges, roads, slight as they were, went through the wilderness in a surprisingly quick manner.

On May 10, 1776, the Congress voted a military road to be built between Newburg, Vermont, and the Province of Canada. This road had already been recommended by General Washington to facilitate the march and return of troops in that area. In forty-five days, a group of one hundred and ten men working for the pay of ten dollars a month, pushed fourteen miles through hardwood forests and steep mountainsides, to make a road suitable for wagons. That is close to two thousand feet a day, including bridge-ways and logways over soft ground, cutting down virgin trees, removing the stumps and piling rocks to the side of the road. Food and a half a pint of rum were thrown into the thirty-cents-a-day wage, and the road which was built at almost the speed of a slow walk was considered no great feat in those days, even though the peril of Indian attack was included.

This road was continued in 1779 by Colonel Moses Hazen (whose name has ever since been attached to it) with a labor force of local militia. The Hazen Road is a military road in design, because it follows hilltops, avoiding valleys and swampy places. The later mill and factory roads which were guided by economic motives, followed the rivers and valley streams where industries settled. Military roads, often a rod wide, crossed water at right angles and sought the protection of ridges and high ground. Both the picturesque road that hugs the river bank, and the rod-wide lane are destined to disappear from the American landscape.

What we now refer to as a country lane was once the minimum width for American private right-of-way roads. The lane land-grant was one rod wide, with an eight-foot roadbed. The same law stated that "private roads shall not be more than three rods wide." Few of the early rod-wide lanes remain with their rows of stone fences or tall trees only sixteen and a half feet apart. The foliage that converged overhead to form a tunnel of green was an unforgettable pleasure: the disappearance of such pathways makes the simple pastime of "swinging down a shady lane" a vanished American delight.

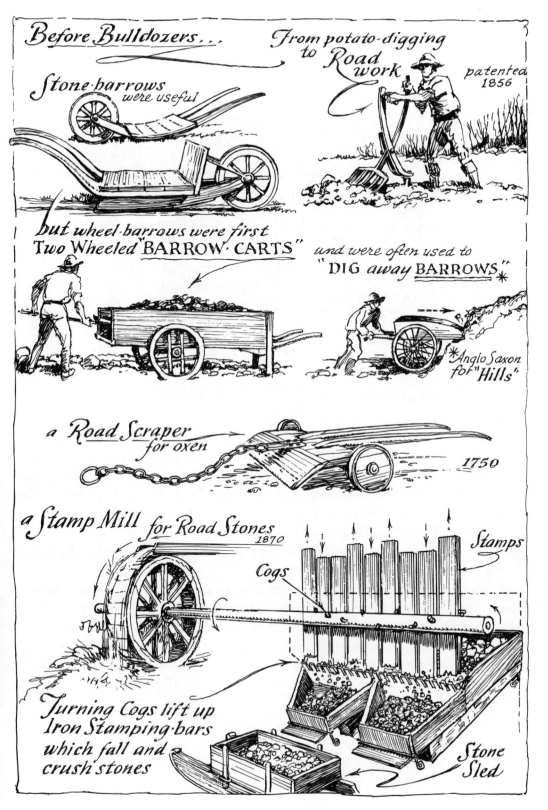

Before Bulldozers...

From potato-digging to Road work

patented 1856

Stone harrows were useful

but wheel barrows were first
Two Wheeled "BARROW CARTS"

and were often used to "DIG away BARROWS"*

*Anglo Saxon for "Hills"

a Road Scraper for oxen

1750

a Stamp Mill for Road Stones
1870

Stamps

Cogs

Turning Cogs lift up
Iron Stamping bars
which fall and
crush stones

Stone Sled

175

Lane-width

← — — — — — *16 ½'* — — — — →

There was once a popular theory that a gently undulating road is less fatiguing to horses than a level one. "The alternations of ascent, descent, and levels call into play different muscles, allowing some to rest while others are exerted, and thus relieving each in turn." This theory was used in New York's subway and elevated railroads but applied to machinery instead of animal muscles. A gentle dip between each station got the train under way quicker, while the upgrade of the next station, worked with the brakes to bring the train to a stop.

It seems strange that in times when our roads were no more than rivers of mud, people should worry about undulating roads or the picturesqueness of their curvatures. Yet those were romantic times when men were both farmers and designers, poets were statesmen and artists were engineers. One of the most controversial details about road design was whether roads should be straight or curved. Coleridge who considered himself a road expert, said,

176

The road the human being travels,
That on which blessing comes and goes, doth follow
The river's course, the valley's playful windings,
Curves round the cornfields and the hill of vines.

"Straight roads over an uneven and hilly country may at first view, when merely seen on the map, be pronounced a bad road," said De Witt Clinton, "for the straightness must have been obtained by submitting to steep slopes in ascending the hills and descending the valleys." "Straightnesss should always be sacrificed to obtain a level, or to make a road less steep," said road expert Dr. Gillespie in 1873, and many others joined the unbelievable fight against straight roads. This, of course, did not pertain to city streets, but it did pertain, for the sake of beauty, to pleasure drives. Some of the best road designers were known for their use of Hogarth's "line of grace," and their ability to put a road through a park or cemetery that deceived the traveler into believing he was traveling over a large area and "lulled him into a relaxation of curves." The Greenwood Cemetery Road shown in the plan from an early road-builder's manual and considered a gem, illustrates this principle. It would be a road-builder's nightmare today.

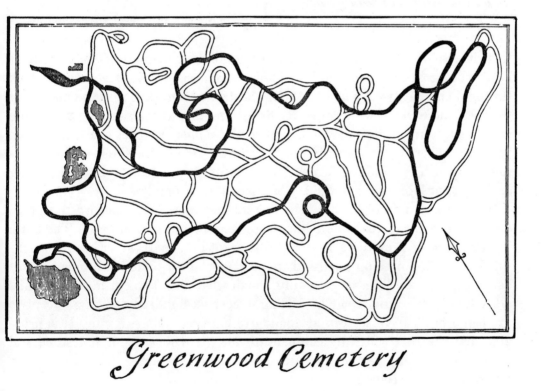

Greenwood Cemetery

177

There are still crushed-oyster-shell roads along the seacoast, left over from the time before the development of plank roads, These shell roads are the only ones remaining from that period of experimentation with everything from crushed coal to corncobs. One material that promised to stay longer

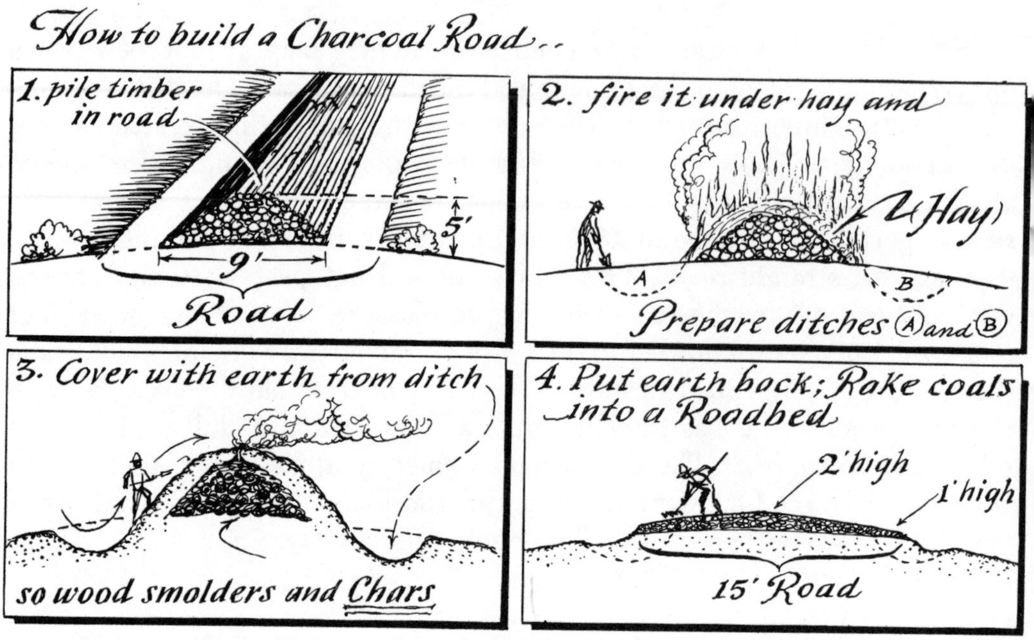

1. pile timber in road

5'

9'

Road

2. fire it under hay and (Hay)

A   B

Prepare ditches Ⓐ and Ⓑ

3. Cover with earth from ditch

so wood smolders and Chars

4. Put earth back; Rake coals into a Roadbed

2' high

1' high

15' Road

than it actually did was charcoal. A road-building manual of 1869 explains how a charcoal road was built. "Timber from six to eighteen inches thick through, and cut twenty five feet long, is stacked lengthwise in the middle of the road and covered with straw. By firing this, and at the same time covering it with earth from the sides of the road, the timber becomes charcoal. When properly charred, the earth is removed to the side of the ditches: the coal is raked down to a width of fifteen feet, leaving it two feet high at the center and one foot high in the middle. The road is then complete."

The manual did not mention the forests that were being laid waste to produce these charcoal roads, but few people considered that anyway. The truth is that more of America's forest wealth went into charcoal, either for smelting iron or for making roads, than ever went into building lumber or for heating purposes. Timber was only worth what it cost to cut it. The manual adds that "a charcoal road in Michigan cost six hundred dollars a mile; two are being built in Wisconsin at about five hundred dollars a mile. It is probable that charcoal will fully compensate for the deficiency of limestone and gravel in western sections where roads are constructed through forests. Charcoal costs a fourth of the expense of limestone."

178

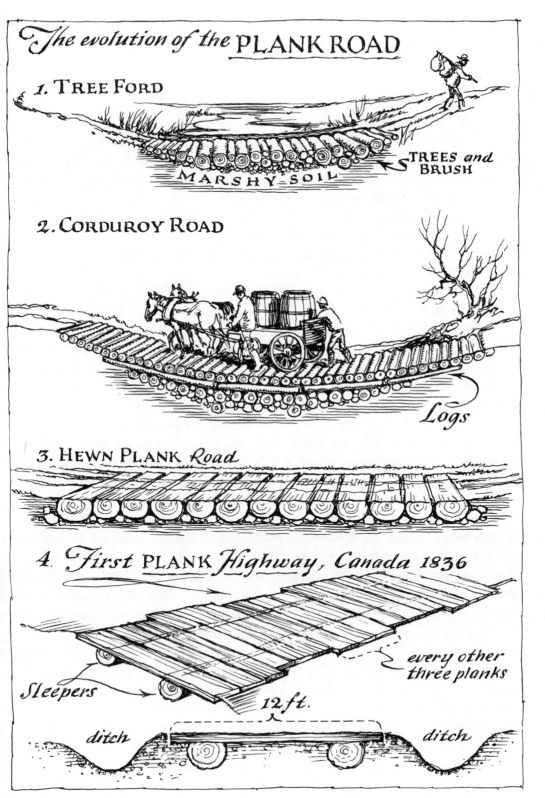

The evolution of the PLANK ROAD

1. TREE FORD

TREES *and* BRUSH

MARSHY SOIL

2. CORDUROY ROAD

Logs

3. HEWN PLANK *Road*

4. *First* PLANK *Highway*, Canada 1836

every other three planks

Sleepers

ditch

12 ft.

ditch

179

WOODEN ROADS

THE ONLY REMINDER of the American plank road might be those highways which still bear the name. The fifteen-mile Paterson Plank Road in New Jersey which was once known as the Farmer's Railroad to New York, is now buried under the modern roadways, yet old residents still refer to the route as the plank road. Only seventy-five years ago, the whole country was webbed with such paths of wood, enough to level forests of pine and hemlock, tamarack, oak, and walnut. In 1875 there were close to three thousand miles of plank roads in New York alone, and by 1880 the idea had spread to every other state.

The first plank road was possibly those short inclined wooden entrances that led to covered bridges, but the first registered plank highway on this continent was the one built in Canada in 1836. This road had twenty-inch planks lying lengthwise, but the next Canadian plank road had "skewed" planks, set diagonally at a forty-five degree angle. When the idea struck the United States, however, the custom was to lay planks directly across the road, at right angles to the direction of the highway.

The word "highway" came from old Europe, where there was always a smooth private road for the King, with an adjoining lower shelf road for commoners. The American plank roads which so resembled that arrangement, with their elevated plank sections and adjoining dirt "turn-off" roads, were at once called Highways and the name has stuck.

Canadian plank roads introduced the idea of using irregular edges, so that wagons could "climb" back onto the planks after having gone off to the dirt turn-off to pass another wagon. A smooth edge would have caused the wagon wheels to just slide along the straight-edge without mounting the planks. At first, every other three planks were set a-jog about four or five inches, but this spacing caused very small wheels to get hung and stuck in the opening. The American plank road at once adopted the idea of projecting every other plank four inches from the edge. This not only enabled wheels to climb back aboard again, but caused an effective series of short warning bumps when the wagon got too close to the edge. Likewise, wherever a sharp curve was approached, planks were set a small distance apart to produce a rumble and awaken the sleepy driver to alertness.

Plank-road design varied, but the design of New York State roads became an average plank-road dimension that was copied throughout the country. The usual road grant was of one chain width (66 feet), with a roadbed of thirty feet and a plank path at least eight feet wide. With ditches for drainage, an earth turn-off track of about twelve feet, the finished plank road was covered with sand or wood shavings. Even today, a well-kept plank road would make a more desirable highway for horse-and-wagon traffic than a modern concrete highway. Horses when given a free rein, on a dirt turn-off, would automatically pull up onto the plank road where the going was perfect both for wagon wheels and horse's hoofs.

The planks themselves were from three to four inches thick and from nine to sixteen inches wide. They were laid on top of "sleepers" or rails. Canadian plank roads put two spikes in each plank, nailing it to the sleeper, but the American custom was more often to lay planks loose and let gravel and their own weight keep them in place. Even when the planks went across a bridge, they were laid loose, and up until a few years ago, the thunder of planks when a car drove across a small bridge, was pleasant relaxation to any cross-country driver.

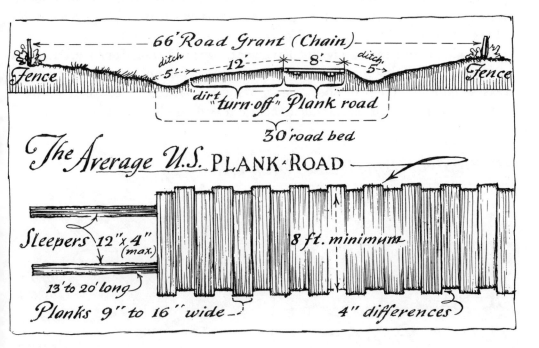

Sleepers varied in size from four by six inches to four by twelve (laid flat) but many small roads left them out altogether. Long stone rollers were used to flatten out the road and push sleepers into the dirt before laying the planks on top. Hidden away in many a barn are still those stone rollers which often baffle the antiquarians.

The cost of a plank road, including gate-houses and surveying, averaged a thousand dollars to two thousand dollars a mile. An oak road was built to last for twelve years and a pine road was considered good for four. The New York Senate reported in 1870 that "plank roads are a more profitable investment than gravel or stone: they never break up in winter thaws or fall away in spring freshets the way paved roads do." Canada reported costs to be four to one in favor of wood.

As plank roads were originally built for profit by tolls, it might interest the student to learn exactly what such tolls were. The New York Plank Road Law established the following tolls in the 1870's:

"Any vehicle drawn by one horse, ¾ cents per mile. For vehicles drawn by two horses, 1½ cents per mile, and ½ cent additional for each extra horse. For a horse and rider, or a led horse, ½ cent. For every score of sheep, swine or neat cattle, one cent per mile."

Plank roads ended where the towns began, but the efficiency of wood paving still carried on its crusade. Every retired man with a flare for engineering and an eye toward an easy income, designed his own kind of wooden brick or patented paving. Most popular was a wooden block pavement set between thin wooden planks and covered with gravel or tar.

"Wood is better than stone for pavement," wrote Frank Johnson, M.D., in a pamphlet for "Nicolson Pavement," in 1867, "for any pavement that increases the destruction of shoe, horse, vehicle, chaise, or decreases comfort and convenience is not economical though it costs nothing and lasts forever."

a Nicolson type Wood Pavement of 1867

Tar or gravel filled into spaces

Oak   Pine

3" wide blocks
¾" boards
Gravel

182

COVERED BRIDGES

THERE ARE THOSE who have the ability to recognize unchanged scenes, who can easily step into the picture of today and listen to the past. To those favored few, covered bridges are always irresistible. Like old watermills, they seem to echo clearer the mood and sounds of the past where in the shadowed recesses of a stream and along the banks of winding dirt roads, American life first developed.

At one time covered bridges were as much a part of any journey as are today's traffic signals. Most country roads followed the banks of a river and at every bend there was one or more of these barnlike structures thrown across the water like drawbridges over a moat to some little kingdom.

Vermont which is known as the "Covered Bridge State" to many, surprises some by being only fifth in number of bridges, with one hundred and twenty-one covered bridges at present. Vermont's interest in caring for her bridges, however, is possibly first. Pennsylvania has the most, with three hundred and ninety; Ohio is second with three hundred and forty-nine; Indiana and Oregon follow closely behind. At least one covered bridge a week vanishes from the American landscape or rots unattended in the shadow of a new concrete structure, but a few are still being constructed!

Although Connecticut has only three covered bridges left, the Housatonic River alone had eighteen fine examples, each marking a community of mills that has since grown into a riverside town. Connecticut was proud of its bridges, particularly because the two most famous names in bridge engineering, Theodore Burr and Ithiel Town were born there. But ambitious men of those days spread their work in far places: although Burr and Town designed hundreds of covered bridges in almost every state, Connecticut never had more than fifty.

The reasons for covering bridges varied with the builder, but they had primarily to do with strengthening the structure and making the wood season properly and last longer. The more romantic reason for making the bridge appear like a barn, so horses would not shy at the running water, is doubtful. But it adds to the rich lore that surrounds the old landmarks. It fooled two inebriated men of Bennington, Vermont, so the story goes. They approached the bridge there, and thought they had come to their own barn. Dismounting and unhitching their animal so it could go to its stall, they soon found their

183

"The Y bridge" at Zanesville, Ohio, 1832

had a Measuring device installed after a Wagon got stuck in it

Hartland, N.B. Covered Bridge,,, called the longest, (1285 ft.) 8 piers

..beat by the Clark's Ferry Pa. Bridge.

1841

184

2088 ft. long! 10 piers

Unusual Covered Bridges

The Humpback Bridge near Covington, Virginia

The Chiselville Bridge, Vermont was insured against being washed out by flood ... built forty feet over the water!

Twin bridges at Rutland, Vermont ... the result of the stream's change of route

185

mistake but lost their horse and had to pull their wagon by foot the rest of the way home.

The closing in of a bridge to make it appear like a barn must have had its merits when drovers passed through with their cattle, for cows led easily into the welcome shade. In fact they often refused to leave and needed urging to come out the other end. Meat was delivered on the hoof in the old days, and often one herd of cattle made up for a week of poor business at the toll bridge. A yearly account book of the Toll Bridge between Windsor, Vermont, and Cornish, New Hampshire, shows about seventeen thousand creatures passing through on their way to Boston. Drovers sometimes came through with mixed herds and the tolls then became so complicated that an itemized bill sometimes had to be made up and sent by post. One story tells of a farmer who included two hundred turkeys in his drove from Dedham to Boston: when he reached a bridge, the toll-taker refused to let the turkeys pass because turkeys were not listed on the bridge's toll-board.

A reason for covering a bridge, which has seldom been mentioned, is for appearances. When toll-collecting was entirely a private enterprise, there was something distinct about using a covered structure which seemed to make a bridge passage worth that much more. The added expense would seem unnecessary today, but bridges were often built for resale and they were therefore made to look as attractive as possible.

Many people think that covered bridges are the oldest kind of American bridge, but the first covered bridges appeared after 1800. Charles Wilson Peale, well known for his paintings of Washington, wrote an "Essay on Building Wooden Bridges" in 1797, in which he stated, "It has been advised to make roofs to cover bridges and some of them are to be constructed in America." Timothy Palmer is given the credit for being the builder of the first American covered bridge, at least the only one of which there is some accurate record. That bridge was over the Delaware at Easton, Pennsylvania, and it bore the words on its portal: "T. Palmer, Bldr., 1805."

Earliest America knew no bridges at all. There were simply stepping stones for foot travelers and fording-places for horses and riders. Stepping stones were once so much a part of every village road that rope handrails were often supplied by the village, and the repair and replacement of stones was included in road-maker's contracts. Bridges were built adjacent to fords so that when a bridge washed out, a crossing by wading or swimming would not be too far away from the road. Over fifty years ago, travelers by wagon often ignored small bridges entirely during summer but drove off the road and crossed at the nearby fording-places so their horses could get a drink at the same time. And twenty-five years ago, these same fording-places were used for washing automobiles. Today small bridges and fording-places are

186

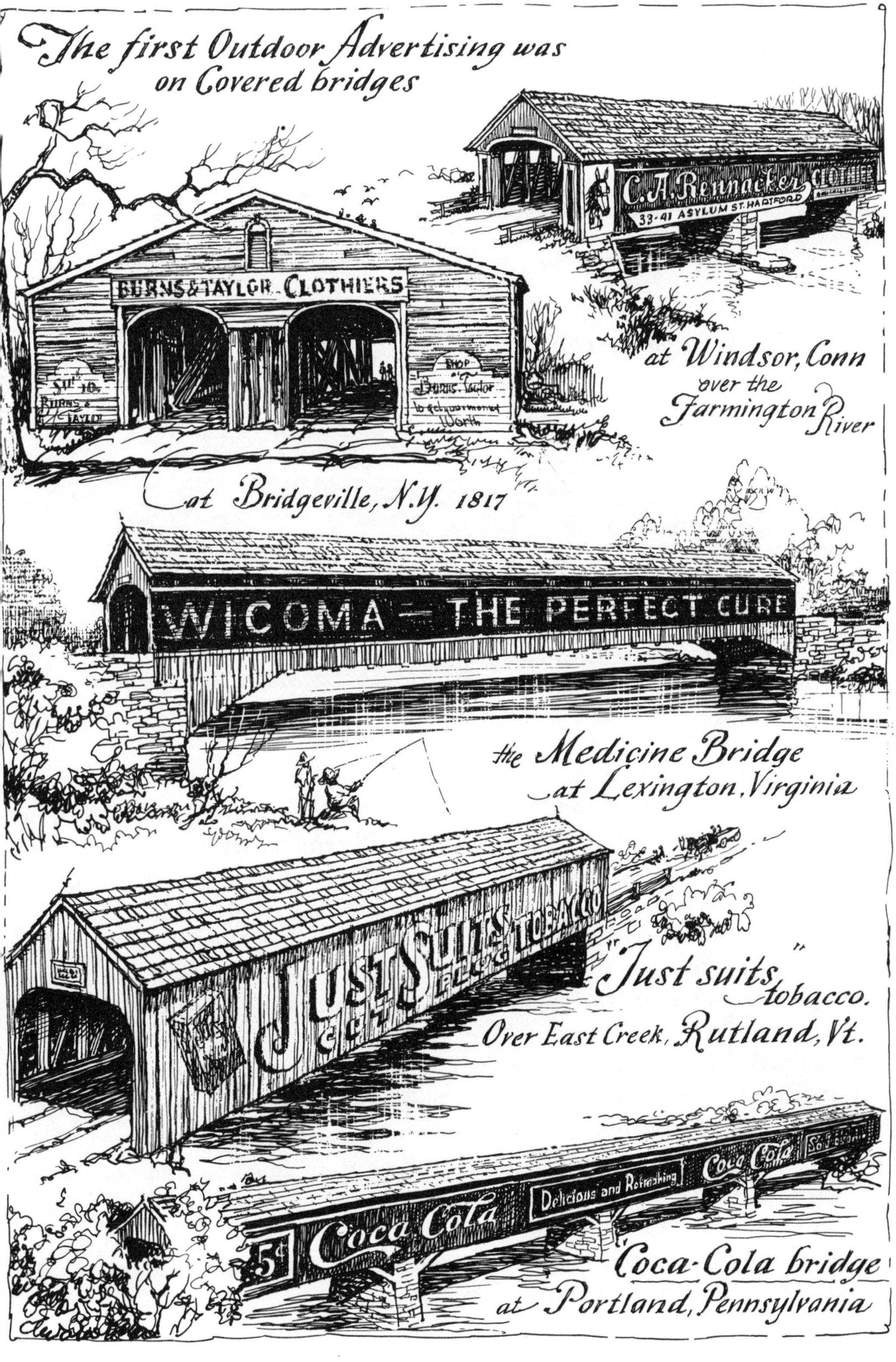

The first Outdoor Advertising was on Covered bridges

BURNS & TAYLOR CLOTHIERS

at Bridgeville, N.Y. 1817

C. A. Rennacker CLOTHIER
33-41 ASYLUM ST. HARTFORD

at Windsor, Conn
over the
Farmington River

WICOMA — THE PERFECT CURE

the Medicine Bridge
at Lexington, Virginia

JUST SUITS TOBACCO

"Just suits" tobacco.
Over East Creek, Rutland, Vt.

5¢ Coca-Cola   Delicious and Refreshing   Coca-Cola

Coca-Cola bridge
at Portland, Pennsylvania

187

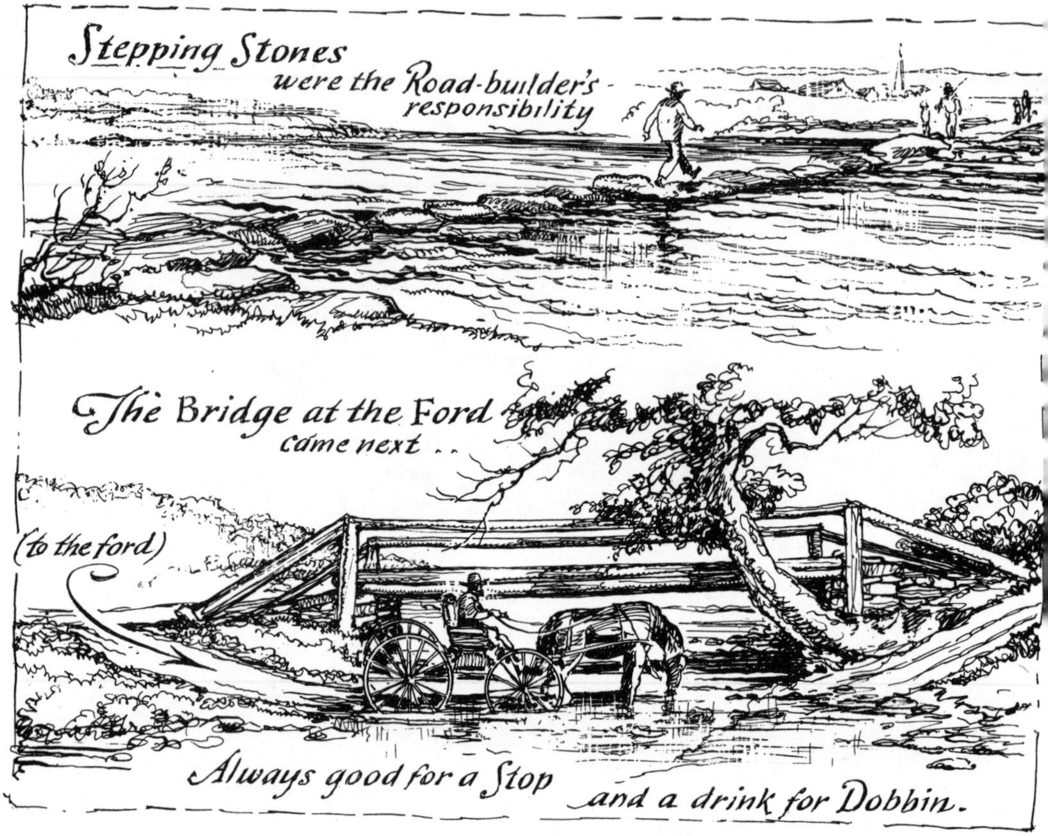

Stepping Stones were the Road-builder's responsibility

The Bridge at the Ford came next ..

(to the ford)

Always good for a Stop and a drink for Dobbin.

only rural memories: motor cars zoom over cement culverts and dried-up streams where a stop at the brook was once a pleasant event of any journey.

Some of America's oldest stone bridges still remain. Even many of the obsolete zigzag or "Z-Bridges" which are now bypassed by new structures, still stand. These erratic bridges which stump the experts with their reason for being, were mostly centered around the old National Road in Ohio, where they persisted into the automobile age, piling up more wrecks than their picturesqueness was ever worth. Some say they were designed in shape of a "Z" in memory of pioneer Ebenezer Zane. Others say it was a method of making horses break from a gallop into a walk while crossing a bridge. Another theory is that they were designed by the builders of the National Road to discourage a new forty-foot freight wagon which was being considered at the time. A forty-foot wagon with horses pulling it, of course, could not maneuver such a crooked bridge without getting caught between the zigzag walls. Whatever the idea of the bridge was, the builders forgot winter when they designed it for snow piled up within the crooked roadway and even sleds avoided Z-bridges during snowy weather.

ONE MIGHT wonder why the inventory of early American implements does not include some sort of road snowplow. The reason is that snow was never a threat but rather was it an asset to the average road traffic of a hundred years ago. The last thing an old-time farmer would think of doing would be to clear snow from his road, for he had looked forward all year to the time that he could use snow-covered roads for hauling his heavier loads. At the first sign of snow, sleds of all sorts emerged from the barns, and the hauling of timber or stones began without the bother of bogged wheels or the slough of mud. When the snow finally began to melt, the farmer put away his sleds and he forgot about further heavy transportation.

The only winter road equipment of yesterday was a machine to preserve snow. The "Vermont snow-roller" packed snow down to make it smooth and to make it last longer. Consisting of wooden rollers and a platform on top for rock-ballast, this machine is now probably one of the scarcest pieces of New England Americana. Shelburne Museum in Vermont unearthed what they believed to be one of the last snow-rollers. But even this book might bring to light others hidden away in barns, that were hitherto listed as unexplainable farm equipment.

Sleds were once used both with or without snow, wherever there was any heavy hauling job to be done. There were "stone boats" for moving rocks, lumber-sleds for logs, pungs for general farm use and innumerable sleighs for pleasure and personal transportation. Children tobogganned down grassy

Z-Bridge

New Concord, Ohio. 1828

189

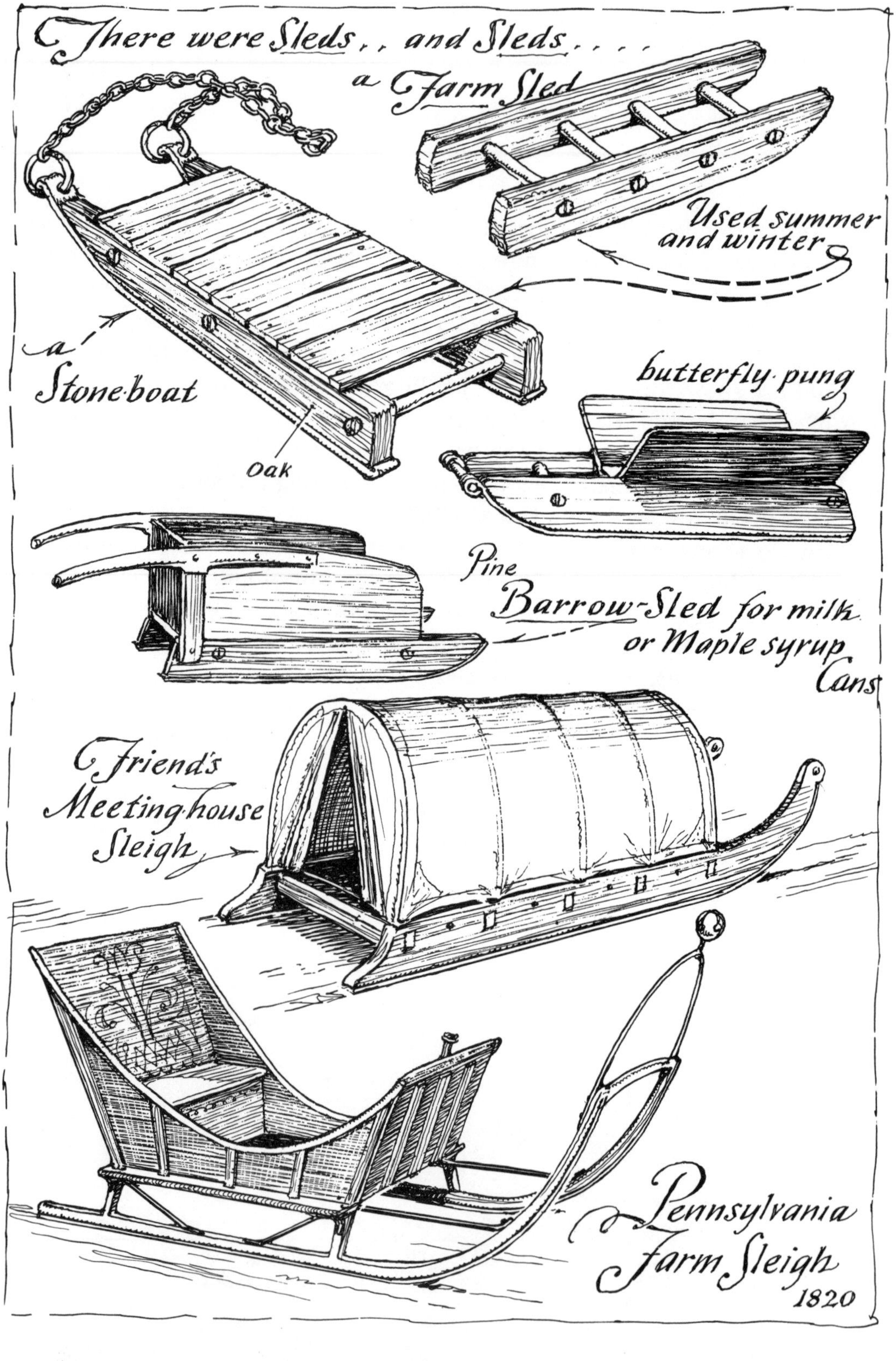

There were Sleds.. and Sleds.....

a Farm Sled

a Stone boat

Oak

Used summer and winter

butterfly pung

Pine Barrow-Sled for milk or Maple syrup Cans

Friend's Meeting house Sleigh

Pennsylvania Farm Sleigh 1820

slopes during the summer almost as easily as they did on snow during the winter. If a farmer of the past could return today, his first reaction might be wonder at the disappearance of sleds from the rural scene.

Far preceding the invention of the wheel, and the crudest vehicle known, the sled is also the fastest. In 1954 a sled was chosen as a rocket-propelled land machine which reached the record of 632 miles an hour. The object was to determine how much acceleration a man can stand leaping from a jet plane. After discarding wheeled vehicles as being too frail, a sled that could have done service in any farmer's barn was built to make the final test. Sleds were

Rocks

Vermont Snow-Roller

..it didn't Clear the Snow..it Packed it

Summer-sledding in South Carolina

191

also the fastest thing in the world of a hundred years ago, for the sail-sled or iceboat was doing sixty miles an hour when railroad trains were still in the creeping stage. One of the most popular Currier and Ives prints shows iceboats racing trains up and down the Hudson River, where there were ice-yachting clubs with memberships in the thousands. The milding winters and disappearance of suitable ice is now making the iceboat a thing of the past, but its record average speed in excess of 145 miles an hour (faster than that of a sports car), testifies to the efficiency of the sled principle. Oddly enough, Oliver Booth who built the first ice yacht in 1790 at Poughkeepsie, New York, predicted that he had designed what would become the fastest land vehicle in the world.

My book, *American Barns and Covered Bridges* drew many critical letters about a drawing that showed two horses hauling a load of sixteen cords of wood on a jack-sled. They said it was impossible and that the drawing looked ridiculous. The drawing, however, was traced from an actual photograph in a New York State *Conservationist Magazine,* and it seems still not to be the record. So here is a later tracing from the October, 1954, issue of the same magazine, showing an even greater load. "The load contains 157 logs," reads the account, "and the number of feet in the load was 35 markets." A market is a lumbering term meaning a log 16 inches in diameter at the small end and thirteen feet long, so 35 markets would be equal to one gigantic log 455 feet long. "The logs were hauled five miles," the account continues, "where this picture was posed with fifteen men besides Mr. Ingram the reinsman, seated or standing on top of the load."

The first Ice Yacht was a box on runners

Thirteen feet above the sled, 16 men aboard!

TURNPIKES

MANY of our busiest modern highways are called turnpikes without those who travel upon them really knowing how the word "turnpike" originated. A turnpike was a turnstile for wagons with horses or oxen: originally it was an actual pike or pole that turned on an axle to admit travelers after a toll had been paid. Long Island's Union Turnpike, Jericho Turnpike, and all the other "turnpikes" throughout the country are names carried over from the past when a pike turned or raised to admit travelers past the tollhouse. There is hardly an old highway today that was not at one time a privately owned turnpike built for profit. The turnpike age was a colorful part of Americana of which little is remembered: it brought towns closer, and made a few men rich, but, more important, it laid out the economic landscape in a manner that has continued for over a hundred years.

193

Turnpike roads were roads built by a company that charged admission, payable at tollgates along the way. The rates were variable and the laws inconsistent until the early part of the nineteenth century when rates were regulated by turnpike commissioners who were appointed by the House of Representatives.

Here is a typical Connecticut act of the year 1836:

> The several turnpike companies in this state are authorized to collect the following toll at each gate where a toll is allowed by law;
>> For each wagon, body not hung on springs, drawn by one horse, *six cents and three mills.*
>> For each four wheeled pleasure carriage, drawn by one horse, *eight cents.*
>> For each wagon for transporting loads, two beasts, *twelve cents and five mills;* for each additional beast, *three cents.*
>> If such wagons are empty, half the sums aforesaid.

The section following reads,

> "No turnpike company will collect these tolls unless voting the following exemptions to wit: all persons travelling to or returning from a meeting of public worship, if such a meeting is held in the adjoining town; also persons going to or returning from military service." It further stated that persons traveling less than four miles on ordinary farming business, were also exempt from paying the turnpike toll.

The turnpike tolls were at one time so complicated that the collector almost had to have mathematical training to survive. A percentage was added during the winter, yet sleighs went by for a cent less than wagons. A mule paid the same as a horse, but two oxen paid the same price as one horse. To add to com-

194

Spear or "pike" used on Long Island's Hempstead Turnpike

Tollgate in Norfolk, Conn. Greenwoods Turnpike

plications, the width of wagon tires regulated the admission to turnpikes because narrow wheels caused ruts, while wide wheels helped to flatten the road. Some of the wagon-wheel tires were six and eight inches wide, designed to save tolls, and even wide detachable tires were invented to put over thin wheels. There were scouts who watched out for those who removed their "cut-rate" detachable tires when out of sight of the toll-collector, and a fine of one extra toll was collected for that offense. Those who knew the countryside, often made "shunpike" trails around tollhouses, some of which eventually became permanent roads parallel to the turnpike. The Lancaster-Philadelphia Turnpike had nine tollgates in all, spaced about seven miles apart, so there was plenty of room for shunpike activity in the Pennsylvania hills.

Before 1800 about seventy-five turnpike companies had incorporated and were selling shares. The Philadelphia and Lancaster Turnpike Road Company was the first, and its road was built at a cost of $465,000, all of which was provided by individual investors. Within an hour after its subscription books were open, the company had sold over twenty thousand dollars worth of shares at thirteen dollars a share. The road was completed in 1806 at a cost of about $7,500 a mile. The success of this road paved the way for a new era in American business, and short connecting private turnpikes sprang up all over the Pennsylvanian landscape. The Dauphin Turnpike in Pennsylvania reported that in one year (and before the snows of winter closed its gates) sixteen thousand people had passed by.

195

In 1800, the first turnpike in Long Island opened for farm wagons, but within a short time there were many pleasure turnpikes leading to the nearby beaches and mountain resorts. The Jamaica and Rockaway Turnpikes in New York were used every day during the summer season, and were filled with carriages that came across on the ferry from Manhattan to Brooklyn.

The success of the turnpike business, however, was short-lived. Public interest leaned toward the railroads, which were more dependable than muddy turnpikes, and private road fortunes disappeared overnight when the government took an active interest in turnpike business. The first road built with funds from the National Treasury was the Great National Pike, once called the Cumberland Road which linked Cumberland, Maryland, to Vandalia, Illinois. It was built in sections from 1806 to 1840, and was hailed as the first link in bringing the east and the west together. The National Pike was America's first great highway and as one historian put it, ". . . the road looked more like the avenue of a great city than a trail through the country."

A full team pulling a Conestoga wagon stretched out to sixty feet in length, so turnpike traffic must have been a problem, even if the going was slow. The custom of leading a horse from the left, and the convenience of having the teamster's seat also on the left side of the wagon, is why turnpike wagons traveled to the right of the road; because of that, Americans started driving on the right side of the road.

The early 1900's found turnpikes taken over by the automobile which unfortunately could not go through mud-puddles or around stumps in the road as horse-drawn vehicles could. Early touring cars that ventured on highways were therefore equipped with spades and wooden planks.

Peru, Vermont 1913
"10 cents a mile but bring
your own mud-planks."

The complaints of the automobile trade and the failure to improve turn-pikes sounded the final death knell of private turnpikes. Typical of this problem was the Peru Turnpike of Vermont which was listed as a "must" in the "Ideal Tour" for vacationers through the Berkshires and White Mountains. The Rutland *Herald* reported that it had 150 water bars on five miles of road. Tourists carried their own "mud-planks" to bridge these handicaps and then complained bitterly at the fifty-cents' admission fee which amounted to ten cents a mile. After five years of such complaints by the automobile tourist trade, the Peru Turnpike gave up, and the road became a free thoroughfare.

BICYCLES

ONE MIGHT presume that the hard-top road was the result of the automobile age, yet the first such roads were designed for the sole use of bicycles. While automobiles were still struggling along back-country dirt roads, bicycle clubs had organized into powerful groups who sponsored hard-top roads, even paying for building them. The League of American Wheelmen was the first organized group of American voters to demand better roads. In fact, many members included demands that automobiles be barred from improved bicycle roads, or at least placed on adjacent gravel road sections.

At the end of the 1800's the bicycle had become a national issue. People were spending over a hundred dollars for a bicycle, often keeping four or five in one household at a time when a fine buggy could be bought for fifty dollars.

197

Hundreds of factories were turning out over a million bicycles a year and many businesses had to gear themselves to the bicycle-age or fail. The clothing industry featured bicycle-wear for everyday street use. Hat manufacturers, after appealing to Congress to make every cyclist buy two hats with every bicycle, settled on making cycling caps for men and women. Whole church sermons were devoted to the bicycle. "Whether bicycle riding on Sunday is sinful or not," the *Wheelman* of 1882 read, "depends upon the spirit and associations of the ride." Amelia Bloomer designed the famous trousers for women cyclers that shook the fashion world, and businessmen came to work in bicycle pants and stockings.

Whatever the social and economic influences of the bicycle were, its influence toward scientific road-building is still felt in present-day America, although we who regard the bicycle as a toy, find it hard to believe.

ROAD SIGNS

MILESTONES were the first road signs. Even highway inns failed to take advantage of road advertising and they depended entirely upon one sign on the building to advise the traveler of their trade, often no more than the name of the proprietor. Covered bridges were first to gather advertising matter. Perhaps they were prompted by their necessary toll-list and "Walk your horse" signs, but by the middle of the 1800's the inside cross-timbers of covered bridges were filled with posters. Kickapoo Indian Oil, Kendall's Spavin Cure, Dr. Flint's Powders and other familiar trade names of the time, printed strips to fit standard eight-by-eight bridge timbers, and out of the shadows of old bridge portals were born the first attempts at American national advertising.

Although we all know that Bull Durham Tobacco, along with Mail Pouch, Carter's Little Liver Pills, Fletcher's (*children cry for it*) Castoria, Bromo-Seltzer, and Miles Laboratories gained first recognition from the sides of old barns, it is strange that there are no historical records left of this fact. "While the writer has been with the concern for twenty years," writes the head of one of the aforementioned companies, "he has no information concerning painting on barns done by this Company in the past. He therefore talked to our advertising manager who came with the Company forty years ago. He neither

198

can recall anything about signs on barns. We regret our inability to give you information about an important milestone in our business and in the industry of American advertising."

Because barn advertisements were first painted to be seen from the trains, and covered bridges existed before established railroads, it may be said that covered bridge signs came first. When bridge signs lost popularity to the thousands of barns that could be seen by train travelers, the entrance walls of covered bridges became place for only local announcements and circus posters. The few ancient theatrical posters that were protected from weather by the wide portals of old covered bridges and are still intact against the sun and snows of a hundred years, have now become collector's prizes.

Perhaps you have noticed during drives through the country, chalked arrows and other strange markings on telephone poles. This is the language of the circus, put there by an advance man to inform and direct the performers

Sharp turn, big hill, Good Coffee

to their next destination. A double arrow means a sharp curve, other lines warn of steep hills, detours, unfriendly policemen, or even good restaurants. Even the performers are seldom aware of it, but these chalked signs are things handed down from the time when the circus was frowned upon, had to hold secret performances, and was guided by such signs to avoid unfriendly towns. Connecticut's Acts and Laws of 1784 ruled that no one "shall exhibit on any Public Stage or Place, any Tricks, Plays, Juggling or Feats of uncommon dexterity, tending to no good and useful Purposes, but tending to collect together Numbers of Spectators and gratify vain or useless Curiosity." Theatrical exhibitions continued to be against the law, even a hundred years ago in many places, and circuses were often named in the Statutes as "public nuisances."

America's barns were painted red because the only paint available at first was that which the farmer could mix himself, using home-grown linseed oil and red oxide of iron. But many of the first paint companies were formed by the sign-painters themselves who painted barns for the privilege of including an advertising sign on the highway or railroad side of the barn. They were armed with printed stories of how paint preserves wood, and sometimes had one half of their wagon painted while the other side was left bare to prove their point. The bare side of course, was in terrible condition with the help of shotgun "wormholes" and "termite" gougings by the sign-painter himself. The real truth is that the oldest barns in America are usually the unpainted ones while those with many coats of paint have long since disappeared. This is no condemnation of paint, which is necessary for most of today's lumber. It is proof of the well-seasoned virgin timber of yesterday which was allowed to breathe and dry by contact with the weather, and lasted longer without the use of paint that might have sealed moisture inside.

The itinerant sign-painter was one of the little-sung artists of America who left a lasting impression on the lore of the countryside. Actually, many of our first portrait and landscape artists were traveling sign-painters. Edward Hicks whose "Peaceable Kingdom" has become a masterpiece of primitive American art, lettered mileposts for country roads, did signs for taverns and painted a gigantic Washington Crossing the Delaware for a covered bridge at McKonkey's Ferry. Thomas Hicks of the same family did coach-painting and commercial signs, yet left his name behind as a master at portraits.

The traveling sign-painter of a few years ago was seldom a recognized artist, but he, too, left an impression behind. With his office in his hat and no more equipment than he could hold in a small box, people got to know his work and waited till the next time he came through town for the signs. Many sign-painters were as much dependent on a bottle which was usually evident in their paintbox, as they were upon their paints. Yet many were quite the opposite, spending their spare time denouncing drink in signs on abandoned houses and barns. Some were evangelists who, instead of signing their own names to a piece of work, added a line or two from the Bible. When they had nothing to do for the moment, and a high rock made an inviting medium, they could never resist putting the word of the Lord there too. You could hardly venture out of town without seeing "Jesus Saves," "The Love of the Lord is Good,"

Signs of Civilization

or whole passages from the Psalms written on whatever flat surface the landscape offered. One such rock on which was painted "Stop and Repent," rolled downhill during a spring freshet and ended near the middle of the road near Brattleboro, Vermont. Wagons drove around it for a long while, thinking it was a religious monument placed there for some good reason, until it was finally removed by the State.

During the winter when the going was hard, the traveling sign-painter spent his time doing cardboard signs which he later carried with him and sold on the road. "In God we trust, all others Cash" was a close favorite over "We'll crank your car and hold your baby, but we won't cash checks and we don't mean maybe." Country banks were always a prospect for ready-made road-warning signs such as "Go slow and see our country; go fast and see our jail," "Drive Slow—you might meet another fool," or "Sharp turn ahead— prepare to meet your Maker."

Not long ago when people traveled slowly enough to read road-signs, most cities had billboards at both ends of town that featured a short history of the

201

a Spreader Sign

place. A tire manufacturer took over this idea and made road-signs in the shape of big history books; they educated the traveler, however, more than they sold tires. In a small village, the sign-painter could always contract as many shopkeepers as there were letters in the name of the town and put up a "spreader-sign." Spreader-signs had one large letter on top of each advertisement so that when seen in a line on the highway by the oncoming traveler, they spelled out the name of the town. Many an eastern sign-painter contracted and collected for a spreader-sign only to find that hard western ground is too stubborn to dig pole-holes into. There was nothing to do then but to place the signs in dents in the ground and get out of town before the wind blew them down. Spreader-signs are still to be seen in the western part of the United States, but the idea took hold in a different version in 1926, when the Burma Shave Company put up a series of signs on U. S. Highway 65 near Lakeville, Minnesota. It said, "Cheer up . . . face . . . The war . . . is over" But it soon changed to a rhymed, "Hinky-dinky . . . Parley-Voo . . . Cheer up face . . . The war . . . is through." Now, the Burma Shave Company changes its seven thousand sets of rhymed signs once a year and finds its idea has become an accepted part of the American highway landscape.

Free water for Autoists

When Taverns where built to be, Taverns, and *looked* like Taverns . . .

The King of Prussia 1709
Pennsylvania

Burnham Tavern
Machias, Maine
1770

The Rising Sun
Fredericksburg, Va
1760

Munford Inn,
Munfordsville, Ky
built of 30 ft. walnut logs, 1800

Salem Tavern, Winston-Salem, N.C.
1772

The Jolly Post-Boy, Frankford, Pa.
1749

Munroe Tavern 1695
Lexington, Mass.

Fraunce's Tavern N.Y.C.

203

ROADSIDE taverns are by no means disappearing from the American land-scape, but their changes are worthy of noting here. Like the big city which has reached a limit in size and has now begun to spread out into the suburbs and countryside, the tavern, too, has reached its limit. Dispersed over the country as motels and houses made into small hotels with "tourist accomodations," the average rural tavern of today is a far cry from that of a hundred years ago.

In the beginning, the tavern was built to be a tavern. It was the club and meeting-place for those who lived nearby and the place where news always arrived first. The first tavern-keepers were nominated yearly. Connecticut's "Acts and Laws" of 1780 read that "the Civil Authority, Selectmen, Constables and Grand-jury-men in the respective Towns of this State, shall some time in the month of January annually, nominate the Person or Persons whom they, or the major Part of them think fit and suitable to keep an House or Houses of public Entertainment in the said Town for the ensuing year." Inn-keepers were not always nominated, however, though they were always looked upon as village officials; to get a license they had to be "passed by select-men, and possessed of a comfortable estate." The tavern-keeper's duties were many, and stiff fines were levied from their cash bond for infractions. For example, the tavern-keeper had to "post the names of tavern-haunters on his door" and refuse drink to those men who were judged by the authorities to be tipplers and idlers at the bar.

In the 1800's when road information became a part of most almanacs, the innkeepers themselves were known more than any actual names of their inns. In fact, they were listed in the following manner:

You will notice that Dedham and Attleborough have two inns listed. In such cases where the coach might have hurried past one of the inns, a flag or a ball signal was used to stop it for a passenger or mail. Although the Americanism "ballin' the jack" and "highballin' through" which is used to indicate a no-stop expresslike speed, is credited to railroad language, it first came from stagecoach slang. A large metal ball was lowered to the ground as a signal to stop, but a "high-ball" hoisted to the top of the post meant "go right on." The same signal continued on into the railroad age and trains "highballed" past no-passenger stations.

In the 1800's a tavern always had its flagpole and religiously displayed the national flag. The American flag and flagpole is unfortunately a characteristic

204

ROADS

to the principal towns, from Boston, with names of the innkeepers and distances in miles.

Boston to Newport.

Roxbury	Whiting	8
Dedham	Ames and Gay	3
	Ellis	3
Walpole	Polly	7
Wrentham	Hall	6
Attleborough	Hatch	5
	Newell	4
Rehoboth	Carpenter	7
Warren	Cole	8
Bristol	Bourn	4
Ferry-house	Pearse	2
Portsmouth	Congden	7
Newport		5
		69 miles

The HIGH BALL

of the vanishing landscape, when almost every country home had its flagpole and every household had an American flag.

Stagecoach-drivers were like truck-drivers of today in finding the best and cheapest place to eat along the highway. Wherever there was an authorized traveler's inn, there was also a teamster's and drover's tavern close by, noted for its food and drink. Our modern version, the "highway diner" has likewise contributed roadside hospitality to commercial drivers and has elevated itself to a top position with the traveler too. Beginning as a "lunch wagon" or "dining car," the first diners were built from discarded trolley-cars. Even now, the proportions and windows and curved roof of trolley-car anatomy have prevailed in the most expensive and plush models. It is odd that long after trolley-cars have disappeared from the American scene, their architecture should live on as restaurants.

The modern American architect has had no fair trial at designing public taverns. There are those who specialize in "Old English" or "Rathskeller" façades and the result is too often a cartoon-effect of overseas tavern architecture. So-called "good taste" was not the most desirable quality in early tavern design, but the vigorous and functional simplicity that suggested the

205

purpose of the building, made it as individual in the American landscape, as the church.

In every big city you will find one or two untouched taverns where people go to enjoy escape from modern neon restlessness. The fact that such places are old is not as important as that the effects of age have been allowed to stay. Friendliness and comfort have not yet caught up with the modern cleanliness and smartness of our new highway architecture, and there are still those who would trade chromium brightness for the dim restfulness of the past.

The first one

COUNTRY CHURCHES

As you approach any unspoiled American village, the first heart-warming sight is the tall white spire of a church. A little slower to go the way of the covered bridge and the little red schoolhouse, the little old-fashioned church remains one of the last symbols of a vanished landscape. Occasionally you will find a fine example left intact, but too often looking out of place in the city that has grown up around it, like an ancient tombstone or monument to the past.

By the early 1800's the American meeting house had reached a degree of architectural elegance unsurpassed by other buildings of that time. As boxlike

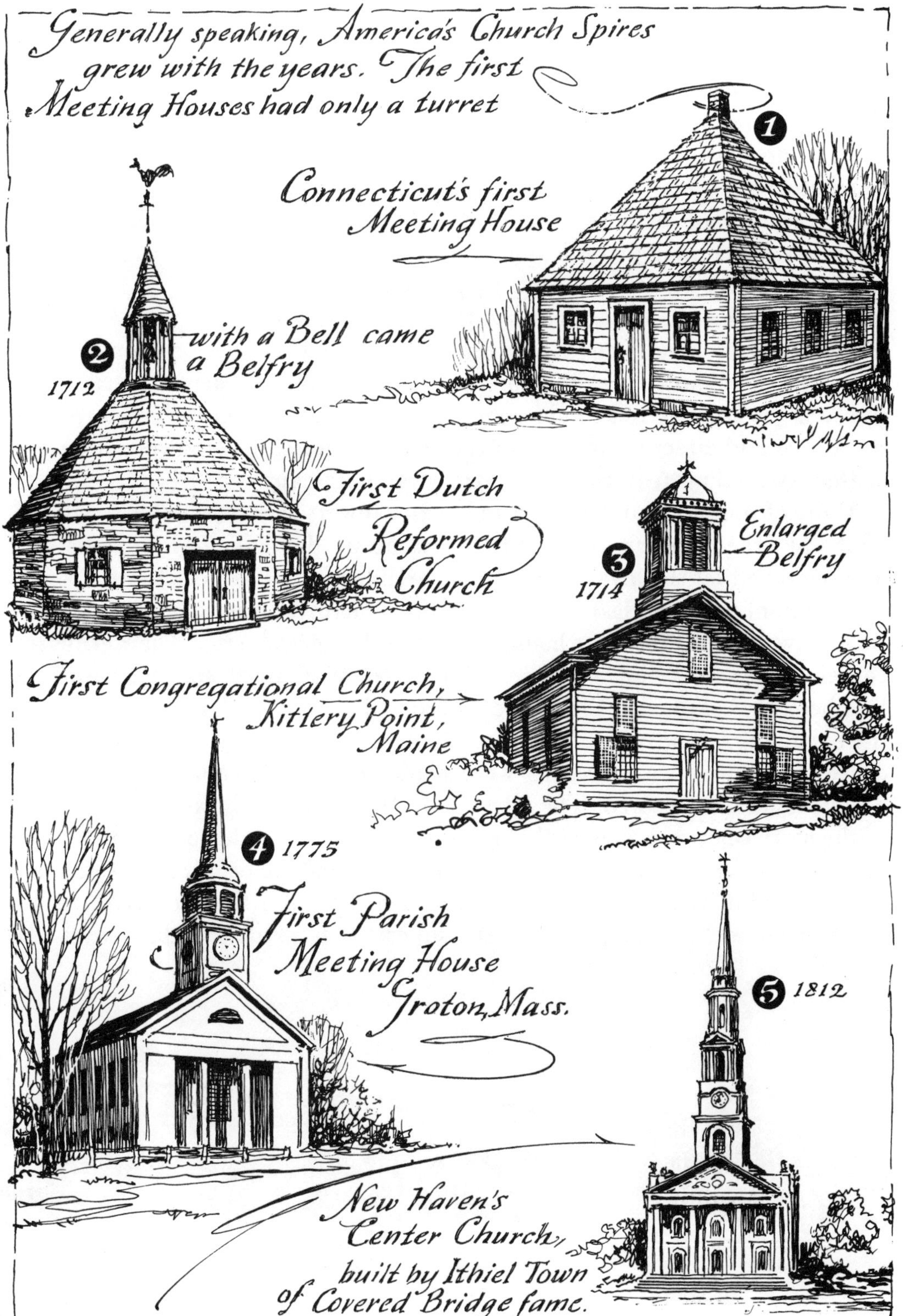

Generally speaking, America's Church Spires grew with the years. The first Meeting Houses had only a turret

① Connecticut's first Meeting House

② 1712 with a Bell came a Belfry

First Dutch Reformed Church

③ 1714 Enlarged Belfry

First Congregational Church, Kittery Point, Maine

④ 1775 First Parish Meeting House Groton, Mass.

⑤ 1812

New Haven's Center Church, built by Ithiel Town of Covered Bridge fame.

and plain as they may have been, they were always classic in their portrayal of their reason for being. At first there was no attempt to copy Europe's monumental stone churches and there was no ornamentation to remind one of the English Church which the Puritans had left behind. But when bells were cast on this side of the sea and a belfry or steeple was built to house them, the tall spire became part of the structure. It took about a hundred years for the steeple to mature in the architecture of the American church, and although there were some early church spires, generally speaking they became bulkier and taller as the eighteenth century progressed.

Before the middle of the century, the vogue for classic formalism swept the country and soon no church was complete without wooden reproductions of stone Greek columns. Yet the quietness and severity of early American design was too striking to be hidden by any ponderous revival architecture. The stark lines and direct white spire of the country church have always been one of the outstanding features of the American landscape.

Many of our old churches have spires and towers that were later additions, built when the pioneer's aversion to "dressing up divine and glorious truths" was tempered by the invasion of classic architecture. The Society of Friends were content with the clean shapes of plain structures; the only major difference between their meeting house and their home was size. They criticized church spires as being poles to hang a fancy weathervane on. "But the weathercock," explained the builders of steeples, "was a church symbol from the beginning." The origin of the weathercock has been hidden in the ages because the earliest weathercocks were made of light wood and have long since decayed and disappeared. The story has it that Pope Nicholas I in the middle of the ninth century ordained that a figure of a cock should surmount the top of every church throughout Christendom to remind the people how Jesus said Peter would deny Him at cockcrow. The Nativity and the Resurrection occurred near cockcrow, and an ancient superstition predicted that when the

Spires like silent fingers
of Faith

cock ceased to crow, the Day of Judgment will be at hand. From these religious symbols, our weathercock evolved, devised to turn with the wind.

There are countless oddities in church steeples, such as the one of the First Presbyterian Church in Port Gibson, Mississippi. Atop its spire there is a twelve-foot hand, pointing toward the heavens. It commemorates a gesture of Rev. Zebulon Butler who founded the church in 1807. In Marion, Massachusetts, the Captain's Meeting House was built with a three-faced clock so only a blank wall faced those towns which had refused to contribute to its construction. The First Congregational Church in Wellfleet, Massachusetts, has the only town clock in the world that strikes "ship's time."

The carriage shed has now almost entirely disappeared. All early church buildings had sheds to protect carriages from rain or snow, but they have been left to rot in an almost deliberate manner. Churchgoers often have to walk in the rain from cars parked blocks away, yet yesterday the protective roof of a carriage shed was always close by the entrance. Even modern gasoline filling stations are usually uncovered: both your gasoline tank opening and the attendant are exposed to the downpour of rain. The old-fashioned carriage shed idea, it seems, would be a welcome and inexpensive piece of architecture, even in this automobile age.

Wherever you see abandoned country churches you will usually find abandoned farms too. The failure of farming and the disintegration of small communities often go hand-in-hand. If we look deeper, as Representative Clifford Hope of Kansas suggests, ". . . it may be that the people's spirit and the failure of their faith brings on the failure and neglect of their land."

The small rural church is much more than an architectural feature of the countryside, and as a vital force of American life its disappearance would be no trivial matter. Politicians argue that churches, like schools, must be built larger to accommodate cities rather than to restore small outlying country churches. There are sixty thousand more churches today anyway, they point

209

out, than there were thirty years ago. But another fact is that twenty-five thousand small country churches have closed their doors during that time and big city churches have taken over their remaining parishes. Many farmers would no more go to a big-city church than they would call in a big-city doctor when they felt sick, so countless country people who are unwilling or unable to make the trip to the city, have stopped going to church altogether. Old-time church suppers and meetings that were once elements of rural culture are losing in popularity or, as some insist, have lost their dignity and meaning by becoming bingo parties.

Yet the country church continues to be a major American force, as stubborn as its white spire against the changing landscape. If skyscrapers are monuments to American industry, the small rural church is symbolic of our heritage. Such symbols preserved by a longing tethered to the past, whether it be a distant church spire, a gracious bend in an old road or just a reverence for trees and the old ways of farm life, become more important as they vanish. But if some good things are destined to be only memories, we can still be thankful that though they have disappeared, the memory has remained.

Cock weathervane,
New Brick Church,
Boston

a little Gallery of Sketches from the Vanishing Landscape

Barns are at their best in Winter. The snow blankets the unheated parts, yet melts over the Stalls, from Animal Heat

...or breaks the back of the weak barn

In Summer, the Barn becomes closer to the landscape...

the old barns blending with the landscape as only weathering wood can

Leaving the scene is the "Summer house"

The ICE·HOUSE

N.Y.

FENCE·STILE,
(Kentucky)

STONE·STILE,
(N.J.)

WELL house

WELL SWEEP ··· New Hampshire

Virginia

Ohio

DRY MOAT to keep cattle from
lawns without a fence.

213

By-passed Covered Bridges are usually closed . . .

CLOSED

and left to decay. Others have
been taken apart and moved. Indiana

The bridge at
Shelburne Vt.

168 ft. long, was
moved 36 miles
from Lamoille River
near Cambridge

Many Covered Bridges rotted in the shadows of Viaducts . . .
Cornwall Bridge . . 1840 - 1936

The Old Yahoola
Bridge

Anderson, Georgia

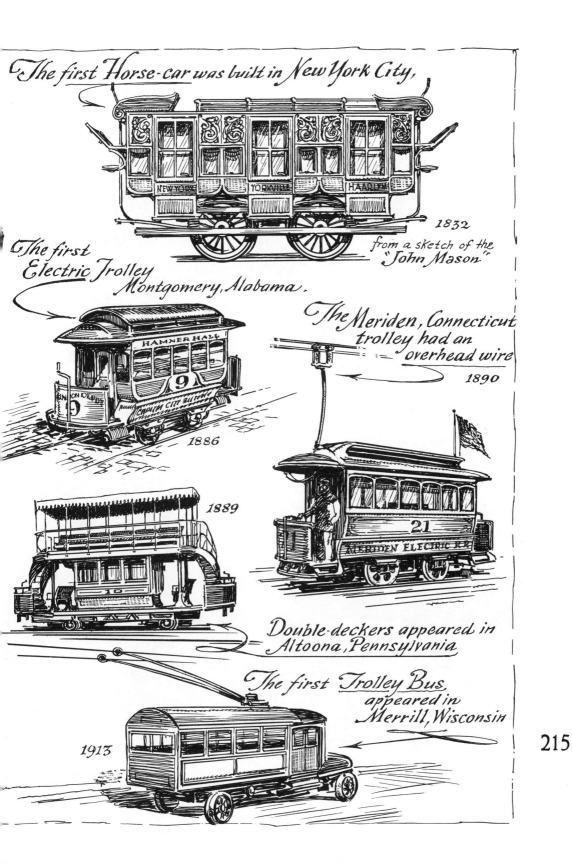

The first Horse-car was built in New York City,

NEW YORK   YORKVILLE   HARLEM

1832
from a sketch of the
"John Mason"

The first
Electric Trolley
Montgomery, Alabama.

HAMNER HALL
9
CAPITOL CITY ...

1886

The Meriden, Connecticut
trolley had an
overhead wire
1890

1889

21
MERIDEN ELECTRIC R.R.

Double-deckers appeared in
Altoona, Pennsylvania

The first Trolley Bus
appeared in
Merrill, Wisconsin

1913

215

Early American

Church design varied ....

First
Presbyterian,
Port Gibson....1859

The Round
Church
in
Richmond,
Vermont

1812

Octagonal
Church
at
Burlington
N.J.

Santa Fé's
San Miguel
1710

Virginia....1690

The
Blackwater
Presbyterian

(like
BARNS)

216

Frankford, Delaware

1796
Meeting House,
South Wardsboro, Vermont

DOORWAYS *as individual as signatures* . . . .

Exeter N.H.

Peacham, Vermont

Providence R.I.

FENCES *were Unique too* . . . .

Fairfield, Conn.

W. Dennis, Mass.

Cape Cod

Even a man's Stone Fence bespoke him

LAID   THROWN   CHINKED

217

Good-bye to BOG MEADOWS . .

and DITCHES . .

and DRAINAGE PONDS . .

. . . . . they have no place in the changing landscape .

218

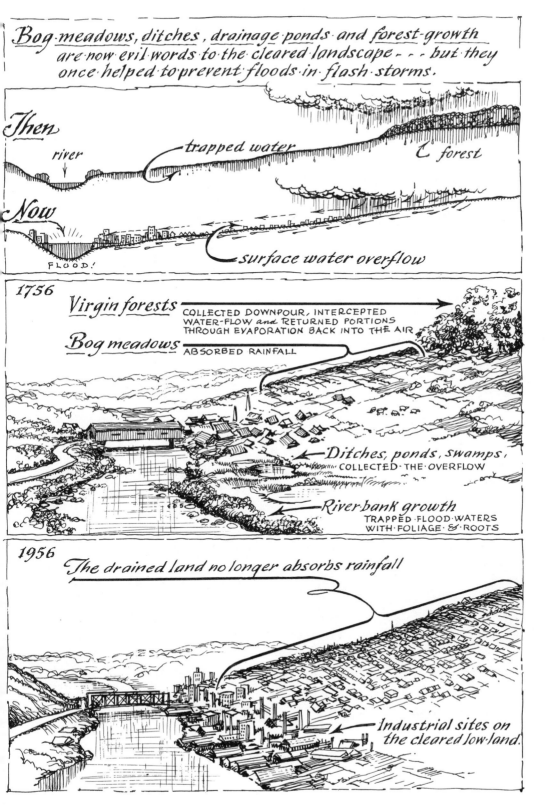

Bog·meadows, ditches, drainage·ponds· and forest·growth are·now·evil words·to·the·cleared landscape - - - but·they once·helped·to·prevent·floods·in·flash·storms.

Then

river

trapped water

forest

Now

FLOOD!

surface water overflow

1756

Virgin forests — COLLECTED DOWNPOUR, INTERCEPTED WATER-FLOW and RETURNED PORTIONS THROUGH EVAPORATION BACK INTO THE AIR

Bog meadows — ABSORBED RAINFALL

Ditches, ponds, swamps, COLLECTED·THE·OVERFLOW

River·bank growth TRAPPED·FLOOD·WATERS WITH·FOLIAGE·&·ROOTS

1956   *The drained land no longer absorbs rainfall*

Industrial sites on the cleared low·land.

219

AMERICAN YESTERDAY

AMERICAN YESTERDAY

by

Eric Sloane

Author's Note

THIS IS A BOOK about our national attic of vanishing ways and obsolete occupations. As always, when sorting through things of the past, we have an uncontrollable urge to save that which we believe to be good and to discard that which we regard as undesirable. Too often, the apparently worthless later reveals its true value.

In observing some of our collections of Americana, a child might picture America's past as a strange world of hand-made artifacts in the possession of people who spent half their lives creating them and the other half living with them. I have collected many of the wondrous things which great-grandfather made, but I have always felt that the old gentleman himself was slighted. If only some of his ways of life might be preserved or his thoughts better recorded, my collection would then be more complete. I am sure that I would prefer that my descendants find in my life a graciousness worthy of perpetuation than simply to decorate their houses with the obsolete implements of my everyday life and regard them only as quaint curiosities.

The antique things and wooden oddities that give me such pleasure do open glorious doors to the past; yet, if I could only meet and speak with the men who made them, an important hunger would be satisfied. The *living* difference or lack of difference between us and our ancestors is a revealing thing; this, and not the change in our attic material, is the proof of progress.

This book is dedicated to those who have kept the past alive, rescuing and sorting discarded objects with fond hands, yet not always knowing exactly why they were doing so; to those who hold to the New England belief that everything comes to good use in time, if one has the patience to wait.

May these pages stir new and urgent voices of ghosts among your relics. May you listen and hear the living heritage of America, and, most urgent of all, may you decorate and enrich your everyday life with it.

ERIC SLOANE

New Milford, Conn.
July, 1956

228

How Different was Great-grandfather?

It is odd what profound thoughts can come to mind when one is not consciously trying to think. There certainly exists no invitation to contemplation while doing sixty miles an hour on a highway or rumbling to work on a noisy morning train, yet some of our deepest thoughts seem to occur at such times. Perhaps it is an American way of thinking, setting us off from the rest of the world. Instead of meditating while resting, as Europeans do, we seem to labor just as hard at our relaxation and often meditate best when we work the hardest. Like our forefathers who created a pattern for a new world while simultaneously splitting rails, building stone walls, and fighting off Indians, many Americans still do much of their thinking while they are busiest.

It seems natural, then, that the thought which prompted this writing should have occurred during a hurried automobile journey to the city. Observing the rush of traffic over highways which only a few years ago were desolate pastures, I found my mind dwelling on the effects of such progress. Exactly what, I wondered, have been the actual effects of this last century on the American man?

We are supposed to be healthier, wealthier, and living in better times. Few of us would argue with that contention. But is the man at the wheel of today's automobile essentially the same man who drove a surrey a century ago? Is he the same kind of man merely wearing different clothes and doing different things, or has he actually undergone a physical and mental and spiritual change? If there is some change, no matter how small, it seems worthy of study. It could be one of the important observations of our time.

229

How much of the American legend have we inherited? One cannot help feeling that there were giants of men walking our land a century or two ago. Yet the crude countryside that gave us our first statesmen should in its present "improved state" produce even greater men. We unconsciously picture ourselves in the image of the early American without realizing that his descendants are subject to change.

We have made a national cliché of the "American way," which unfortunately has in so many minds become synonymous with capitalism. But the American way is no recent industrial-age invention. It flourished as vigorously perhaps, or more so, in the early days when most of our needs were satisfied through barter and money was a strange giant just invading the scene. If the American has altered during that period, or if we have created a different national philosophy, we should certainly be the first to realize it. Changing industrial eras are as normal as new-model automobiles, but a shift in the attitude toward life is a symptom to be watched.

There are those who cannot conceive that a single century can exert a noticeable effect on mankind. If it were impossible, however, there still would be no reason for not discussing the impossibility. However, time and change have already affected plant and animal life. The quality of our average landscape can be scientifically proven to have been altered from that of a century ago through erosion and exhaustion. The rich earth and moss and the first-growth trees that sprang from it have changed to a poorer soil and a different grade of wood. Man may well have changed to a lesser or greater degree.

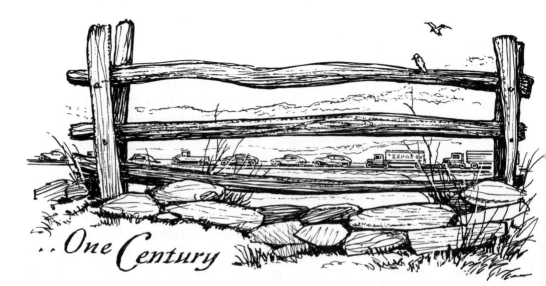

230

.. One Century

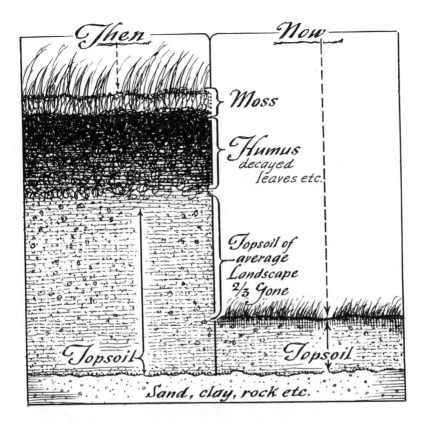

It is easier, however, to analyze a physical alteration in a nation's soil and wood than it is to isolate a less tangible change in its people. In analyzing great-grandfather scientifically, we would have to take into account such physical elements as heat and moisture, gases, dust, noise, and the various other environmental factors that make modern life different from that of the past. We would have to compare changes in manual labor, habits of sleep, and the character of food. These things exert their effect upon people and all these conditions have altered during this one century.

It has almost been forgotten, for example, that the world in which we move about today is much drier. The early American farmer invariably wore boots because he continually walked on moist ground. Even the village worker lived in a wet world because all factories were mills built over water-power. The consequence of two centuries of reclaiming wet lands and building cities on the sites of former marshes and meadows has been the creation of a far different workaday climate.

Despite this distinct climatic alteration, the weather during the last hundred years has not changed as much as the landscape has. The virgin forest

231

and mossy topsoil of a century ago were a natural sponge, absorbing rains which now roll across the surface of "tired," dry landscapes and into abnormally swollen rivers. A New England farmer put it nicely by comparing today's landscape with a modern blotter. "It used to be," he said, "that blotters were just made for absorbing ink. Now they are money-makers with one whole side advertising some darned thing instead of doing the job they were intended to do. That's the way the whole countryside is getting. Bulldozers are covering over the good bog-meadows with money-making real-estate developments. When a good rain comes, it runs over the top of the ground, just like ink on the wrong side of a blotter."

Boots
for the wet world of yesterday

A century ago, towering first-growth trees broke raindrops into tiny particles, turning a large portion of rainfall back into the atmosphere by evaporation before it reached the ground. The trees' great roots braced the soil and made a framework for moss and peat that held as much as ten to fifteen times its weight in water. The farmer, who never ventured outdoors without his traditional boots, accepted moisture more contentedly than does the man of today. The swimming hole, the pond, the creek and ditch and bog-meadow were a necessary adjunct to his farmland operations. Now they are regarded as nuisances of nature to be filled in and "improved." Such are the changes that have come to the average American landscape in a century.

According to collectors of early American clothing, it is evident that over this period the average American woman has grown taller and the man a bit shorter. An estimated ten million American men sit their way through life, either at meals, coffee-breaks, at the office, in automobiles, before the TV, or at the baseball stadium; the average American male's waistline has changed accordingly. A hundred years ago, the American would have done an average day's work as morning chores before starting his actual occupation. The few people who now walk to work or to the morning train are regarded as physical culturists. According to reliable research, American men live so much in a sitting or "relaxed" position that they use up less than half the calories they did seventy-five years ago. To illustrate how rapidly changes in the human body can evolve, consider the findings of Dr. Wilson T. Sowder in *The Journal of Lifetime Living,* who agrees that American men are becoming physically inferior to their women. In 1920, the mortality rate of white men between 45 and 54 was already ten per cent higher than that of women; in 1950, it was seventy-eight per cent higher! The outdoor clubs, to which the average business man belonged seventy-five years ago, have vanished. Bicycling and hiking are now "for Boy Scouts." It seems that America's most disastrous invention may be, not the atomic bomb, but the easy chair.

In another hundred years, barring war or pestilence, there will be seven billion people on this earth, or about three times as many as now exist. The land will be proportionately that much more worn out, and its mineral content that much more depleted. Irrigating the deserts and de-salting the sea water will enable farming to feed the seven billion, but how different will be the average American's life and diet from those of the first settlers! In the refined diet of the present day, about two-thirds of our calories are supplied from food which has been stripped of nutrients. A few generations ago, the very poor were deriving more nutritive value from their food than do the very rich today.

It is important to remember, when comparing the past with the present, not to allow modern wonders to awe one into believing that all changes are synonymous with progress. "The old way" is not necessarily an inefficient way. William Morris said, "The great achievement of the nineteenth century was the making of machines which were the wonders of invention, skill, and patience and which were used for the production of measureless quantities of worthless make-shifts." However rash this statement may appear, the more one analyzes it, the more truth one will discover in it.

It is difficult, perhaps impossible, for anyone to believe that progress and improvement may be accompanied by inconvenience or danger. Nevertheless, consider the average modern electrified house. If the current went off for a week during the winter, the oil furnace would fail to operate, water pumps would stop, lights would go out, cooking would cease, and the plumbing might burst. The house would be rendered unlivable unless it also contained an old-fashioned fireplace, a cook-stove, and candles or kerosene lights. Consider a modern metropolis such as New York City. If it were completely shut off from outside territory, its food supplies would last only a matter of days, and starvation would overcome its population perhaps in one or two months. The ancient farmhouse, without plumbing but with a large woodpile and its own source of food, gave its owner a better sense of security than we might suppose. The smallest village with its own water-powered mills was actually more self-sufficient than the average metropolis of today! Progress and speed become more treacherous as they increase.

An early London newspaper once criticized us for our haste. "Speed kills five hundred people a day in America," it said. A New England paper retaliated good-naturedly, but with a great deal of truth, "It isn't the speed that kills us, you know, it's the quick stop." And so in modern everyday living, the pace is often of less importance than is the dilemma of having to stop.

Great-grandfather did things always with a purpose. He did them conscientiously because he did them himself. That is why he so often put his name and the date on his belongings. Today we might do the same thing for sentiment, but the dates one sees on old things were put there in pride, as if to say, "In this year I was satisfied with this piece of work which I myself created."

The awareness of life and time which seemed to permeate the early days shone brightest in the home. When a man built his house, he might not put his name upon it, but the date seemed all-important. His position in the stream of time and a consciousness of the part he was playing were part of a rare experience that few of us are now privileged to enjoy.

Often there was special sentiment connected with a date such as "E.A.C., 1781" carved in a topmost rafter of a house built by Ebenezer Clark and his wife Abigail, near Washington, Connecticut. Whenever they built substantial houses, the Germans in Pennsylvania made date-stones which not only incorporated the owner's name but included a blessing on the house. A typical inscription upon a 1771 date-stone reads, "To Thy care, O Lord, are commended all in this household going in or out."

Dates were often mosaicked into brick walls. They were put into fire-place backs, twisted into the anchoring irons of brick sidewalls, carved into some main beam of the house, and even designed into the over-all pattern of

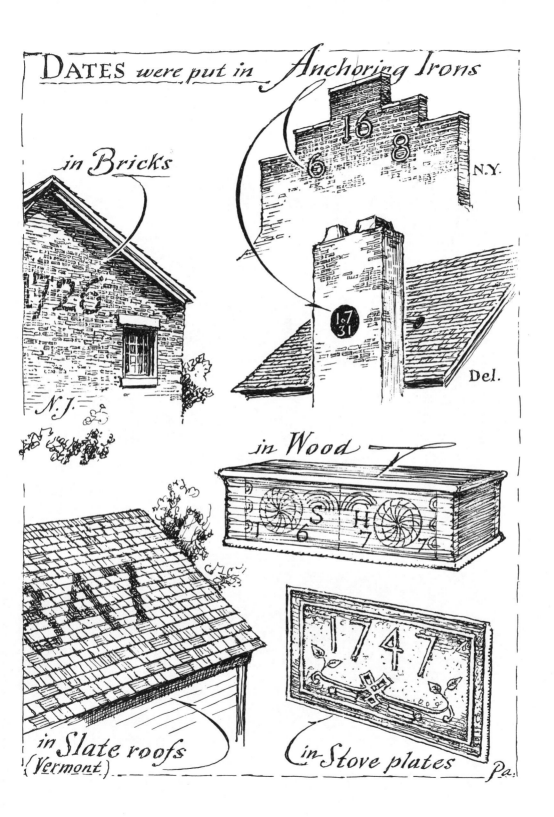

DATES *were put in* *Anchoring Irons*

in Bricks

16
6 8

N.Y.

1728

N.J.

1731

Del.

in Wood

S H
6 7 7

in Slate roofs
(Vermont)

1747

in Stove plates

Pa.

NAMES were put on Tools.

German felling Ax 1800

GUTH

Broadax
R.I., 1817

FELDE
1817

. . . . . on Boxes
and Chests . . .

Sarah Hopts

Ja. HuBER, his hand

EBENEZER T

and Barns . . .

H. SCHULZE

and any creation of which the maker was proud

slate roofs. It is always obvious that they were put there for others to see in some distant future. The old-timers firmly believed that those who fail to look backward at their ancestors seldom look ahead to posterity. The pioneer looked both ways in those days, and the knowledge of his own relative position created a gratifying American philosophy of content.

It is a pity that a man's work should outlive his identity, yet many of the old barns and farmhouses had identifying information which was obliterated when it became the vogue to "preserve wood with paint." The better timber of those days did not, of course, require a preservative coat, and the oldest surviving wooden structures are still the unpainted ones. Paint eventually has a decaying effect on moist wood; unless it is kept in constant repair, soft wood actually seasons better without it. In addition to this scientific reason for keeping wood bare, for a long while it was considered vulgar to paint one's house. The red barn of New England is comparatively recent. Not until Pennsylvania barns had sported paint, fancy weathervanes, and decorative designs for almost a century did the conservative New Englander dare to alter the appearance of the naked seasoned wood of his farm buildings. But the paint era evolved suddenly and barns with names and dates upon them soon lost that valuable information under many coats of paint during the years which followed. There is now hardly a barn with positive identification left in America.

The early American's urge for identification was born of pride, both in himself and in his time; but we are now so taken up with progress and money-making that identifying ourselves and our time has become almost meaningless. For example, you will not find a date on any part of your automobile. Its year, which represents nothing but depreciation, can be found only hidden away in a used-car price book. Trade names are on everything about the home, but the name of the designer and the date on which it was made can scarcely be found.

It is interesting to note that things made nowadays with "do-it-yourself" kits are almost always identified by the maker's name and date. Only a few do-it-yourselfers make their own things to save money; it is the thrill of recapturing that lost satisfaction of creativeness that really makes it worthwhile. At the turn of the century, when "do-it-yourself" kits were sold to burn pictures already traced into leather postcards, *Harper's Weekly* predicted that "such mechanized art will sound the death-knell for the creative urge of our young artists." Today's painting kits, with numbered colors and pictures outlined ready to fill in, would really insult great-grandfather. He had no inferiority complex about creating, and he conceived all sorts of original and primitive designs, just as did his wife with quilts and his daughter with samplers.

237

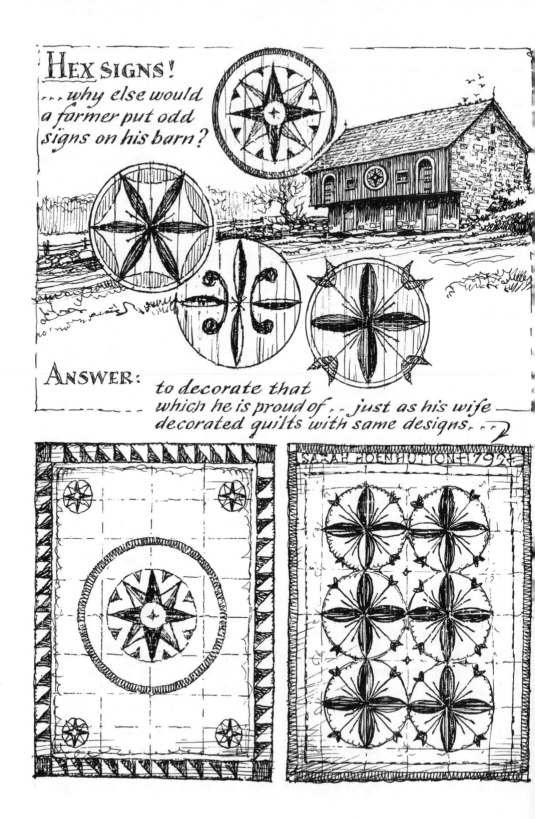

HEX SIGNS!

...why else would a farmer put odd signs on his barn?

ANSWER:

to decorate that which he is proud of ... just as his wife decorated quilts with same designs...

SARAH HOENSHUTTONER 1792

Great-grandfather enjoyed the proud life of an artist living among artists; everything about him he had created himself. He made farms out of forests and he built his house with tools fashioned by his own hands. In simply living his own life, he was creating villages and towns. But, alas, everything we touch nowadays has been created by others. We have been robbed of our creativeness and the result is often a moral emptiness. Yet, like unemployed actors who continue to live in the glory of their pasts, modern men will never give up the dream of returning to that wonderful world of great-grandfather. Meanwhile, most of us must be content to be the healthiest and wealthiest audience to mechanical greatness in all history.

Only a few years ago everyone carried a folding knife called a penknife. Many men still carry penknives, yet few know that they are so called because they were designed for sharpening crow quills before the time of steel pens. Aged men enjoyed whittling with their penknives, but nowadays you will seldom see anyone whittling. It was a joy to keep a knife sharp and clean, just as it was to keep an ax in perfect condition. Creativeness need not always be a thing of splendor: there is sufficient beauty in a pile of well-stacked kindling or a clean-cut pile of cordwood to make a man feel good. The satisfaction of seeing rich pine split into sweet-smelling sections of kindling was only a small part of life's pleasures, but it was also a part of boyhood training that a man enjoyed remembering.

...even the wood-pile is a Creation on the farm.

239

Our dilemma of emptiness lies in no lack of ability; it lies rather in a lack of understanding. We are led to believe, for instance, that to be creative we must be original. The early American artist naturally adopted classic and ancient design wherever he could. His architectural ability lay in understanding and recognizing the best things of the past and in making use of them, *not in being an inventor*. His special genius was more often his ability to refrain from being original! He preserved the good art of the past by incorporating it in everything he built, but our idea of preservation has sadly changed. Now we preserve buildings of *historic interest,* with only secondary consideration of their design. We save things of the past by putting a proud date upon them so that they become poor servants of nostalgia. A sense of history thus becomes a national apology wherever a sense of beauty is lacking.

If you were to define briefly the difference between the man of today and the man of the past you might find the word "awareness" very descriptive. Fiorello LaGuardia, in praising air transportation, said that he dozed into slumber in a plane at Chicago and landed in New York without being aware of having left the ground. A century ago you would have been conscious of every mile of travel, counted by the bumps and turns and stops and starts. Uncomfortable, indeed, but you would have been awake to the experience of the trip. One of the wonders of jet-plane travel lies in the fact that there is no sensation of movement and the passenger remains unaware of speed. We have relegated the inconvenience of travel to the past, but we have also lost our wonderful awareness of the experience.

A cross-country trip, an air flight, or a sea voyage once called for much thought and some strength, but things are made easier now. The day of great pilots has passed because the need for great pilots no longer exists. A push-button flight to the moon will some day become boresome, but the Davey Crocketts and Wyatt Earps and the Lindberghs will always excite the American mind.

A jet-plane test pilot was asked to recount his greatest thrill in flying. His reply is interesting. "Years ago in an air circus," he said, "I flew an old Curtiss-Wright pusher as a stunt. It wasn't the danger of flying an old crate that gave me the thrill; it was being out in the open with wires whistling all around, the way the first flyers did, feeling each updraft and flying almost as birds do. I did only about thirty miles an hour, but I still make that flight in my dreams."

240 The antique automobile fans who go on trips in their obsolete cars are not exhibitionists. In fact, they would happily dispense with spectators. They are enjoying a slice of the past and the unique experience of making a trip in one age, with an awareness that belongs to another.

Great-grandfather was intensely awake to everything about him. He knew where his clothes came from, because the cloth was made in his own home. All the things in his house were more than familiar to him: he had made them himself. Today the average city person has not the slightest idea where his tap water or heat or light and power or food come from. He knows only the location of faucets and switches; he takes the rest for granted. He cannot conceive that he might derive some satisfaction from knowing where these conveniences originate; to him, the most important thing is the ability to pay for them. The satisfaction of being completely aware of all that goes on around us has become a lost art.

It is typical of America today to say, "If I only knew *then* what I know *today*," or "I certainly didn't appreciate what I had," or "I didn't know when I was well off." Such afterthoughts are the result of having lived without a full consciousness of life. We are often in such a hurry to get somewhere that we don't care too much where somewhere is. As long as we are working and on our way, we are morally and economically content.

Satisfaction with one's lot was to great-grandfather something to be learned while very young and remembered for the rest of one's life. But it has now become an American virtue to be dissatisfied! It is acknowledged that dissatisfaction results in improvement or the invention of something new; that is good. But satisfaction has its benefits, too, and should least of all be ignored. When you accept dissatisfaction as a virtue, you trade in your good automobile when the lines are slightly out of style, or anything else that becomes "dated," in spite of its continuing efficiency.

Progress has become so involved with dissatisfaction that modern salesmanship and advertising depend largely upon instilling discontent with what one already possesses. Any given product is advertised one year as "what you should be satisfied with" and advertised the year following as "what you should be dissatisfied with." It is now regarded an insult to a person to say that he is "easily satisfied!"

It might not be considered progressive to be satisfied with last year's model, but it is certainly a worthwhile adventure in contentment.

a Dissatisfied American, 1902 style.

Great-grandfather's Church

"THANK GOD," say the antiquarians, "the church is one thing which hasn't changed." But great-grandfather would be saddened at some of our new church buildings, particularly those which have been built in the so-called progressive style of modern architecture. There is a brave school of thought among designers which holds that man should try not to look backward, even if the view is pleasant. If a church can be made to appear to be farthest away from what all other churches have ever resembled, we are supposed to have reached a goal, especially when we have created a church which resembles nothing ever built before in this architectural form.

The church, of course, is not the only architecture attacked by "progressive creativeness." The average filling station, deprived of tanks and signs, could often pass for a modern home; many of our apartment buildings resemble penitentiaries; some banks might double for automobile show rooms, and dog hospitals for inns.

Two hundred years ago, when twenty men built their homes in one group, there was a common source of inspiration; although each house was individual, they all were traditionally correct and they blended into one pleasing composition. Twenty men given free reign to build their dream houses today would produce twenty more efficient buildings, but a revolting group of architectural contrasts. On the other hand, when a modern development is planned for one particular style, the result usually looks like something from a mechanical production line.

243

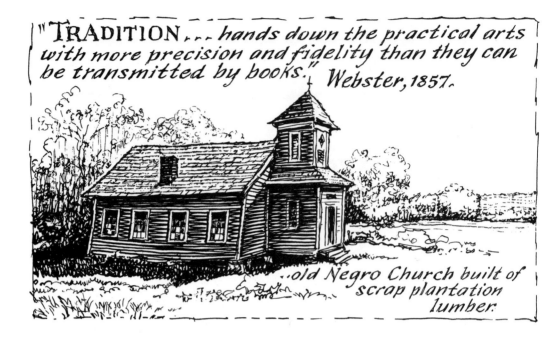

"TRADITION ... hands down the practical arts with more precision and fidelity than they can be transmitted by books." Webster, 1857.

..old Negro Church built of scrap plantation lumber.

During the past few years many roadside shopping centers have grown into villages. "They become a village," real-estate developers say, "when a bank building joins the group." It used to be the rule that the church was the center of the village, with homes and shops spreading outward from it. Ironically enough in this age, if great-grandfather were seeking the village center, he would be directed to the bank building instead of the church.

Great-grandfather did not go to church simply because he enjoyed the service; he enjoyed discipline and he was aware of its benefits. The appreciation of discipline seems to be another vanished grace; the actual meaning of the word has even changed within one century. Webster defines it as: "obsolete) teaching, instruction"; the other and more modern definition is: "punishment, chastisement." Discipline was originally an ecclesiastical word, derived from the word "disciple," and it referred to a set of rules for good conduct with no reference to punishment. The newer use of the word discipline and the American interpretation of freedom clash, so in that round-about way discipline itself has become a distasteful thing to many of us in the present day.

Freedom without discipline in the old sense of the word was deplored by the old-timers. Alexis Carrel said: "Emancipated man is by no means comparable to an eagle soaring in the sky. He far more closely resembles a dog escaped from its kennel and dashing hither and thither among the traffic. He can indeed, like a dog, do exactly as he pleases and go wherever he wants. He is

244

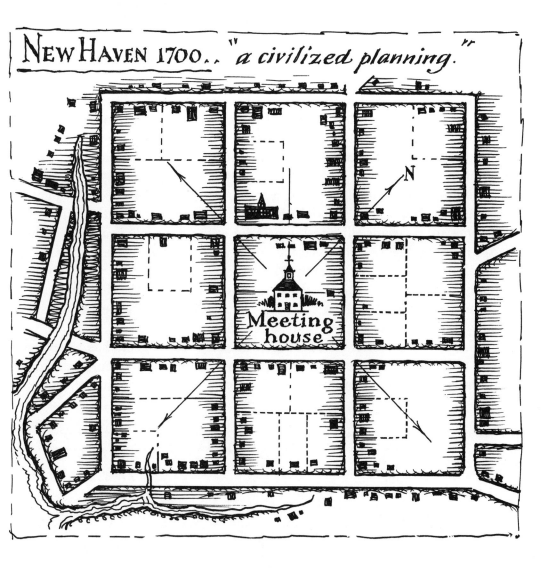

New Haven 1700.. "a civilized planning."

none the less lost because he does not know where to go or how to protect himself from the dangers which surround him. How is he to discover once again the moral security his ancestors knew when they built the Gothic cathedrals?" A telling point, indeed, for old-time religion!

Psychiatrists explain that people who dwell in the past are escaping from a present with which they are not content. Perhaps that simplification explains why so many of us find it pleasing and comfortable to decorate modernistic houses with bits of early Americana, often incongruous in the surrounding décor. Even more interesting is the possibility that many antiquarians are escaping from religious insecurity because in their ability to "dwell in the past" they are automatically assuring themselves of a hereafter!

The idea is not new. The preface to the *Connecticut Historical Collections* of 1830 begins: "The power by which we recall past scenes, the rapidity

245

with which they are brought in review before us, the faculty by which we can range o'er creation, and dwell upon the past and future, demonstrates that man was indeed formed in the image of his Creator, and destined for immortality. By the contemplation of the past, we feel our span of existence extended: we enter into the thoughts, hopes, and aspirations of generations before us, and in such moments hold communion with the departed spirits of antiquity."

Escaping the present to recapture the past's religious security may be inconvenient, but it is not at all unhealthy. If there is any truth to the belief that some antiquarians cling to the past for such a psychological reason, there is still no cause for regret. Once the truth were known to them, they would suddenly find themselves collecting art, whereas previously they were collecting only historical curiosities of the past. They might, for the first time, see in a room in which Washington slept the beauty that was previously overshadowed by the picture of a great man asleep there.

The Christmas-card interpretation of early churchgoers has never been a true picture. Very often, for example, the familiar tall steeple was added years later, after bells were cast on this side of the sea. The first church was

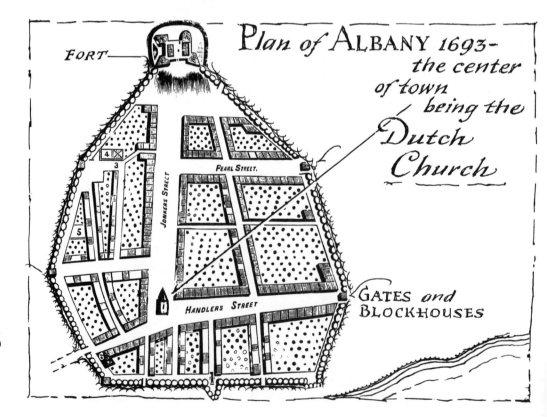

246

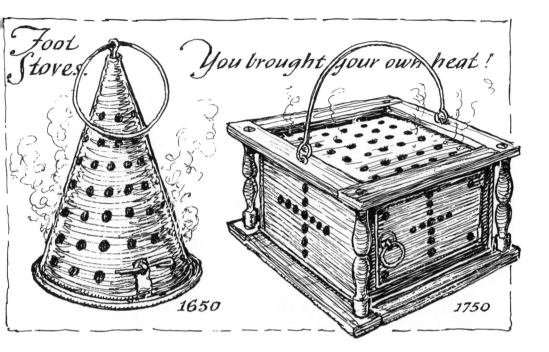

Foot Stoves. *You brought your own heat!*

1650   1750

called a meeting house and it resembled exactly that. It was used for all sorts of town meetings during the week and it became a church only at sundown on Saturday, when the Sabbath started, and lasted until sundown on Sunday. Sunday night was not the quiet eve that it is today, for as soon as sundown occurred, fasting ended and the partying began. Because no cooking or other utilitarian work was allowed during the Sabbath, mother labored all day Saturday, but stopped at the moment the sun dropped below the horizon.

Churches were unheated primarily because of the dread of accidental fire. There were no chimneys, as you may have noticed in pictures of the early church buildings. In any event, an open fire built in a large building that had been closed overnight during winter would do little more than thaw the walls out.

Church services used to start at nine in the morning and lasted until dusk because by town vote no lights were allowed in most early American churches. The first lights in church buildings appeared about 1820. The first stoves were installed at about the same time, but against much protest. Churches were the coldest houses in town during the early days, and many a preacher's winter diary included such a phrase as "bread was frozen at the Lord's Table today." Bread used in celebration of the Lord's Supper was kept in a charcoal heater in most Maine churches to keep it from freezing. Baptismal water was kept under the parson's coat in a warm flask.

247

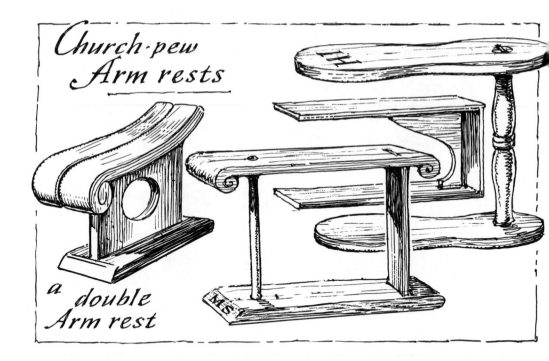

Church-pew Arm rests

a double Arm rest

The fact that children were taken to church to be baptized the Sunday following their birth, even in winter, is typical of early religion. If the church happened to be nearby, it would be bad enough, but there were often long rides by sled to the unheated church, which sometimes actually caused the child to "die of baptism." On January 22nd, 1694, Judge Sewall wrote, "A very extraordinary Storm by reason of the falling and driving of the Snow. Few women could get to Meeting. A child named Alexander was baptized in the afternoon." He did not, however, record Alexander's death a week later.

The "hardest seats in the world" were church seats. Cushions were frowned on as improper for use in church, and some of the early carpenters found play for their sense of humor by billing for "church planks of ye softest pine for comfort." Arm rests eliminated some discomfort during the tedious all-day services, but few churches supplied them. There are still many wooden arm rests with names carved upon them, indicating that owners often left their arm rests in the pews rather than carry them between home and church. There must have been many things taken to church, what with foot-warmers, pillows, blankets, arm rests, often spittoons and other conveniences. One church built in 1843 by the whaling men of Sag Harbor, Long Island, was equipped with a brass spittoon in each of its mahogany-trimmed pews.

It is strange to think of the early preacher giving his sermon with great-coat and ear muffs on and a muffler over his head, yet this is precisely what he

248

did during winter. When he pointed heavenward, it was often with a mittened hand, or with a hand that was immediately afterward plunged into a fur wrapper. House stoves were, for some strange reason, considered sacrilegious in a house of God, but one Vermont pastor made a giant foot stove upon which he stood all the while he preached. House stoves finally had to be voted on, and one of Connecticut's finest anecdotes involves two old maids who were opposed to a stove in their church. They were outvoted by the rest of the parish, however, and *two* big stoves were installed. One autumn day, after fanning themselves vigorously and complaining loudly about the overheated room, the ladies fainted from the "unnatural heat." But the stoves, they learned after being revived, were not even lit!

A description of the early American church worth remembering was given by the pastor of Longmeadow Church in Massachusetts almost a century ago:

"It is the Sabbath Day; the second bell, first peal. The population comes from all angles, on foot, in carriages, in farm wagons without springs. Some are drawn by horses, some by oxen. Women and younger children and older men sit on straight-backed chairs and milking stools set on the green; young men and maidens, and the boys, line the wayside, talking in whispers. Having walked all the way barefoot to keep their shoes shiny (and save them from wear, too), boys and girls are now putting shoes on and buttoning them.

"This day belongs to the church and nothing is done aside from that. No wagon or stage-coach or man afoot is moving except in accordance with the Lord's Day. Bridge and highway tolls are forbidden. New England statutes as late as a century ago put a twenty-dollar fine on any 'driver or proprietor of any coach, wagon, or sleigh upon the highway on the Lord's Day, except for necessity or charity.'"

The bell begins to toll and the congregation throngs the meeting-house steps. It is the day of greetings, the social exchange, the news day. Dr. Williams emerges from the parsonage in gown and bands and powdered wig, three-cornered hat, knee breeches, woolen stockings, and silver shoe buckles. The bell will not stop tolling until he passes through the double door and goes into the high pulpit under the great sounding board. The deacons are seated in their railed pew beneath the pulpit.

There is no stove. For fifty-one years the frosty air of the new meeting house was mitigated only by the women's foot stoves and the cracking together of frozen boot heels. The parson sometimes preached in a heavy homespun cloak; at the nooning, grateful indeed was the roaring fire in the great kitchen of the parsonage, at the tavern barroom, at all the hospitable neighbors' open houses.

The congregation stands up to pray—bodily infirmity alone prevents. If one sits down in prayer time, it is a sudden and emphatic protest against the parson's praying for the king and royal family—not that he is a Tory or inimical to the liberties of America, only an old man to whom the times look dark and fears are in the way. In due time he reads from the pulpit, though not without some misgivings, the Declaration of Independence.

For fifty years the congregation sat down to sing; but after the pitch pipe no longer toots, and the singing master has organized the choir, and the bass viols and flutes conspire with young men and maidens to make a joyful noise, they now rise up and face about to see the choir.

The gallery of the meeting house runs around the east, south, and west; square pews line the gallery walls. The Negro pew is in the southwest corner; the boys of twelve occupy the next pew, the boys of fourteen the next, those of eighteen the next (it having the advantage of a window), and the boys of sixteen the last pew on that side. A similar arrangement for the girls obtains in the eastern gallery; the single men and women of discreet age occupy the pews lining the south gallery wall. The choir seats run all around the gallery front, and the smaller children sit on benches directly behind the choir. In such an arrangement, the necessity for tithing-men is great. The seats of honor are in the broad aisle pews, below and nearest the pulpit. The pews are all free, but the seating committee assigns them. They are first instructed to wait on Dr. Williams and to know his pleasure, what pew he chooses his family to sit in. But, after that, "dignifying the house" is no easy task. Age is one consideration, property another, standing yet another.

The vanished customs of the early American church could fill a lengthy book. Because the church was the center of all village life, it seems odd that its ways have changed as much as they have. The church bell, for example, was once a sort of town crier; it spoke to tell of births and deaths, of fire and war. After a death, the bell greeted the morning with "three times three for a man, and three times two for a woman." Then after a short silence, the bell pealed out the number of years the dead person had lived. All church bells rang three times a day, at seven o'clock in the morning, at noon, and at nine o'clock for curfew. Striking each hour is a recent custom. At evening, the last ringing was followed by strokes indicating the day of the month, a signal for many a farmer to turn to his farm diary and complete the day's entry.

The tone and range of its church bell was the talk and pride of every village. The ways of the weather were often sensed by the sound of the bell. Any old-timer could tell you which way the wind was blowing, whether the barometric pressure was up or down, and what tomorrow's weather was going to be by the church bell's muffled hollowness or its crisp clarity. When one of the

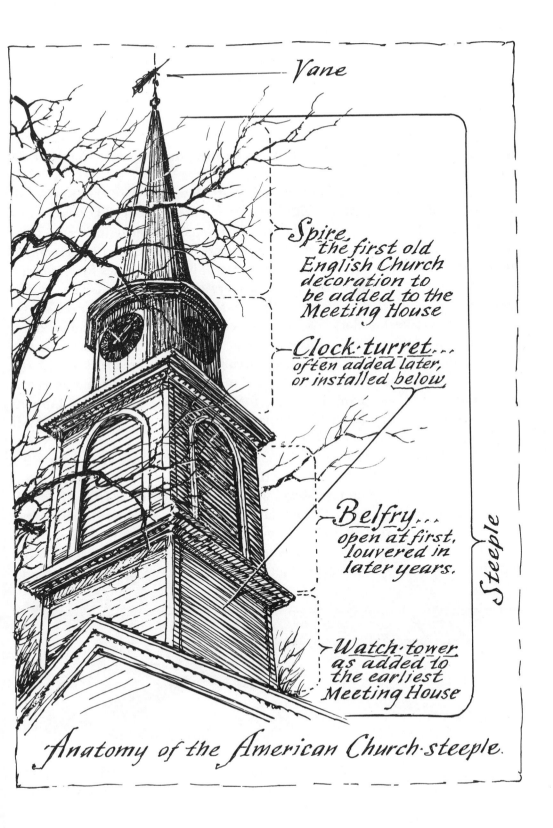

Vane

Spire, the first old English Church decoration to be added to the Meeting House

Clock-turret... often added later, or installed below.

Belfry... open at first, louvered in later years.

Watch-tower as added to the earliest Meeting House

Steeple

Anatomy of the American Church-steeple.

better-known early bells cracked and was recast with silver from donations of coins, the parson told everyone that the good act had added a special quality to the bell's tone. From that time on, cracked bells were usually recast with donated silver "to make ye tone clearer." During the Kennebunk fire of 1824, the town's church bell was heard clearly in Alfred, Maine, eleven miles away. The limit of thunder's carrying power is supposed to be ten miles, so the Kennebunk bell had set a record! It was called the only bell "louder than thunder."

Collecting taxes was a full-time job yesterday, and the tithing-man had a varied set of jobs to contend with, even during the Sabbath. There were special fines to collect from people who left their dogs unleashed during the summer Sabbath; dogs often followed their masters into the church, where a dog fight might upset the quiet of the proceedings. There were fines for those who left burning coals behind in their foot-warmers after the services. The tithing-man was always given a convenient place in the first American churches, and it was his job to keep order. His badge was a long stick with a rabbit's foot on one end and a fox tail on the other. The heavy end of the stick was used to waken nodding boys; the faces of slumbering matrons were brushed with the softer end. This was always good for a laugh, but undue noise was reprimanded by the tithing-man's holding a forefinger across his lips and tapping his stick with the other hand. The "finger-to-the-lips" sign for quiet may well have originated from the church and the tithing-man.

At first, there were square pews, sometimes curtained off to keep the draft out and to keep body heat in. Bearskins, carpets, and blankets were brought into the pews, and foot stoves were kept fed with coals from "Sabbath Day Houses" nearby. Sabbath Day houses or Sabbaday houses, as they were more often called, were little buildings put up at a respectful distance from the church and equipped with stools and blankets. Fireplaces were built in the center. A caretaker or servant was left in charge to keep the fires going and

Tithing-man's Church-stick

Children   Adults

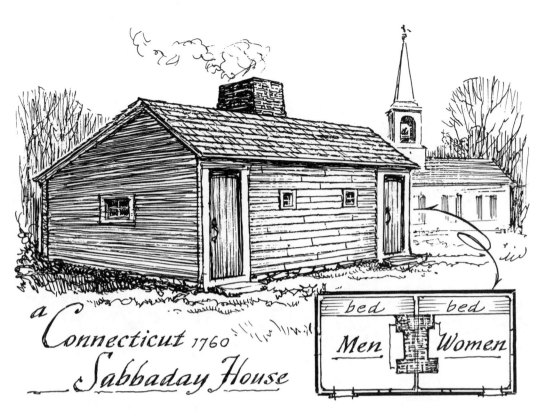

a Connecticut 1760 Sabbaday House

bed | bed
Men | Women

coals were continually carried into the church pews to replenish the footstoves there. When churchgoers were unbearably cold, they went out during intervals of the service and warmed themselves in these Sabbath Day houses.

When stoves were later added to the old churches, some of the Sabbath Day houses still remained, but people sold refreshments and meals from them. Money was never allowed to pass hands on the Sabbath, so food was either paid for during the week or contributed free by the congregation. In either case, the convenience was appreciated because many churchgoers lived so far away that the weekly trip was a brave overnight pilgrimage which always induced hearty appetites. When there were no Sabbaday houses, local homes were usually thrown open for the purpose, and many a "house on the green" was known as a Sabbath Day house a century ago.

Great-grandfather's church has been condemned as embodying too much "hell fire and brimstone," but those who criticize forget that everything was done with more zest in the olden days. When Sunday came and the meeting house became a church, the preacher forgot all business and politics of the week and became an ardent revivalist. There were few quiet preachers. As a matter of fact, if you want to imitate an actor, preacher, salesman, or other character who might have lived a century ago, you can get the proper effect by

253

a Sabbaday House New Jersey, 1820

Four fireplaces

simply putting your everything into your act. In modern parlance this is known as "overdoing it."

The earliest colonial church services were solemn and quiet, much like a court of law. Both, incidentally, were announced by a roll of drums. But when church bells arrived and organs were installed, nineteenth-century sensationalism found expression even in the church. Revival meetings were particularly noisy, and when the national anthem was sung, drums and bells and even guns usually accompanied the singing.

In 1872 a religious festival advertised a chorus of twenty thousand voices and an orchestra of two thousand. Musical concerts could not survive without tableaux and spectacular sound effects. One concert had a hundred real anvils for a hundred men to pound on during the anvil chorus. Circuses by this time carried actual cannon with their bands. Here, for example, is the wording from a P. T. Barnum poster:

"National anthems by several hundred trained voices, accompanied by music and roar of cannon. I carry my own park of cannon and a large church bell. This circus fires a national salute of thirteen guns each morning accompanied by public bells, while the national anthem at night is sung to a cannonade of my whole park of cannon, a display of patriotic fireworks of Washington, American flags, etc., in red, white and blue."

One accomplishment of modern life is the art of not overdoing things. Another is doing several things at the same time. Many of us cannot enjoy breakfast nowadays without cereal-box labels to decipher while we eat. Some fathers seem to get the most out of the newspaper over the breakfast table and some mothers do their housework best with a soap-opera TV background. All this double action might be regarded as an amusing accomplishment if great-grandfather could come back and observe it. But still he would frown at such goings-on as letting a TV play or a speech by our President serve as the background for parlor conversation. Such present-day "accomplishments" are really bad habits. The child who can't sleep unless some program—any program!—is coming over the air will too often in later life be the slave of habit who removes his hat when a lady enters the elevator and puts it back on again when the elevator stops.

Theodore Roosevelt said the greatest thing he learned in school was to "do one thing at a time, and to concentrate on it." When great-grandfather removed his hat for a lady, he really put his heart into it, and the lady loved it. When the old-time minister preached, he really "went to town," and great-grandfather heartily approved.

From the day great-grandfather learned his alphabet, the discipline of the Bible became a part of his everyday life. Even the first alphabetical toy blocks were painted with Biblical illustrations. Wherever a reference to the Bible could be used, it seemed a natural accompaniment, no matter what the subject matter.

If there is any difference between the American churchgoer of today and his brother of a century or two ago, it might involve their reasons for going. Now that churches tend to decorate city life instead of being its hub, church learning has become more of an embellishment to living than its source.

The first churches were considered to be the main support in the structure of American life. An old New England name for the summer beam—the strongest beam of a house—was the "church beam"; it was this now-waning importance that the colonists gave the church. Today, if you ask an average person why he goes to church, he will invariably say, "To gain something." But when you ask him exactly what he expects to gain, he gropes for an answer. Great-grandfather did not go to church expecting to gain anything more than he already had; he went there to give thanks for it. In these competitive times, where the love of gain has penetrated everywhere, we are led to believe that we are going backward as soon as we cease to gain. It seems incredible to do anything, even to attend church, without profiting materially from it. Great-grandfather had mastered the magnificent art of standing still.

Today we have all but forgotten the many religious sects which once

A In ADAM's Fall / We finned all.	**N** NOAH did view / The old world & new
B Heaven to find, / The Bible Mind.	**O** Young OBADIAS, / DAVID, JOSIAS / All were pious.
C Chrift crucify'd / For finners dy'd.	**P** PETER deny'd / His Lord and cry'd.
D The Deluge drown'd / The Earth around.	**Q** Queen ESTHER fues / And faves the *Jews*.
E ELIJAH hid / By Ravens fed.	**R** Young pious RUTH. / Left all for Truth.
F The judgment made / FELIX afraid.	**S** Young SAM'L dear / The Lord did fear.
G As runs the Glass, / Our Life doth pass.	**T** Young TIMOTHY / Learnt fin to fly.
H My Book and Heart / Must never part.	**U** VASTHI for Pride, / Was fet afide.
I JOB feels the Rod,— / Yet bleffes GOD.	**W** Whales in the Sea, / GOD's Voice obey.
K Proud Korah's troop / Was fwallowed up	**X** XERXES did die, / And fo muft I.
L LOT fled to *Zoar*, / Saw fiery Shower / On *Sodom* pour.	**Y** While youth do chear / Death may be near.
M MOSES was he / Who *Israel's* Hoft / Led thro' the Sea.	**Z** ZACCHEUS he / Did climb the Tree / Our Lord to fee.

It began with your A, B, C's in those days

Summer or "Church Beam" which supports the *Jacents* or joists

sought to found their own little independent "nations" within America. Driven from Europe because of persecution and inspired by the success of the Pilgrims, these people built almost countless little "paradises" in almost every state. Pennsylvania possibly has the greatest scattering of such lost Utopias, although its Mennonites and Amish are the only commonly known "plain people" left.

Picking one of the old American Utopias at random, we might choose Harmony, Pennsylvania, where the Rappites built a complete town in ten years and sold it at a great loss. Or we might follow the Rappites to New Harmony, Indiana, where they built another town in ten years and sold it at another loss. Their next Utopian town was ironically named Economy, in Pennsylvania, but the end of the Rappites was by then already in sight when George Rapp, who had inspired the movement and believed in a second coming of Christ within his generation, died. Because the Rappites were bound to strict celibacy, with their men and women sleeping in separate dormitories, there were no children to replace the Rappites who died. But the empires of trade to which they gave birth and the towns they built will live on despite their pathetic contribution to the religions of vanished America.

Today, the white spires of yesterday's churches are among the few remaining symbols of America's past. The church and the farm were once pieces of each day's activity, but now they are becoming refuges. Whether it is the suburbanite whose big church day is Sunday or the city person who stops

257

by during lunch hour to pray, there is always an element of escape from the business world. Perhaps great-grandfather overdid his religion with long graces at the table and group Bible readings before bedtime, but he derived more of God as a way of life than he could by regarding Him only as a refuge.

The Rappites, who didn't believe in marked graves, were buried in walled enclosures

Great-grandfather's Home.

IT TAKES A THOUSAND men to get a load of fuel oil from the raw material to your furnace and probably as many to deliver a load of coal. It takes only one man, however, to make a pile of cordwood. Unlike a mess of oil or a heap of coal, a stack of wood is a living and a gladdening thing to behold. It has long been the symbol of the double benefits of farm life, warming you twice —once when you cut it, another when you burn it. Actually there is a third warming which is hard to define; an old almanac says, "City homes are warmed by coal, but country hearths do warm the soul."

The happy fact that the early American home and farm were one is much more than a casual commentary on colonial life. It was the pioneer's creed and a basic American belief until only a century ago. Today it has all but vanished. Like every American, Jefferson truly believed that "those who labor in the earth are the chosen people of God" and that "the farmer is the most noble and independent man in society."

Whether you were a banker or shoemaker in colonial times, you were always at the same time a farmer: whether your home was large or small, it was also a farmstead. Even princes and politicians and poets of the eighteenth century were ardent agriculturists or posed as farmers and rural philosophers. Not having a rural background and a farming philosophy in those times was perhaps as bad as not being a church member.

259

To a great extent, the size and condition of your land and barns influenced your standing in the community. This in many cases resulted in barns

The fuel that heats you twice.

being much bigger than necessary, particularly among the Dutch and the Germans who were least conservative architecturally and most competitive in spirit. Some of the Dutch and German barns were bigger than the great tithe-barns of ancient Europe, a fact which gave their owners great pleasure as New World farmers.

We think of George Washington as being a "gentleman farmer," which now describes a hobbyist, but Mount Vernon followed the tradition of all homes of that time. The General had the exact knowledge of farming that every American enjoyed as part of his daily life. How strange and foreign to modern living is a notation from the diary of John Adams: "Rose at sunrise, unpitched a load of hay and translated two more 'Leaves of Justinian.'"

Farming now is an occupational pursuit. Farmers raise stock to sell, but two centuries ago they farmed almost entirely for themselves. Instead of a pursuit, farming was then a way of life. The philosophy of farming, which was once a recognized American principle, was based upon three beliefs:

1. That agriculture is the fundamental employment of man upon which all other economic activities are vitally dependent.

2. That the farmer enjoys economic independence.

3. That farm life is the natural life and, being natural, is therefore good. (This belief implies that the completely city life is necessarily a corrupt one.)

260

The inference that city life is inescapably corrupt seems so foolish as to be childish. Yet only now are psychologists wondering how to return to the American morality of a century ago. Without our realizing it, the laws and regulations of city and industrial living have stripped us of the habit of taking

Dutch Barns were big....

Schenectady
New York
1715

German Barns were bigger!

Pennsylvania
1760

responsibility for our own moral judgments. Guiding ourselves by polls and unions and what other Americans think, we base our decisions entirely upon what the majority does. A century ago when everyone took pride in being individual and different from the rest, the fact that many people cheat on income tax, practice race segregation, or use politics for their own personal gain would have been the last argument to justify our doing likewise. That would be just the time, in fact, for great-grandfather to polish his personal honor.

It is perfectly true that today's automobilist believes himself free to drive fifty miles an hour in a forty-mile zone, provided everyone else is doing the same, while the typical country driver is more careful about adhering to the law. It is true that the farmer would blush at the practice of putting down on his income tax report the "entertainment" and similar "expenses" which the city man enters. So, as childish as the remark might seem, your psychologist will prove that the city conformist is morally far behind the rural individualist.

Many features of the American home, from framing to shingles, were first used in barns. Barns, however, were designed to shrink and allow for ventilation during dry hot weather, but as homes improved, they became tighter and less drafty. The clapboard was the first refinement over barn design to grace the farmstead home. Clapboards, which are the simplest of outside house coverings today, were at first considered "dressy." Their earliest use was on the fronts of houses, while sides and backs were covered with

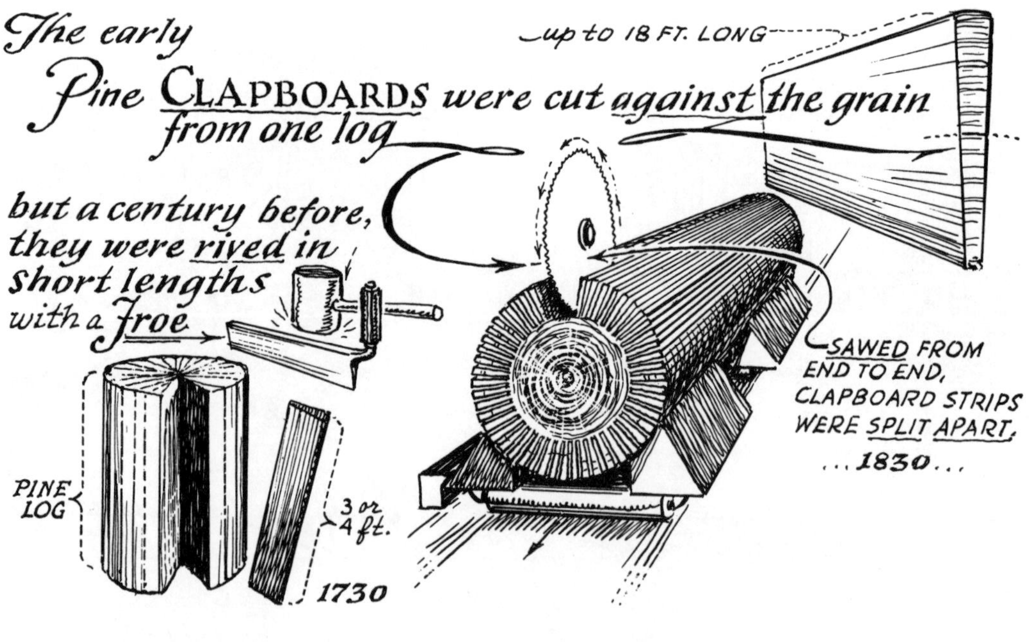

The early Pine CLAPBOARDS were cut against the grain from one log — up to 18 FT. LONG

but a century before, they were rived in short lengths with a froe

SAWED FROM END TO END, CLAPBOARD STRIPS WERE SPLIT APART.

...1830...

PINE LOG

3 or 4 ft.

1730

262

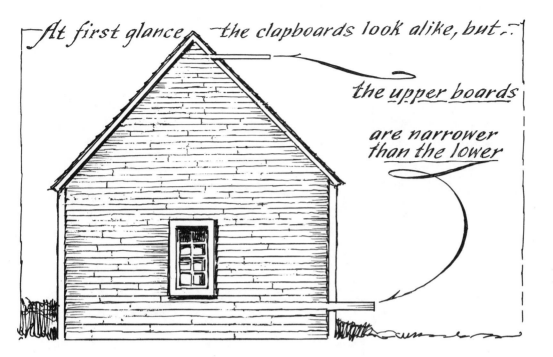

At first glance, the clapboards look alike, but... the upper boards are narrower than the lower

rough shingles. There is confusion about the origin of the word "clapboard" as the New England version was at one time called "clayboard," and some antiquarians insist clapboards once covered clay walls. But as the early Germans called them "Klappen Holz," the derivation seems more likely to have come from that source. ("Klappen" means to place or fit, while "Holz" is wood.)

The practice of clapboarding included such lost arts as cutting boards inward from one log (so there could be no warpage) and placing them upon the house in graduated widths. For example, many early gables were clapboarded according to dynamic symmetry, the widest boards at the bottom of the gable and lessening in width toward the peak. The difference is usually so slight as to be almost imperceptible, but that subtlety makes the difference all the more important and the builder that much more an artist. An effect of height is obtained by graduating clapboarding in this manner and many otherwise squat farmhouses have narrower boards toward the roof to give a pleasing effect. You might need a ruler to prove the difference, for perspective is deceptive. It is interesting and revealing to realize that the so-called simple farmer of yesterday knew these classic rules of symmetry, and that he considered them more important than does the average builder of today. Such variations have often been mistaken for the "imperfections of primitive carpentry." Consider the

263

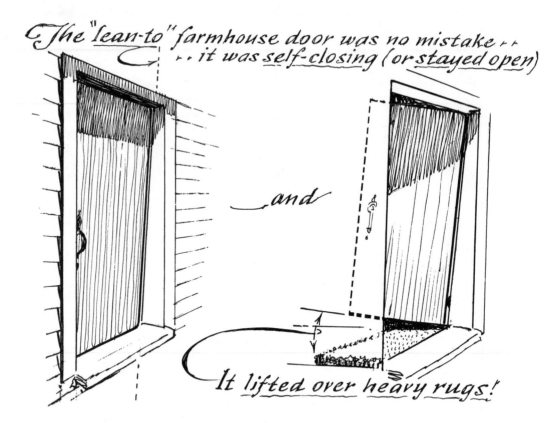

The "lean-to" farmhouse door was no mistake ··
·· it was _self-closing_ (or _stayed open_)

and

It lifted over heavy rugs!

plight of the New England lean-to door which is usually regarded as a mistake and replaced with a new door. It leaned so that almost no doorsill was necessary, and so it lifted itself over the heavy foot-wiping rug which was usually within the room. When you can't open a door because of an interfering rug, take the trouble to recall how great grandfather solved the problem.

At first the farmer had no more uniform of his profession (such as overalls, boots, and straw hat) than a business man would have now. It was the great divide of the Civil War and the machine age that shook the philosophy of farming and separated the farmer from the business man and the farm from the home. Those few who would have no part of change and continued in the old way became the "farmers" we knew only a few years back. They became the chin-whiskered, heavily booted Abners and Zekes who have so long been caricatured as "the American Farmer."

Farming is no longer a philosophy, but a full-time occupation. Whereas every American fed himself two centuries ago, only ten per cent of the population now feeds the other ninety per cent—and some portion of the rest of the world, too. Silas and all his things "down on the farm" are passing from the scene to join the vanished American landscape.

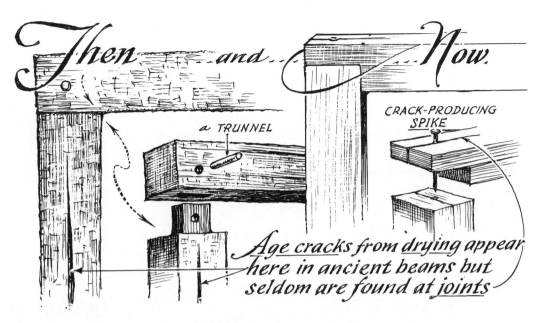

a TRUNNEL

CRACK-PRODUCING SPIKE

Age cracks from drying appear here in ancient beams but seldom are found at joints

If the covering were removed from old buildings, you would find the framework of the home and the barn exactly alike. The early method of fastening beams has never been improved upon; despite the contention that the "old fellows had all the time in the world," it is we with our time-savers who actually have more time. Using mortises and wooden pins is not just a slower way or a primitive way: it is the best way.

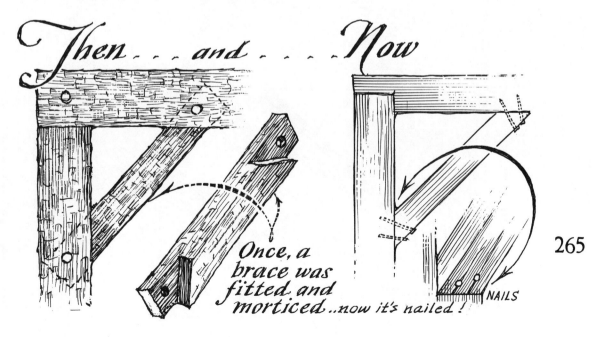

Then ... and ... Now

Once, a brace was fitted and morticed ..now it's nailed!

NAILS

265

History students are told that early settlers put timbers together with wooden pins because there were few nails to be had and those few were taxed by the Crown. The scarcity of metal and the taxes on hardware were real, but even if nails and spikes had been available, the wood-wise pioneer would have still used wooden pins. Much mention has been made of early houses being burned for their nails, but this occurred only during wartime. Often the nails remaining were not used as hardware at all, but melted down for bullets and implements. In all furniture and paneling, even when nails became plentiful, wood pins were still used, some as small as present-day brads. Most wooden nails or trunnels (tree-nails) were put in place hot and dry so that they might swell up with normal moisture and "weld" the joint together as they aged. As the drawing shows, nails tend to crack wood, while trunnels never cause cracks.

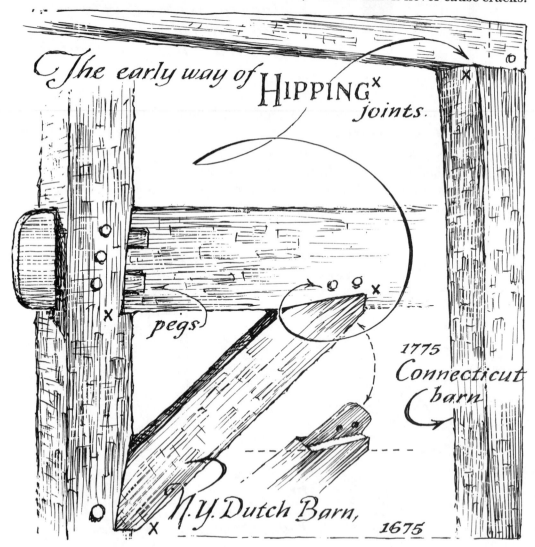

The early way of HIPPING^x joints.

pegs.

1775
Connecticut
barn

N.Y. Dutch Barn,
1675

266

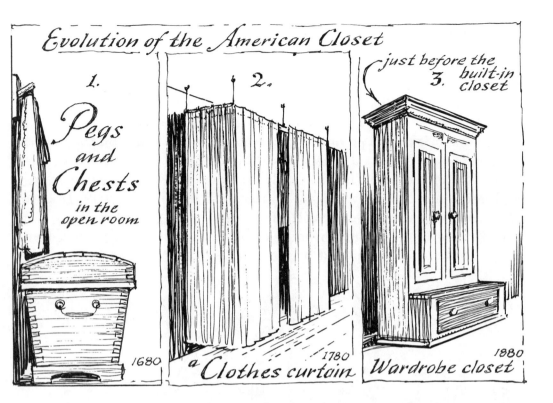

Evolution of the American Closet

1. **Pegs and Chests** *in the open room*

1680

2.

a *Clothes curtain*

1780

just before the **3. built-in closet**

Wardrobe closet

1880

Ancient timbers split with the dryness of age, but their joints and fastening-pins are usually left hard and crackless.

The ancient art of "shouldering" or "hipping" joints for extra strength was evident in the earliest pegged framework. The drawing shows hips at places marked X. The hip was often so slight as to be mistaken for an error in beam width: only the fact that all the rest of the beams were so treated reveals the truth.

Not long ago, few people were without an old homestead in their childhood background. But now when many people seem to change their home as often as they change their automobile, homes have become apartments or apartment-sized. Big homesteads have disappeared into rarity. Before the next century has passed, the typical American homestead will have become past history.

The average home of a century ago had twice as many extra rooms (most of which are now obsolete and forgotten) as are in the complete house of to-day. The smoke room, food cellar, borning room, milk room, chapel room, keeping room, summer kitchen, wash room, and corn room are just a few rooms that were as standard to an old house as a coat closet is to a modern one. Such a maze of rooms must have been fascinating to children; there is little

267

wonder the old houses have lingered through growing-up memories and haunted us during later years.

By the 1900's most of the old homesteads' rooms had been eliminated. Some had become bedrooms for that "new institution," the servant girl. Others became closets, which were unknown before 1800.

The clothes closet as we know it today is an American invention. The "closet" was originally a private or secret room. Clothes were either hung in the open on pegs or folded into chests, each person having a personal chest, often at the foot of the bed. The only early American household enclosures were cupboards, and even they did not appear until the middle 1700's. In about 1780, American farm wives invented the idea of placing curtains (hung from a wire) to cover the clothing hanging on pegs. This arrangement waited only for the curtain to be replaced by wooden doors to give birth to the clothes

Plumbum-man 1700's or *Plumber* 1800's

Beating a Lead Pipe with a Lead-man's hammer

Pipe-mold   *Sheet Lead*

closet. If you have ever seen small iron hooks hanging from ancient bedroom ceilings and wondered what they were, they were probably there to hold "clothes curtains" during the pre-closet days.

Privies entered the house about 1800 by way of abandoned clothes closets and were appropriately called "water closets." When tubs were installed, however, a whole room became necessary and the American bathroom was born. Tubs were all different at first; they were designed entirely by carpenters and installed before adding lead covering and lead-pipe outlets.

In early days, when you wanted to buy lead, you used the Latin word and asked for so many pounds of "plumbum." The man who worked with lead, making rain gutters, surveyor's weights (plumb bobs), and kitchen sinks was called a "plumbum-worker." When sanitary engineering appeared just before the 1900's, everything metallic connected with it was made of lead. All metal pipes were made of lead; sinks and bathtubs were wooden boxes lined with sheet lead. Pipes were not threaded and screwed together, but joined with an overlapping layer of lead and "wiped" together. Wooden pipes were still being manufactured in 1875, but the lead worker or plumbum-man of the nineteenth century ended that industry and became the plumber of today, by way of the bathroom.

It is startling to realize that the bathtub, as we know it, is very recent. Many persons now living were once children in a world of no bathtubs other than small portable ones. One of the things that impresses visitors at the Sagamore, Long Island home of Theodore Roosevelt is its lonely tub. The President of the United States had to share one tub with his large family and the great number of notables who visited the estate. The fact, of course, was not that the President was stingy, but that tubs were rare then. Made to order and quite a new thing in the early 1900's, the President's wooden-boxed model was probably the envy of all who wallowed in its watery confines.

The first built-in bathtub is supposed to be that of Adam Thompson at Cincinnati, Ohio. It was seven feet long and four feet wide, cased in mahogany and lined with sheet lead, weighing close to a ton. It was filled with water through a hand pump. On December 20th, 1842, Thompson had a tub-christening party and all the guests were invited to try out the new "indoor bathpool." The newspaper stories that followed were characterized by attacks by doctors who said the practice of bathing in winter would cause chronic colds. However, the idea took hold among the wealthy. In many towns where the water supply was small, a thirty-dollar tax was levied on each bathtub, designed, of course, to discourage their use.

269

The change from lead worker to plumber came almost overnight. Although mass production built-in bathtubs did not appear until a couple of

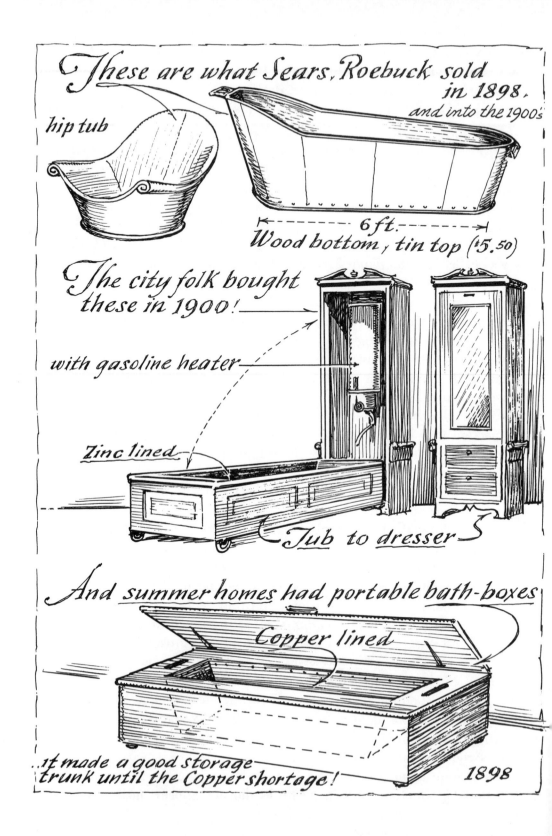

These are what Sears, Roebuck sold in 1898, and into the 1900's

hip tub

6 ft.

Wood bottom, tin top ($5.50)

The city folk bought these in 1900!

with gasoline heater

Zinc lined

Tub to dresser

And summer homes had portable bath-boxes

Copper lined

...it made a good storage trunk until the Copper shortage!

1898

When tubs were New...

drain

1890
Rocking-tub

Sheet tin
Cradle-tub 1900

years before the 1900's, by that time the word "plumber" had already come to mean the same as "sanitary engineer." Lead is still used by plumbers for soldering connections, and their ladles and equipment are unchanged from those of two centuries ago. Today few plumbers know the origin of their title.

It seems that Saturday evening has always been bath night, but few of us know that it stems from a religious beginning. When the Sabbath started at sundown on Saturday, many people followed the adage that cleanliness and Godliness go together and bathed only at that time. Before bathrooms existed, cedar tubs were placed before the fireplace on Saturday, half-filled with cold water, while the kettle of hot water to be added later hung over the fire. Some of the first portable tin tubs even had Biblical quotations painted upon them, but not many people would now associate a bathtub with the Sabbath.

The first tubs, like any other new-fangled gadget, assumed strange shapes. Some were made with "hips" to fit the shape of the body. Some were

271

painted with scenic designs, some were decorated solidly with floral patterns. Among the oldest was the cradle-tub for children to splash and rock in while taking their bath.

The cradle, which is one of the earliest standard pieces of furniture, has now passed into obsolescence in America. If you went out to purchase a cradle you would be disappointed, for they are no longer made. The last cradle manufactured was made over fifty years ago. The reason for the disappearance of cradles from the household scene is an American mystery, for they are still made in Europe and children need and enjoy the pleasant motion of rocking. Books on child care suggest rocking, but they do not say how they should be rocked, unless they imply that the child is to be held in a rocking chair!

At one time or another, cradles have been attached to butter churns, turnspits, dog mills, and even windmill gears to give them automatic movement, but the simple rocker cradle remained in the American household for over two centuries before its disappearance. People now prize antique cradles for storing magazines; it seldom occurs to them to put them to their proper use.

One of the more disputed examples of early American rocking furniture is the "adult cradle." It is sometimes argued that a few examples which are over six feet long were intended as cradles for twins, arranged so that the babies could lie end-to-end instead of side-by-side. Some have been used by new mothers and babies at the same time, while others have been occupied by senile or invalid persons. At any rate, they are known as "adult cradles"; they are just about the size of a single bed, but built closer to the floor.

The rocking chair is a purely American idea. We have had them since 1774, whereas the earliest known foreign rocker was made in 1840. The word "rocker" did not mean a chair until recently, but it did refer to those curved pieces of wood beneath cradles. Originally rocking chairs were called rocker chairs.

The step from cradle to rocking chair is lost in the complexity of American inventiveness that flourished between 1750 and 1775. There was once a combination cradle and settee known as a "rockee" or "rocking settee" that might have been the missing link between the two pieces of furniture.

Almost all of the early straight-backed rocking chairs are converted chairs with rockers added. Benjamin Franklin had experimented with an iron rocker to fasten to any chair. He also had a most remarkable "chair with rockers, and a large fan placed over it with which he fanned himself, keeping flies off, etc., while he sat reading, with only a small motion of his foot."

272

One of great-grandfather's achievements was his discovery of comfort. Colonial comfort, like its medieval interpretation, was mostly in a "satisfaction of space and proportions." Chairs were all hard and flat, while beds were

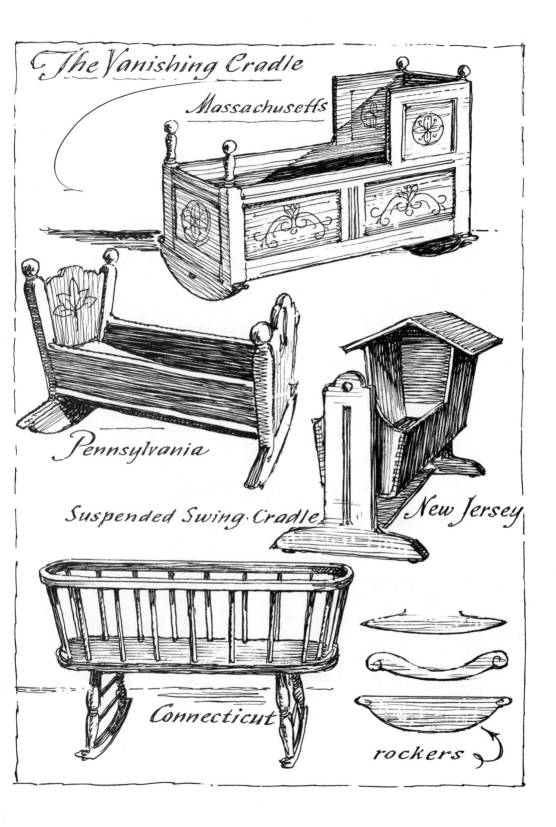

The Vanishing Cradle

Massachusetts

Pennsylvania

Suspended Swing Cradle

New Jersey

Connecticut

rockers

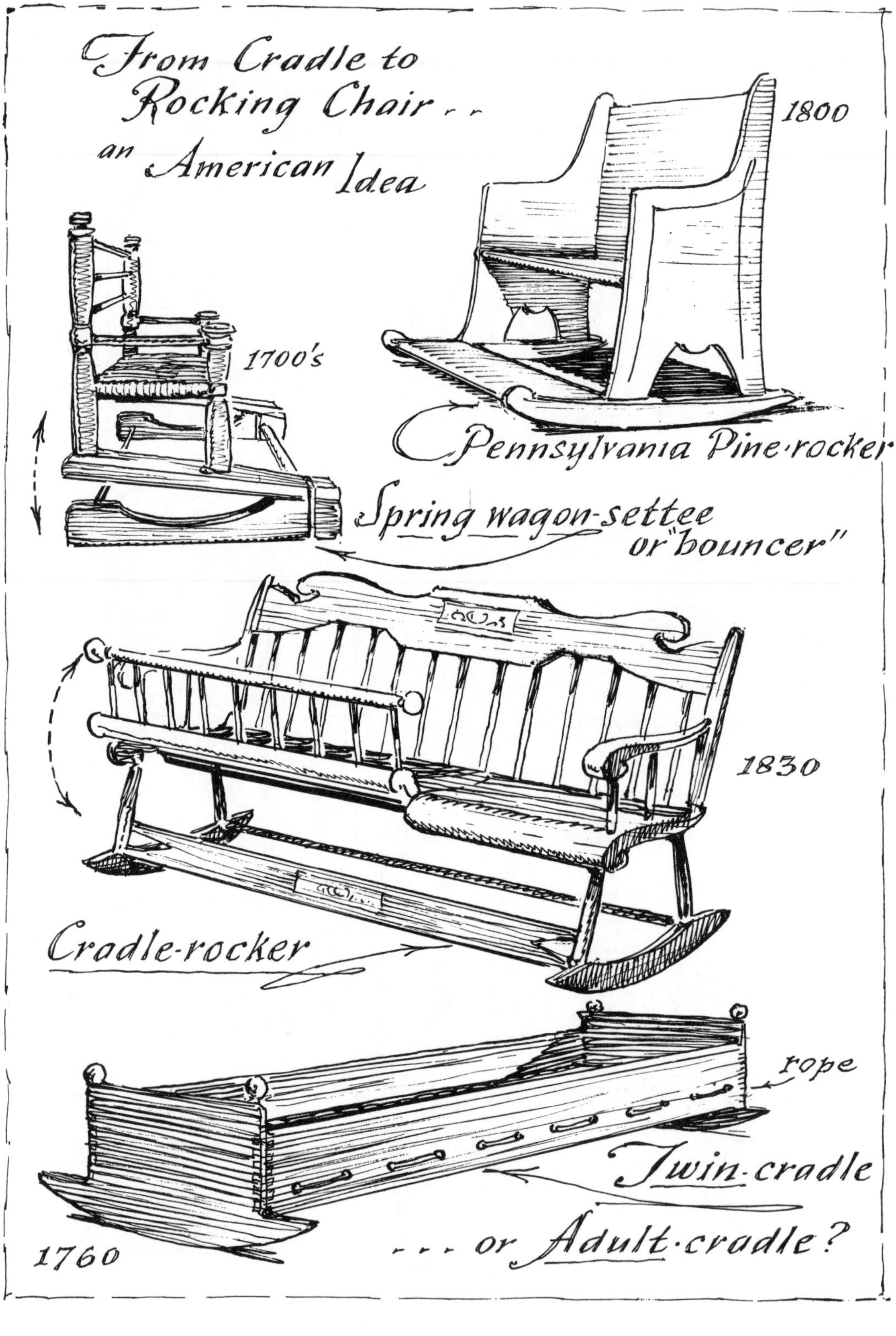

From Cradle to Rocking Chair...
an American Idea

1800

1700's

Pennsylvania Pine·rocker

Spring wagon-settee
or "bouncer"

1830

Cradle·rocker

rope

Twin·cradle

... or Adult·cradle?

1760

not much better. The American rope bed was considered the ultimate in comfort.

The rope-strung torture machine in which our ancestors slept suited the times very well, and it likewise seemed to suit its occupants. When you realize that most of the early beds were entirely home-made, their slight efficiency and comfort seem all the more remarkable. The early days were so much more active than the present ones that sleep fortunately must have been quicker and sounder.

Many antique shops sell wooden "butter paddles" with handles that slant to one side instead of extending straight outward. This is often confusing until one realizes that they are not butter paddles at all, but bed-patters. Feather

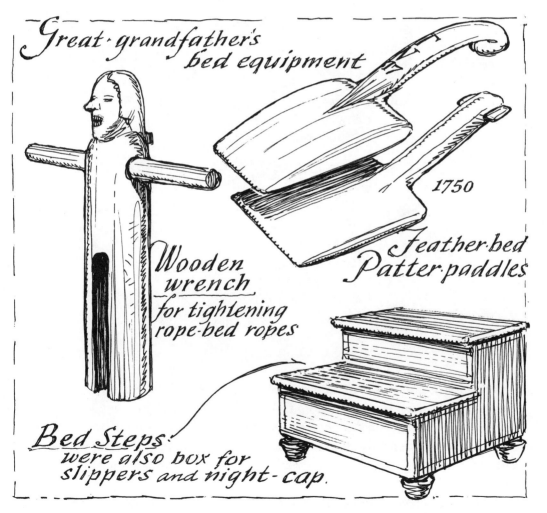

Great · grandfather's bed equipment

Wooden wrench for tightening rope-bed ropes

1750

Feather-bed Patter-paddles

Bed Steps were also box for slippers and night-cap.

275

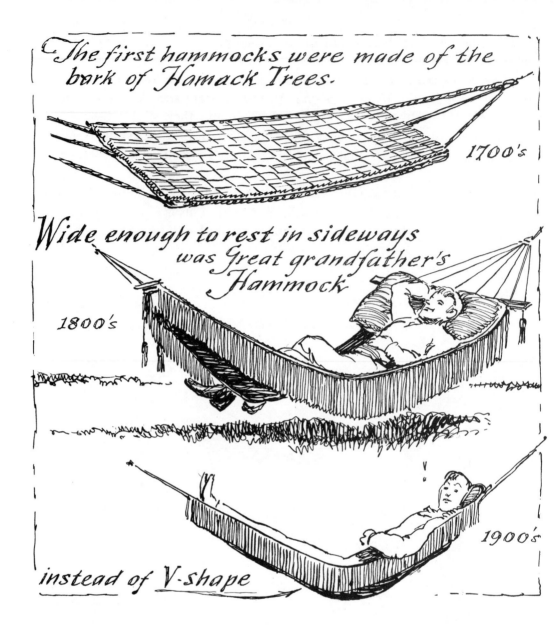

The first hammocks were made of the bark of Hamack Trees.

1700's

Wide enough to rest in sideways was Great grandfather's Hammock

1800's

1900's

instead of V-shape

beds needed a good deal of banging and patting to get them back into shape after a night's sleep on them, and a flat paddle to do the job was part of bedroom equipment. If you find a large paddle in your collection of wooden kitchenware, and wonder why it is dated or initialed, it is probably an eighteenth-century wedding gift, for bed-patters were once a favored present for the new bride.

The oldest rooms looked finished even when they were unfurnished: their comfort was visual rather than physical. The early twentieth century added

276

lounging porches to farmhouses, with rocking chairs and cushioned furniture to match. It became an age of featherbeds and padding. Indoor and outdoor comfort was the nineteenth-century order of the day.

One of the delights of those times was the hammock, which was a fringed joy compared to the skimpy examples available today. Perhaps it is a scarcity of trees for support that makes the old-fashioned hammock nearly obsolete, but the fact that the hammock is possibly the only type of furniture entirely native to the American continent should make it worthy of preservation. In 1492, when Columbus reached the western shores, one of the things which impressed him about the natives was their hammocks, in which a whole family often slept. When we rest in our present model, we recline lengthwise and assume an uncomfortable V shape, but the earliest hammocks were much wider and made for resting partly crosswise and nearly horizontal.

The early American house design is immediately recognizable by its outline or silhouette alone, and the reason is interesting. Houses used to be shapes divided into rooms, whereas houses have since become rooms massed into shapes.

The result of this early method of house-planning was a completely serviceable design. It gave immediate thought to roof slant, dynamic proportions, and pleasing over-all form. The modern method of planning often results in a ramble of disconnected shapes, in a one-story model or a two-story box-like shape with an unrelated roof. Today, when we design a home, we first decide the number and sizes and arrangements of rooms, then fit them into "a proper shape." Yesterday, Dutch gambrelled-squares, Duxbury-barn types, Cape Cod fisherman boxes, Pennsylvania penthouses, Virginia five-part mansions, New Hampshire joined houses, adobe ranch houses, New England garrison houses, and Southern plantation houses were all *basic shapes* to be divided into rooms. The major contribution to standard home design today is possibly "ranch house modern," which is less a style than it is an identification for a one-floor grouping of rooms.

So-called modern design is too often less inspired by the times than it is an escape from things traditional. Pure beauty is seldom the result of escape. With nothing to escape from, the good old homes were inspired by satisfaction of life and heritage, and revealed this quality. The finished product was lasting and good to look at, outliving architectural vogues.

Designers who have used the word "functional" as an explanation for their modernistic efforts have often been embarrassed to find their work identical to early American things which were functional without being at all obvious or calling for explanation. It is like a man traveling far in search of what he needs and returning home to find it there.

277

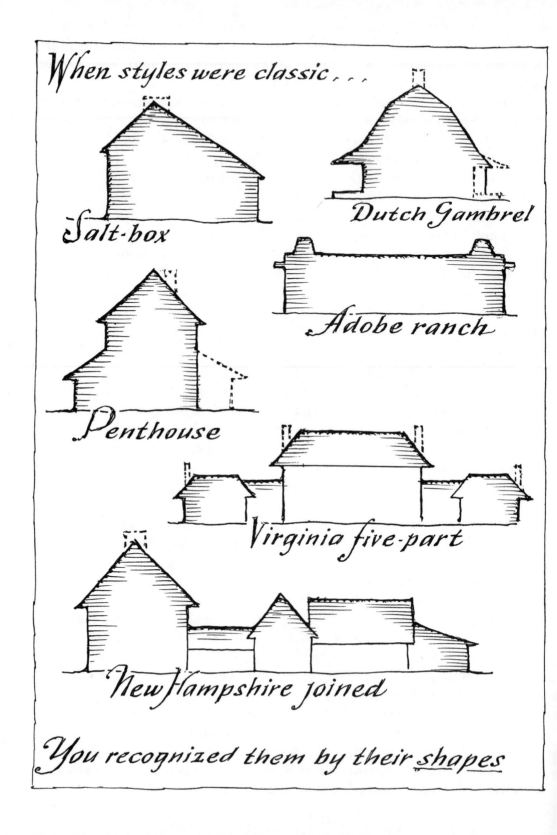

When styles were classic . . .

Salt-box

Dutch Gambrel

Adobe ranch

Penthouse

Virginia five-part

New Hampshire joined

You recognized them by their shapes

The nineteenth-century architects who produced what we call "Victorian" were important factors in America's first industrial era. The machine age seemed to call for a change in architecture; true to the American fallacy that any escape from the past or anything new must necessarily be progressive, the change was made. What resulted was a battle of styles that produced somewhat theatrical interpretations of Tudor, Gothic, Italian villa, Swiss chalet, Egyptian, and so on, into an endless list of the historical garbs of architecture. It even invaded the engine room and the plumbing.

There seems to be one outstanding characteristic of American Victorian, however (and one which has not been satisfactorily explained), called "gingerbread." We call it that because there is no definite word for the fretwork of scrolled wood that adorns most examples of this style of architecture. It has been called "Steamboat Gothic," "Belvidere," "Ice Cream," "Bargeboard Scroll," "Carpenter's Gothic," and other terms which denote ornateness in wooden trim. Its true name still remains as hidden as the identity of the forgotten carpenters who created it. Very often gingerbread scroll was not included in the building plans any more than rubber plants or bric-a-brac would be included in interior plans, but was added during construction. In some cases, it was even added years later to "modernize" farmhouses. The fact that gingerbread scroll appeared at the same time as the carpenter's ribbon saw (later to be known as the bandsaw) explains much.

The early northern farmhouse bedrooms and our present-day bathroom had much in common in both size and shape. A farmhouse room in those days

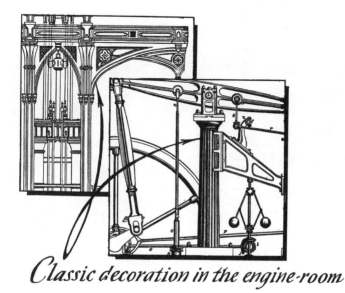

Classic decoration in the engine-room

279

was just what the word "room" denotes—space for a purpose: every room was self-contained and maintained its own integrity. Halls which allowed a cell-like division of small rooms have since been eliminated wherever possible; the old "bedroom hallway" is joining the list of vanishing rooms. This list has just about reached its maximum now that homes have achieved a uniform minimum of size. Here are some of those rooms which were all-important yesterday, but which will never find their way back into an architect's plan:

Wash Room:
Laundry. In the South, this was situated outside the house and under a shed. In New England, it was a room or shed off the kitchen, often within the breezeway between the kitchen and the woodshed.

Smoke Room:
Always next to the main chimney, often on the second floor between bedrooms, more often in the attic. Here hams and meats were smoked over smoldering hickory shavings and ashes. Even farms which possessed outdoor smokehouses often had an attic smoke room.

Keeping Room:
A "heart-of-the-house room" where, during great storms, all living could be confined. Often the kitchen, but sometimes a general sitting room.

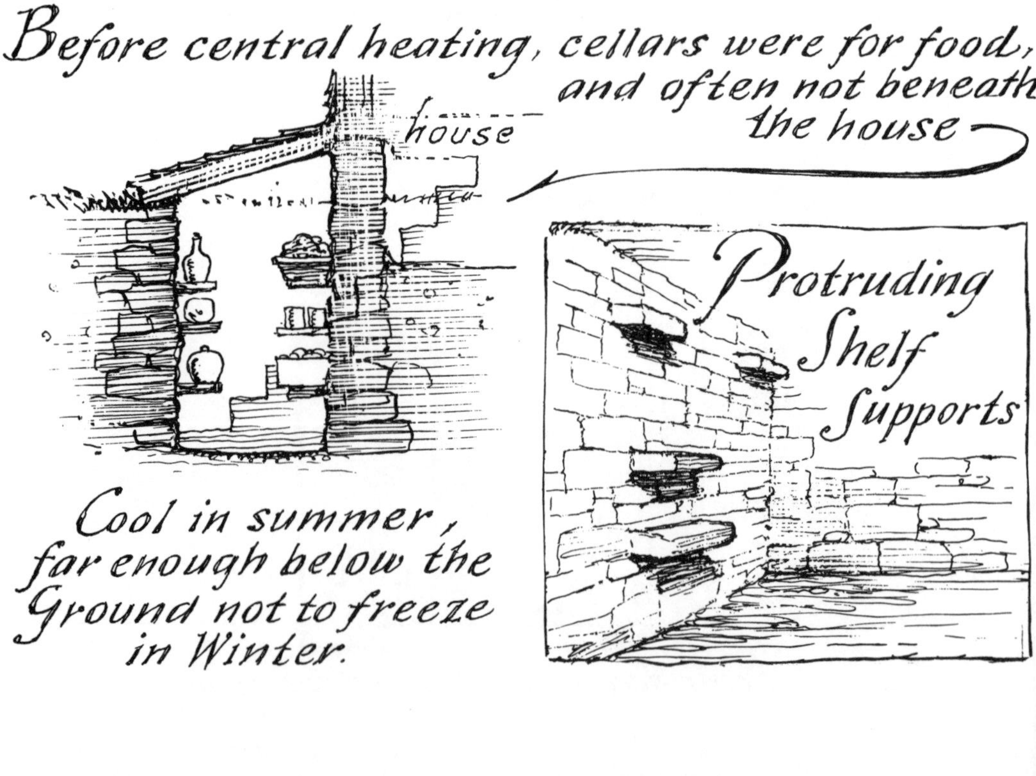

Before central heating, cellars were for food, and often not beneath the house

house

Protruding Shelf Supports

Cool in summer, far enough below the Ground not to freeze in Winter.

280

an Attic Smoke-room

L.I.N.Y 1780

— main Chimney

Pillion Room:

On the first floor, near the kitchen. Used for women's saddles, whips, harnesses, blankets, and riding accessories not associated with farm horses and farming equipment.

Powdering Room:

The smallest room. Not the "powder room" of today, but used for the keeping and powdering of wigs. Once equipped with wig stands.

Loom Room:

Where weaving, spinning, and reeling were done. Usually a separate house in the South, often found in the back or under the great northern slant of New England saltbox houses.

Cellar:

In its true use, cellar is a word from the French meaning food storage room. It was located beneath the house only to keep food cool during summer and to protect it against freezing in the winter. The first cellars were not

281

under the house at all, but a few steps away from it. They were underground rooms, sometimes with an opening into the well pit so that cool, damp air could enter. You will find evidence that ancient cellars served as storage pantries by the discovery of protruding stones in the cellar walls designed to support massive shelves.

Cock Loft:

A room above the garret. Garrets were used for so many things that a ceiling was often put in, making them separate rooms in their own right, with a small garret overhead.

Open Chamber:

Sometimes referred to as the season room. The large unfinished upper story of a house which was left to whatever use might arise, according to the time of year. In winter it stored corn and hides. In summer it was the hired hand's room, the "boy's room," or the chest room for clothing. Often referred to in Vermont diaries as the "corne loft."

Chapel Room:

A small room-closet, usually at the front of the house, used for meditating. A surprising number of plain farmhouses had chapel rooms which have since become forgotten and converted into closets.

Invalid Room:

A room hidden away in the back of the house with entrance only through the kitchen; intended for invalids, but most often for the member of the

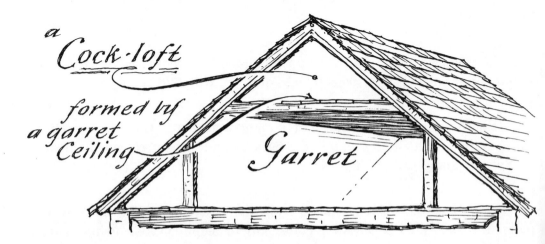

a "Cock·loft
formed by
a garret
Ceiling

Garret

family "not quite right." It was considered better to keep weak-minded relatives at home with the family instead of committing them to institutions, particularly when they were aged. In many old farmhouses these rooms were known only by the invalid's name, such as "Aunt Jenny's room" or "Old Pete's room," etc.

Captain's Room:

A small room on top of a flat-topped monitor roof. Originally used by sea captains or their wives for watching ships arrive in the harbor. When railed around, it was called a "captain's walk" or "widow's walk."

Buttery:

A room for provisions off the kitchen, often a milk room or place for the making and storing of cheeses. Here the churn and cheese cloths were kept. Milk rooms were missing in the earliest houses, and so was milk. Cows were kept mainly to breed oxen; cider and beer were drunk at the dinner table, even by children, who seldom tasted cow's milk.

Dumbwaiter (or Butler's) Pantry:

A turn-of-the-century room off the dining room for the "dumbwaiter" or rope elevator which transported food and dishes from the kitchen below to the upper floors of brownstone-type houses in the city.

Borning Room:

Usually off the kitchen, an ancient room reserved for births. Often used as a sick room and for placing tubs for Saturday bathing.

Hot-Water Pantry:

A closet near the kitchen where water was heated in a big iron pot. This pot was often located over the fire where the coals for baking ovens were prepared. The pantry (from the French word for bread) was also a room for keeping bread. The moist effect of heating water kept bread fresh and tasty, so the two rooms were combined and bread was stored in the hot-water pantry, along with dough and baking equipment.

Summer Kitchen:

A room separate from the house, but usually attached by a breezeway, where all cooking was done during the warmer months. The kitchen fireplaces and ovens operated twenty-four hours a day, causing considerable heat during the warm months. Breakfast, which was usually indistinguishable from supper, was often started at night so it might be cooked by morning.

283

Spring Room:

Often a part of the kitchen, sometimes a dropped room just off the

Hot-water Pantry

Stone shelves

Hot water pot

FLUE

Fire for preparing Oven Coals

kitchen. Here spring water constantly flowed into a giant barrel and over-flowed into an outlet that carried it downhill and away.

As the farm grew and the family increased, many of the old rooms became outbuildings and they, too, were placed with some forethought and planning. When great-grandfather chose his home site, he built into a plot of air as well as upon a plot of ground. Weatherwise and aware of the effects of weather on buildings and farm stock and humans, he determined the position of his home

284

and barn and outbuildings by the disposition of the land with regard to the prevailing winds and to the arc of the sun.

Wind dictates the mechanics of all fireplaces; therefore, it governed the comfort of early houses during winter. Long before the pick and ax fell, weather sites were researched and planned carefully. You will still find houses and barns molded into the weathered contours of the land, their roofs slanted steepest toward winter winds and their most lived-in rooms facing the warm south.

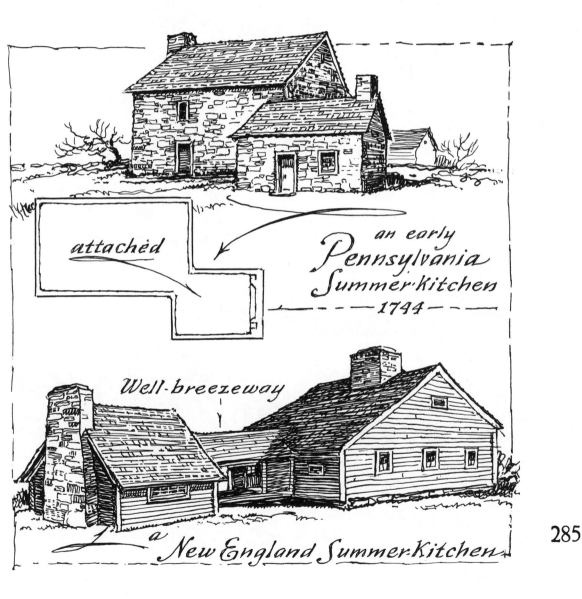

attached

an early
Pennsylvania
Summer-Kitchen
— 1744 —

Well-breezeway

a New England Summer-Kitchen

285

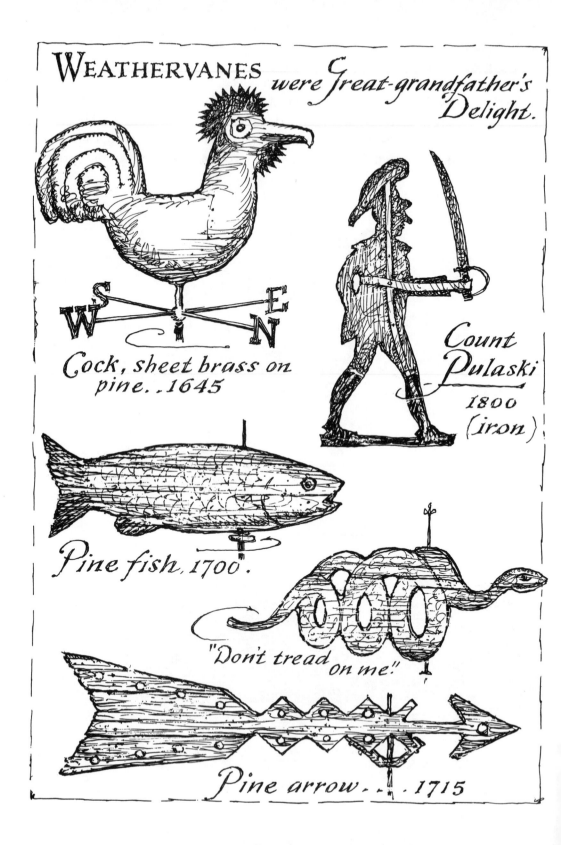

WEATHERVANES *were Great-grandfather's Delight.*

Cock, sheet brass on pine.. 1645

Count Pulaski 1800 (iron)

Pine fish, 1700.

"Don't tread on me."

Pine arrow.... 1715

The weathervane which decorated all ancient barns was not a decoration as much as a farm implement. When to plant, when to cut hay, almost every act of farming in some way or other involved the direction of the wind. Barns, farm outbuildings, and privies were placed where prevailing summer winds could carry odors away, while honeysuckle and herb gardens were put where the same wind would carry sweet scents into the house.

The earliest weathervanes were made of dry, light pine, which explains why so few of them are still in existence. It was the custom for settlers first to use a strip of cloth as a wind pennant (vane is from the early word "fano" for flag), and to whittle a fine wooden weathervane during the first winter. The quadrants indicating north, east, south, and west were not used on early farm vanes because the barn itself was placed with its sides to the cardinal points and the farmer knew his wind directions instinctively.

When the 1800's brought in the vogue of painting houses, all sorts of decorations were added and iron weathervanes appeared by the thousands. Sheet copper was hammered over pine to make molded figures, but they were heavy and swung poorly in the wind. Later, however, after pounding the metal to a wooden shape, the inner wooden shape was removed; the result was a lighter hollow copper figure which swung easily. So the hollow weathervane, such as is still made today, was born.

The second most important thing about choosing a home site and arranging the early buildings was the water supply. Dug wells are comparatively recent, and the oldest houses had a constant gravity supply of spring water. Some farmhouses still have gravity spring water and they enjoy a supply even when the electric power fails or ordinary water systems become frozen. The contentment of hearing your own clear spring trickle into your house is fast becoming a vanished pleasure of the olden days.

A few antique shops still have examples of wooden pumps, but there is little interest in or market for them. Within another decade or two they will have become forgotten Americana. The pumpmaker was a very important man in the early village and he was always looked to for having special "water-finding" abilities. He was always an expert dowser.

"Dowsing," "divining," or "water-witching" was carried on as a regular occupation, although most farmers professed some ability to locate underground water. They held a forked willow stick in both hands and walked over the spring site; a sudden mysterious pull was supposed to be exerted upon the witching-stick, directing one to the nearest water. The first sticks were made of swamp hazel (hence the name witch hazel), but when willow (which English dowsers had always used) was imported to America, witching-sticks were then fashioned from this wood.

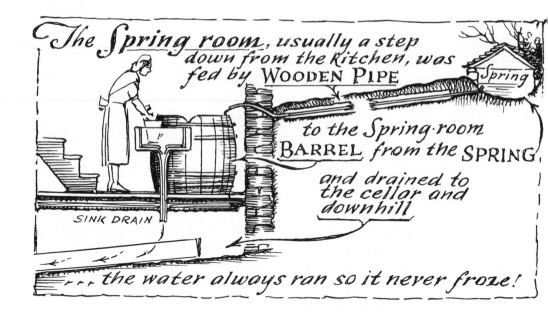

The Spring room, usually a step down from the Kitchen, was fed by WOODEN PIPE to the Spring-room BARREL from the SPRING and drained to the cellar and downhill

Spring

SINK DRAIN

... the water always ran so it never froze!

Well-building was not always a full-time job, particularly when the ground was frozen, so the pumpmaker spent his winter turning pump stocks and handles. He also specialized in dry-wall building. Dry-masoning began to disappear when cement entered on the American building scene. Hitherto, a good dry mason could build a permanent foundation wall without any bonding cement at all and could make it so tight and strong that two centuries have left the old foundations unmoved. Ask for a dry mason in any rural dis-

Well-diggers were expert with the Divining Rod

WELLS dug by GEO. OTT

Old sign from Roslyn L.I.

288

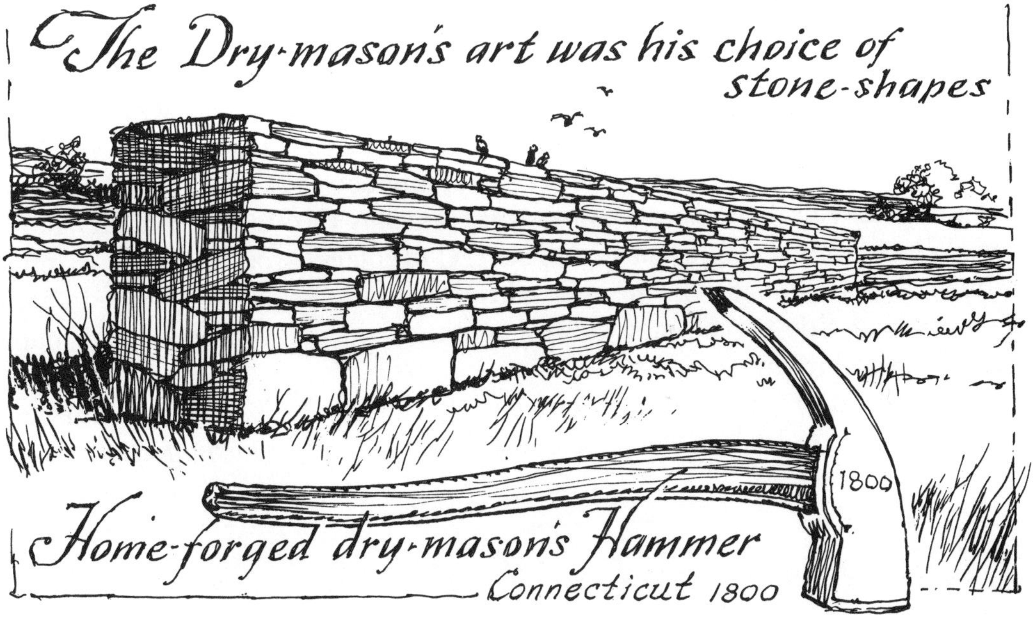

The Dry-mason's art was his choice of stone-shapes

Home-forged dry-mason's Hammer
——— Connecticut 1800

trict in America and people will know what you are talking about. Furthermore, you will still find these men have the inherent knack of placing the right stone in the right place. Yet the art is a vanishing one and the name "dry mason" has already disappeared from dictionaries.

You might wonder why dry masonry and other obsolete occupations are not properly gone and forgotten. But we are not comparing building styles as much as we are discussing the builders themselves. It is revealing that the common worker of a few years ago did all his jobs "the hard way" and with an eye toward their lasting qualities, thinking almost less of his own lifetime than that of his successors. Our white population now averages two or three children in a family, but in the early nineteenth century women produced an average of eight, which might explain the passion for permanency.

Today one could hardly build anywhere and be certain that the area would not change within a few decades or that a highway might not come through sooner. There is no doubt that people used to build for their children's children, while the basic philosophy of present-day building (outside of immediate needs) is "What will I lose or gain if I sell?" It is interesting to learn from the termite-control companies how well some of the older places were built. "In houses of about two hundred years," they say, "the decay or eaten wood almost always has started in newer additions. Woodsheds or other structures added within the last fifty years are the source of our biggest business."

289

The first dry masons learned their art by making chimneys. Chimneys were made of mud and sticks when roofs were thatched, making both roofs and fireplaces dangerously flammable. With a little political pull, a dry mason could get the job of chimney-viewer and earn about eighty dollars a year (at present-day values) checking all the chimneys in town to prevent fire hazards. The first chimney-viewers were appointed by the Crown and they also became tax assistants wherever houses were taxed by the number of their chimneys. When colonists built houses and several fireplaces around one monstrous chimney, it was probably fireplaces and not chimneys which were taxed. But the work and title of chimney-viewer continued in many places until long after the Revolution.

Great-grandfather had his own special windows. We still use shutters "for decoration," although they once were opened every morning and closed

Even chimneys had Individuality...

N.Y. Dutch 1700

Virginia

Snow hoods

Maine, New Hampshire

Maryland, Delaware

290

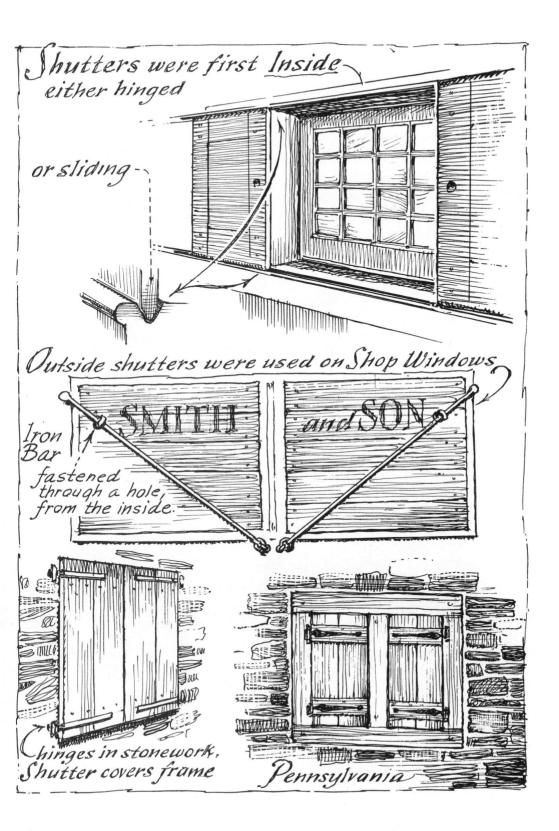

Shutters were first Inside
either hinged

or sliding

Outside shutters were used on Shop Windows

SMITH and SON

Iron
Bar
fastened
through a hole
from the inside.

hinges in stonework,
Shutter covers frame

Pennsylvania

every night. Storekeepers "put up the shutters" as soon as night arrived; being too large for hinges, they were kept in back of the store during business hours. The scarcity of glass made early windows poor substitutes for what we have today, but, architecturally speaking, the beauty of old American windows will never be recaptured by the mass-production methods that seem necessary for modern building. We might think it strange or quaint to learn that the old-timers sold their houses or even rented them "less windows," carrying these around as special possessions. Yet the building wreckers' most prized merchandise now comprises old casement windows and attic "lights": modern builders buy them quickly, for they cannot be reproduced today with the same grace and workmanship.

292

a Window Sundial

The small New England windows with sashes that are never fastened but cling with nails half driven into the side casing were made thus so that windows could be removed or tightened easily. Most people hammer the nails in all the way with some annoyance at "the old way of doing things," but find trouble during winter when wood shrinks and the rattling windows need tightening. Others wonder at the cuts on window sills, often accompanied by numbers. These were indoor sundials for use in the days when a stopped clock could not be reset as easily as it is today; the shadow of a window strip on the sill could be depended on to tell fairly accurate time.

Great-grandfather's house would certainly not be sufficient for present-day living, but we might wonder if present-day living is sufficient itself. As time unwinds the clock, old houses are still sound emblems of gracious living. We may live more easily or casually nowadays, but there is a graciousness in hard work and chores that is beyond present-day comprehension. The building of a log fire and the task of watching and poking it is a pleasure which no steam radiator can replace. And the nervousness created by company moving from place to place in a room, glasses in hand, was missing from the early living room where everyone gravitated to the fireplace group.

Some ancient houses seem to speak like humans, even though they are empty. Yet most modern houses without furniture or people in them have no more character than a closet or a bathroom wall.

"The severe simplicity of the ultra-modern living room," says one designer, "is a suitable theatre for the dynamic character of today's personality." Such a statement causes one to pause and reflect.

Great·grandfather's Town.

A BLIND PERSON might say that living in the city is almost unbearable, while living in the country is a great adventure. Of course, in thinking of country living, we immediately recall its scenic values. Yet places, even one town from another, can also be identified by sound. Most of us are unaware of such slow change, but any age, even the decade we live in, may be identified by its sounds.

In the 1700's, the tread of heavy boots on wide plank floors, the ring of felling axes through the hills, the occasional roll of drums, the call of peddlers and town criers in the square, all identified the time. Each room had the sputter and hiss of fireplace logs; the kitchen had a tiny, comforting tinkle of water into a spring barrel. The whirr and clatter of spinning wheels and farm mills lasted throughout the day, but the wash of water through mill sluiceways and the faraway booming of back-country plumping mills lasted throughout the night.

In the 1800's there were church bells and door bells and bells on horses and cows and oxen. Lighter-weight button shoes were quieter as they walked on carpeted floors, but hoofbeats in the street clattered hollow and sharp on the new cobblestones. The sound of travel became one of wagon wheels over gravel roads and the booming roar of plank roads. Every bridge thundered its loose planks as the stagecoach passed over it. Kitchen stoves clattered their iron lids, the noise of plates was more brittle than the soft clash of pewter. All the noises of the early ovened fireplace were absent. The walking of people on stone sidewalks was the first "big city sound," second to the metallic

"Home, Sweet Home"... Long Island, N.Y.

screech of street car rails or the whistles of trains and factories. "The noise of the city," an 1850 *Harper's Magazine* said, "is so strange to the farmer that it takes a few days of country quiet for him to get over the nervous tension."

The 1900's introduced new machine noises. The suburban clatter and clack of lawnmowers, the sputter and bang of the first automobiles, and the tinkle of pianos invaded the noises of rural home life. The city had by then developed its own noise—a hum which reached a nervous roar by day and settled to a more slumbering breathing hush by nightfall.

Spring-Barrel Symphony

...the tiny comforting tinkle of water...

295

We are already accustomed to jet-plane noises. What would have troubled us twenty years ago has become no more than a sound backdrop for normal conversation today. We accept radio sounds without even analyzing them; only when they become so loud as to drown out conversation do we begin to notice them. Indeed, there is considerable sound-difference between the world of yesterday and the world of today.

It might be believed that great-grandfather enjoyed the sounds of his world more because he knew what they were. Today when we accept the pattern of city noise as an undercurrent or unnoticed sound of living (like that of our own breathing), we do so because to listen and identify each individual sound would be impossible. But the past joy of having to contend with only a few uninterrupted sounds made bird song, farm sounds, hearthside sounds, and each person's voice the appreciable music of everyday life. Yesterday there were sounds; today there is noise.

The noisiest part of yesterday's community was the town market. The best salesman was usually the loudest crier; if you had no "crying" ability, you could always hire it. Professional criers were the vaudevillians of their day, sometimes dressing in strange costumes, throwing in whatever talents they possessed, and often selling on a commission basis. You will hear about

Crying in the Market

The Head-House of Philadelphia's Second St. Market

old-time street vendors who "cried their wares," but these were usually professional criers who worked side by side with the actual salesman.

New York and other big cities still have a few crying vendors, such as the flower-wagon man who cries "flower plants," the rag merchant who cries "I cash clothes" (frequently just an abbreviated "I cash!"), and others selling ice, vegetables, etc. But all such "salesmen" were once frowned upon in any place but the town market and it was there that you could choose, from an always available group, the man to cry your wares.

Often in early records there will be mention of a "market master"; antiquarians have found little clue as to the meaning of this occupation. In 1952, while plans were under way to demolish Philadelphia's "Head House" in the Second Street Market, the office of market master was brought to light and as quickly eliminated from the city payroll. This long, narrow one-story structure had been in operation since it was built by the first mayor of Philadelphia, Edward Shipen, in 1745. It was one of the last of the old "middle-of-the-street markets."

Few people know that the very wide streets in the old business sections of some cities are wide because there was once a middle-of-the-street market there. Philadelphia and Boston and New York owe many of their wider streets to these outdoor markets which were managed by market masters. The city market master, like the country miller, was lawyer and banker to the farmer, who usually preferred trading merchandise instead of selling it. The market bell sounded the end of the business day but, because farmers usually drove all night to arrive near daylight, there was no opening signal for the day's trading. Every market had its bell, however, which closed the market day at sundown. Selling after hours was punished by a fine, imposed on both buyer and seller and payable to the market master.

Selling on the Sabbath likewise drew a strict fine and that was the only Holy Day or "Holiday" so observed by law. Holidays will never vanish from the American scene, but their meanings often become distorted with the years. Like the little boy who remarked how nice it was "that Christ happened to be born on Christmas Day," many of us are ignorant of the meaning of our holidays. The "Christmas rush," the "Easter parade," the "Thanksgiving feast," and all the other descriptive American holiday phrases convey meanings which are sometimes the opposite of their original significance. It is revealing to compare our present holidays with those of a century or two ago, before commercialism intervened.

Knowing that this country was founded on early religious principles, most people believe that Christmas is one of our first and greatest holidays. But the holy days of the English Church were completely ignored by the

Puritans and the one they hated most happened to be Christmas! When the Church of England established Christmas services in Boston, the majority rose against it, forbidding their children to attend. The Christmas celebration took a long while to evolve in America, and the Noël we know could not be regarded as a New England holiday until the nineteenth century.

The first New England Thanksgiving service was performed in the Church of England by the Popham colonists at Menhegan. Neither the Plymouth Pilgrim nor the Boston Puritan observed Thanksgiving at that time, although everyone seems to think they did. The final Puritan Thanksgiving lasted a week (not a day) devoted to feasting and gaming, without any record of special religious services.

Thanksgiving Day was never New England's big holiday. Writing in 1699, Ward does not even name it. "Election Day, Commencement Day and Training Day are their only Holy Days," he explains. "If the college die," the theory went, "the church cannot live." So Commencement Day was one of America's favorite holidays, although few of us are now aware of it. Much of our present holiday cooking originated with Commencement cake, Commencement puddings, and other Commencement Day delicacies.

Training Day, of course, was a military exercise, although it came closest to our present Fourth of July. When the Fourth came into being, many of the public shooting matches, "exercising of arms," and military din-

298

Independence Day was America's Picnic Day.

ners of the old Training Day were carried over into the new Independence Day celebration. The first Fourth of July in many ways resembled today's Thanksgiving Day, except that the feasting was in the form of outdoor picnicking.

In a New Milford, Connecticut barn there is an old newspaper, glued to cover the wall cracks, in which there is an account of a Fourth of July military luncheon. The toast mentioned therein gives insight into the average villager's conception of that holiday:

"July 6, 1822.

". . . at one o'clock a number of Officers dined at Patton's Tavern, and then drank the following

"TOASTS.

" '1. THE PATRIOTS OF '76. —May we ever cherish their principles and imitate their virtues.

"2. THE ARMIES OF THE UNITED STATES. —The laurels acquired by them in honorable war have never been sullied by outrages like those of our enemies at Hampton and Frenchtown.

"3. OUR DECLARATION OF INDEPENDENCE. —A beacon to the friends of liberty and a terror to monarchs.

"4. INDEPENDENCE. —May we not lose its substance and court its shadow.

"5. THE NEXT CONGRESS. —May they encourage Domestic Manufacturers and be contented with forty-two dollars a week.

"6. THE LEGISLATIVE AND EXECUTIVE DEPARTMENTS OF THE UNITED STATES. —May they think less about the next Presidency, and more of our National concern.

"7. THE AMERICAN FAIR. —Their smiles animate the soldier's bosom; their virtues awe him into respect.

"A prayer by the Chaplain of the First Regiment followed, then a volley of gunshot from the Common, and the dinner commenced."

Election Day was possibly the loudest and least religious of early American holidays. Although an election sermon was supposed to start the day off, the sermon was most often about the evils of the day, and warnings about the use of election beer. Our present Election Day is strangely mixed up with Guy Fawkes' Day which was observed for many years in America by the burning of bonfires and with parades of children in fantastic costume. In Newburyport, Massachusetts, and Portsmouth, New Hampshire, Guy Fawkes' Day is still recalled. In New York and Brooklyn, the bonfires on the night of election are descendant of those for Guy Fawkes' Day. Fires are still lit on November 5th by some of the back-country children, although they do not know why.

Holidays were once signals to get away from the farm and come to town. Now holidays are times for getting away from the city and rushing to the country. Unfortunately we seem to have less time for one-day enjoyment and relaxation than people used to; even in ox-cart days a ride to town took less time than a present-day trip to the country on a traffic-filled highway often does.

Going to town was once a pleasing experience to the eye when villages were nestled comfortably in valleys and the outskirts were unmarked by road stands and advertising. There was a turn in the road, it always seemed, where the town suddenly came into view. Now roads are straighter and the pattern of the town spills over into the highway for miles before you come to it.

The twisting of old roads was usually intentional. Horses (and humans, too) found "the longest way 'round the sweetest way home" because it eliminated hills. We now go in a straight line up and over hills, whereas we used to

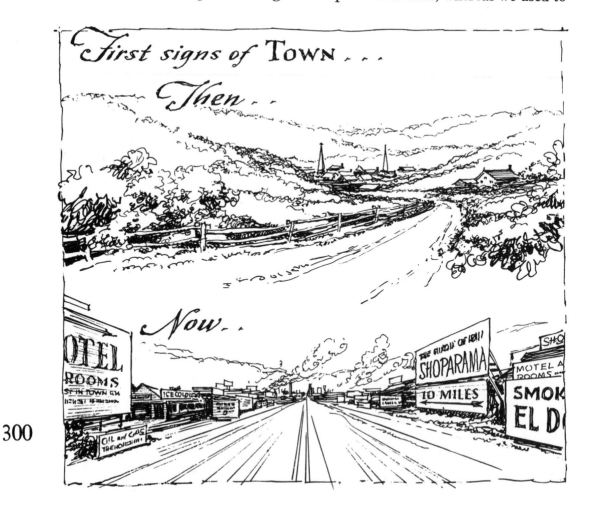

First signs of TOWN . . .

Then . .

Now . .

300

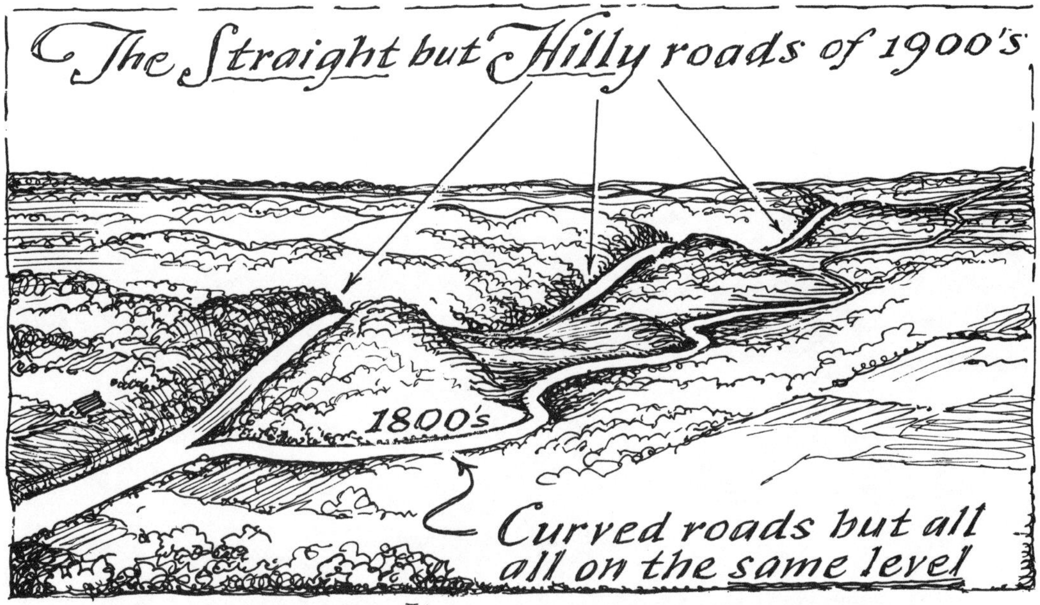

The Straight but Hilly roads of 1900's

1800's

Curved roads but all
all on the same level

..like cowpaths along the side of a ridge

keep on the same level and wind around them in much the same manner that a cow travels on a hilly farm.

One of the outstanding changes occurring in small towns during the last few years is the healthy tendency to abandon valleys and move to higher levels. Actually, most cities are built around the principles of two centuries ago, with electrically run mills still crowded over ancient river-powered mill sites. Even regular and devastating floods have not discouraged this practice or persuaded the mill owners to give up their real estate and move to higher ground. Only within the last two decades have highways by-passed valley towns and has small industry built with highway philosophy, avoiding rivers and valleys and floods.

Actually, valley locations are damper and less adaptable to many industries, as well as being areas in which heavier cold air from the hills gravitates and collects. Pollen and smoke and smog, such as you will see over many low-lying industrial cities, likewise settle in the valleys.

One of the greatest differences between the town of the past and the

301

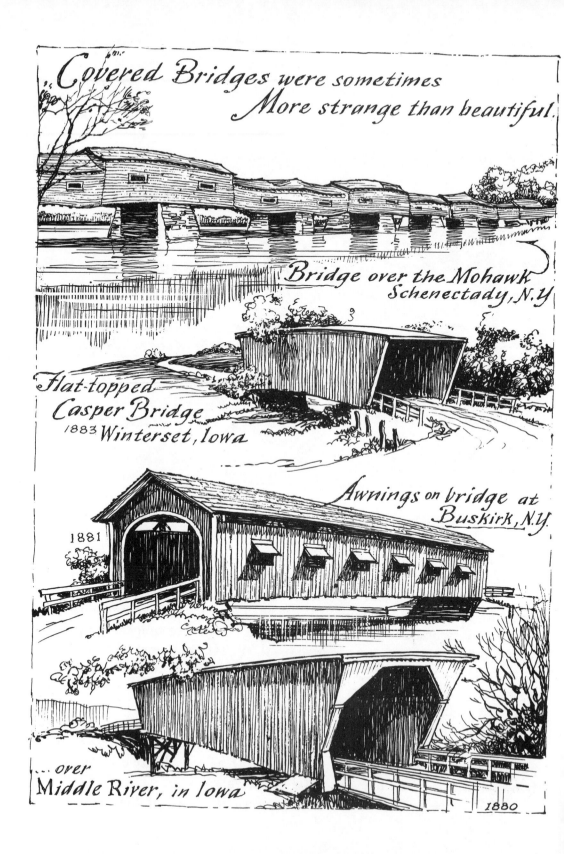

Covered Bridges were sometimes More strange than beautiful.

Bridge over the Mohawk Schenectady, N.Y.

Flat-topped Casper Bridge 1883 Winterset, Iowa

Awnings on bridge at Buskirk, N.Y.

1881

...over Middle River, in Iowa

1880

city of today is to be found in the atmosphere. The sky seems of limitless height, yet the truth is that one-half of all the atmosphere above sea level lies below a height of 18,000 feet. The average "settling area" of quiet city air is below a thousand feet. Although we are so used to it that we do not notice it, you will actually see the settling level of dirty atmosphere when you fly from a big city airport and almost immediately climb into clear air. New York receives an airborne layer of a half ton of dirt on some city blocks each month. Chicago reported an average of 71.6 tons of dust and dirt on each square mile per month. Sending thirty million tons of soft coal a year into the atmosphere, Chicago finds that most·of its dirt is soot, but any big city has the same sewer in its sky, no matter what the character of the foreign matter happens to be. Recently an epidemic of "disintegrating" nylon stockings occurred in major cities, and the phenomenon was found to be caused by "coal and oil in combination with an oxidizing agent within polluted city air"—the same air, of course, that the nylon-wearers inhaled. Some of the chemicals in city air are known to cause cancer in experimental animals, but what we can't see doesn't worry us, so we are mostly concerned with the dirt that rims our shirt collars and makes city apartments dingy.

Never to be left out of the early American picture are the wooden bridges that led to town. Only the covered ones seem to be revered and "collected" by antiquarians, but the uncovered ones were of equal importance.

America's covered bridges are known by the few examples remaining. Those are the ones which were built soundly and which have therefore withstood the ravages of age and the strain of ice floods. But the uncovered bridges which have disappeared or even those which lasted perhaps for only a few months were often as interesting as the longer-lived covered structures.

The idea of collecting a dollar a foot royalty on your own bridge patent became a delightful and fashionable inspiration to all retired men of the 1800's with architectural leanings. By simply adding a brace here or an arch there to your neighbor's patent, you were in business with your own design. Printing houses were soon kept busy making posters and leaflets extolling the virtues of new bridge designs, and men who thought they were destined to the easy chair of old age were suddenly traveling as far as Europe with patented designs for "American-type" wooden bridges. But not everyone could be a Town or a Burr, and many a strange new creation of trestles and arches fell into the river when the builder's scaffold chocks were knocked out.

303

The number of covered bridges which were carried away during floods, yet were floated back and put into place again, is astonishing. Some were even set on new supports where they came to rest downstream and the road itself

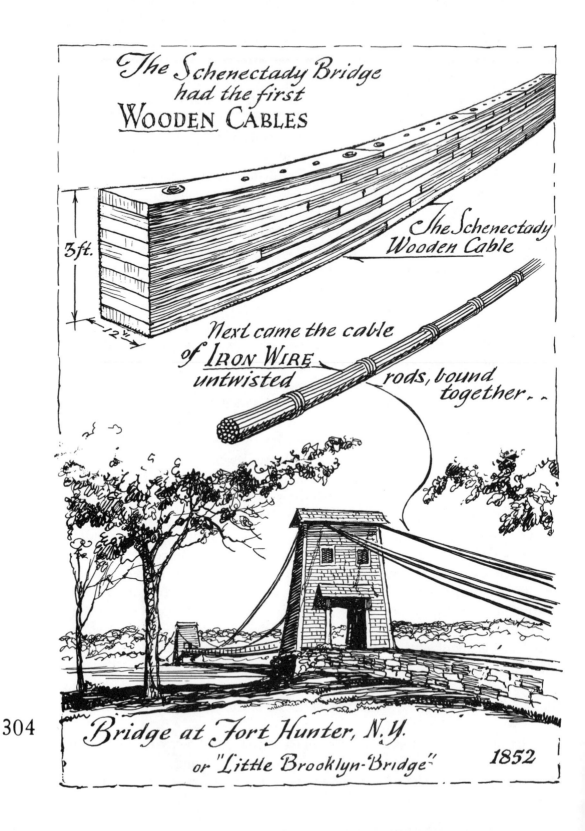

The Schenectady Bridge had the first **WOODEN CABLES**

3 ft.

2"

The Schenectady Wooden Cable

Next came the cable of IRON WIRE untwisted rods, bound together..

304

Bridge at Fort Hunter, N.Y. or "Little Brooklyn-Bridge"

1852

was changed to suit their new location. After any good flood, most of the old covered bridges acquired new addresses. There are even records of capsized bridges, the upturned sidewalls of which were used as roadways until a new bridge was built.

America's first suspension bridges were made of rope and chain, as early as 1801, but they were only experimental foot bridges. In 1816 the first wire suspension bridge, using two cables of only three wires each, was thrown across the Schuylkill River at Fairmount in Philadelphia. The wires were only three-eighths of an inch thick and they supported an eighteen-inch footpath of pine. Stretched four hundred and eight feet between some trees and the upper windows of a wire mill on the other side of the river, it was built

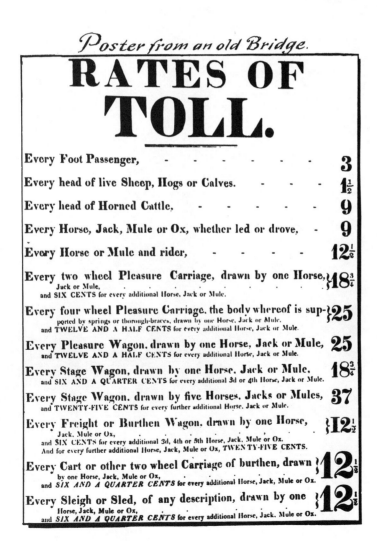

Poster from an old Bridge.

RATES OF
TOLL.

Every Foot Passenger, - - - - -	**3**
Every head of live Sheep, Hogs or Calves. - - -	**1½**
Every head of Horned Cattle, - - - -	**9**
Every Horse, Jack, Mule or Ox, whether led or drove, -	**9**
Every Horse or Mule and rider, - - - -	**12½**
Every two wheel Pleasure Carriage, drawn by one Horse, Jack or Mule, and SIX CENTS for every additional Horse, Jack or Mule.	**18¾**
Every four wheel Pleasure Carriage, the body whereof is supported by springs or thorough-braces, drawn by one Horse, Jack or Mule, and TWELVE AND A HALF CENTS for every additional Horse, Jack or Mule.	**25**
Every Pleasure Wagon, drawn by one Horse, Jack or Mule, and TWELVE AND A HALF CENTS for every additional Horse, Jack or Mule.	**25**
Every Stage Wagon, drawn by one Horse, Jack or Mule, and SIX AND A QUARTER CENTS for every additional 3d or 4th Horse, Jack or Mule.	**18¾**
Every Stage Wagon, drawn by five Horses, Jacks or Mules, and TWENTY-FIVE CENTS for every further additional Horse, Jack or Mule.	**37**
Every Freight or Burthen Wagon, drawn by one Horse, Jack, Mule or Ox, and SIX CENTS for every additional 3d, 4th or 5th Horse, Jack, Mule or Ox. And for every further additional Horse, Jack, Mule or Ox, TWENTY-FIVE CENTS.	**12½**
Every Cart or other two wheel Carriage of burthen, drawn by one Horse, Jack, Mule or Ox, and SIX AND A QUARTER CENTS for every additional Horse, Jack, Mule or Ox.	**12½**
Every Sleigh or Sled, of any description, drawn by one Horse, Jack, Mule or Ox, and SIX AND A QUARTER CENTS for every additional Horse, Jack, Mule or Ox.	**12½**

Jericho Mill, Vt.

"..when mills were
delights to the eye."

in about two weeks. At a toll of one cent per person, it had almost paid for itself within a year, but it collapsed during the first ice storm and was soon forgotten.

Bridge-builder Burr erected a suspension bridge at Schenectady, using great wooden cables one foot wide and three feet high. These spans were no architectural gems, being odd lengths of 160, 190, 180, and 157 feet each. Originally there were three piers in the river to link the four spans but later, when the spans sagged, an extra pier was added under each span, adding to the irregularities. Finally the narrow shingled roofs over each cable were abandoned for a complete bridge housing of hemlock boards, making it one of America's most unique and wavy covered bridges, as shown in the drawing. Although the bridge was unlike any other in America, its toll rates were typically complicated. The list as shown on the opposite page would be enough to drive a modern toll collector mad; between the varying tolls and fines, a bookkeeper and mathematician would have been better suited for the job.

Although the Ramshackle Bridge (as it later came to be known) ended its career dilapidated and uneven, it was once hailed as being "unsurpassed in beauty by any structure in America." It lasted sixty-five years and when it was taken down in 1874 to be sold to a match manufacturer, the massive wooden cables were in perfect condition.

The first metal-cable suspension bridge at Fort Hunter, New York was a Roebling creation of rods or wires lying side by side and bound together. It was supposed to be a small model for the Brooklyn Bridge, and was more an experiment than a finished design. When you walked over it, the floor "came up to meet your feet." In the mildest wind it swayed as much as four feet, and under a fair load it sagged by about the same amount! Between the sway and the sag, many a horse and wagon found itself trapped in the middle and needed a towline and pull to "climb the hill" and reach the other end of the bridge.

Yesterday our city waterfronts were preserved as spots of beauty, but today bridges and docks are often areas of the greatest squalor and evil odors. The country mill and riverside business building were once delights to the eye. However, our consolation lies in the fact that man finds it more difficult to change water areas; rivers and inlets may be less clear, but they still exhibit the same anatomy they possessed a century ago.

Man's inhumanity to the land reaches its peak, it seems, in America's giant sand and gravel pits. Some of them are so permanent and huge that they have become landmarks on aviation maps. Usually near valuable waterfront or along approaches to a city, these scars on the landscape have become

307

"typically American." Zoning boards are usually helpless to bar them because courts have ruled that the sand and gravel business is "farming" and have affirmed the right of any landowner "to remove earth from his own property." Obviously, however, a business which destroys farming and removes the farm itself is not really farming. Today's concrete world needs sand and gravel, but we stand in great need of laws forcing people to level off mining activities when they are finished, so that a worthless scar will not be the heritage of the future landscape.

The word "street" immediately characterizes the city. Originally it had nothing to do with road surface; it measured the distance between two rows of houses. In 1656, when New Amsterdam had one hundred and twenty houses, streets were ordered set off and laid out with stakes, but these streets were measurements without names. Within two years, however, New Amsterdam gave America its first named streets, many of which have now been duplicated in almost every town across the country. It was William Penn who chose a system of naming streets in accordance with the Quaker love of botany, and Philadelphia streets were once almost entirely named from "things that spontaneously grow in the country." Because the early American was familiar with Latin and with the scientific names of plants, some of the old Philadelphia streets became tongue-twisters which it became necessary to change. But enough botanically named streets remain to make intelligible the famous rhyme for remembering their order:

"Market, Arch, Race and Vine,
Chestnut, Walnut, Spruce and Pine."

Streets were often named after some tavern which has long since been forgotten. A great many American towns with strange names were named after an inn famous in the neighborhood. Inns were named for some emblem that could be painted on a signboard and well-preserved in a traveler's memory. Such Pennsylvania towns as Blue Ball, Cross Anchor, Rising Sun, Bird-in-Hand, Broad Axe, King of Prussia, Red Lion, and White Horse often set people speculating as to how their names originated, and what appropriate names they are, at least for a local tavern. Therein, of course, lies the answer.

In 1819 an Act of Congress formally established the Territory of Arkansaw. It was William Woodruff, a Long Island printer, who rebelled against the word Arkansaw. He set up a newspaper press in Arkansaw and reprinted the Act of Congress, changing the name of the new territory to Arkansas. The population of the territory was only about ten thousand, and a great many could not spell, anyway, so Woodruff's version was immediately accepted. Nevertheless, confusion followed, particularly in Kansas and Arkansas City. To this day, although Webster says it should be pronounced "Arkan*so*" and many Kansas people have their own ideas, most people prefer the original form of pronunciation.

Pronunciation was a lesser worry to hundreds of American towns with such strange and unexplainable names as Igo, Peanut, Intercourse, Goodnight, Lovelady, Ticklenaked, Skunk's Misery, and so on. Some continue with their baffling titles; a few have changed their names. But if you want to know the origin of one of these rollicking American town names, and you are certain that it is not derived from the Indian, you will most often find a tavern behind it all, and a sign painter not far away.

Many apparently meaningless names on the ancient taverns were corruptions of familiar phrases of the day, often perpetuated by the successive mistakes of sign painters. The "Pig and Carrot" was originally the "Pique and Carreau"—the spade and diamond of playing cards. A familiar north country tavern name was the "Bell Savage" and the tavern sign usually showed an Indian alongside a large bell. Actually this was a corruption of a popular French book character of the day, a beautiful woman found in the wilderness and called "La Belle Sauvage." "The Bag O' Nails" was originally "The Bacchanalians"; the "Cat and Wheel" was "St. Catherine's Wheel." The "Goat and Compass" came from the motto on an ancient bar, "God encompasseth us." Sign painters renamed many an American town or tavern either by wit or by misspelling.

The American passion for unique advertising signs is no new one. There were slat signs of tavern days that read two different messages, tin signs cut to hammer on covered-bridge rafters, signs cut to put on stair risers, signs with actual animal heads or horns attached to them, even very fat men who were paid to stand outside restaurants with "I Eat Here" signs on their hats or depending from cords about their necks.

Some of the richest American street names live only in people's minds. They are permanent because they are not on the map and therefore cannot be stricken from it. Hell's Kitchen, Back Bay, The Gas House District, The Loop, Harlem, Chinatown, and thousands of others will live on long after the place has changed character entirely. Like the great men of the past, their names remain long after all else has vanished.

People were once required to clean the streets within a certain radius of their own homes. But Benjamin Franklin, who was responsible for so many "firsts" in America, hired the first street cleaner. "After some inquiry," he reported to the Philadelphia Assembly, "I found a poor industrious man who was willing to undertake keeping the pavement clean by sweeping it twice a

309

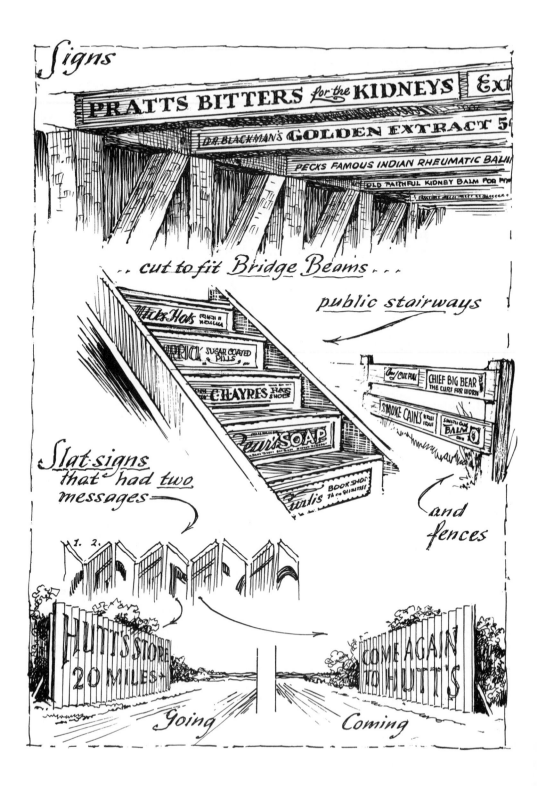

Signs

PRATTS BITTERS *for the* KIDNEYS   Ext

D.R. BLACKMAN'S GOLDEN EXTRACT 5

PECKS FAMOUS INDIAN RHEUMATIC BALM

OLD FAITHFUL KIDNEY BALM FOR PYM

. . cut to fit Bridge Beams . . .

public stairways

CHIEF BIG BEAR
THE TURF FOR WORN

SMOKE CAINS

Slat-signs
that *had* two
messages

and
fences

HUTTS STORE
20 MILES

COME AGAIN
TO HUTTS

Going

Coming

week, carrying off the dirt from before the neighbor's doors, for the sum of six pence per month, to be paid by each house." Franklin's bill for this first street-cleaning service was put through in 1757. The barrels carried on cart-wheels remained identical in design until they disappeared about twenty years ago, along with the famous city "white wings" or street sweepers.

Street sweepers did not disappear from the big cities only because horses vanished; they faded away mostly because of the congested automobile traffic. European towns still find good use for street sweepers; Russia has all-women crews working on twenty-four-hour shifts, still wielding hand-made twig-and-stick brooms.

Street cleaners and Water wagons...

1800

The first lord of the street was the Town Crier. He was also the lamp-lighter. In town-crying days, street lights were bunches of burning pine knots held in an iron cage and suspended from a pole. These had to be fed with fresh pine throughout the night, and it was the town crier's work to do this. The lamplighter of romantic memory and song was a later American of the gas-light era. The writer of this book does not regard himself as ancient, yet he can recall lamplighters in New York City. He likewise recalls that it was they who also delivered the evening paper.

"Extra-boys" are still used in some towns when special news breaks, but they, too, have all but vanished. Fifty years ago their calls of "Wuxtra, read-

PINE-KNOT CAGE
the first American Street Light
1650

all-about-it!" was as commonplace as the clang of trolley bells. Things change quickly in the big city.

Early newspapers were folded into four pages, but consisted of one sheet. This was somewhat for convenience, but primarily because the postal laws demanded extra postage for each extra sheet of paper. Before envelopes came into use, letters, for instance, were written on single sheets, folded over and sealed, and sent for one stamp. A letter of two pages would legally require double postage, and newspapers were dealt with in the same manner. A few publishers came out with "bedsheet papers" that were nearly twice ordinary size; when unfolded, they were the size of a full bedsheet.

The old-time newspapers look different and seem inadequate by comparison with those we enjoy today. Yet few of us consider that the readers of those times could have been equally different, and that a twentieth-century paper would not have fitted into the eighteenth-century picture at all. In going through old attics, one will often find trunks full of old newspapers. That in itself is not unusual, but the fact that they are usually complete day-by-day collections for a year at a time should make one reflect. You will seldom hear of anyone outside of the public library keeping such files today. Why did the old-timers do it?

Of course, if we saved our daily papers we would be collecting more advertising matter than news. It seems regrettable that the life of a newspaper now depends upon paid advertising to such an extent that many small-town newspapers must gather news for the main purpose of creating an advertising medium. A New England publisher jokingly commented that "there is so much news in the papers nowadays, you can hardly get around to the ads."

The greatest change in newspaper stalls lies in the array of magazines added to them. Despite the good publications, most of the space is often taken up by "girly" magazines. These cheap publications are attacked by righteous moderns as "endangering our youth." Great-grandfather would not only have spanked his children for reading them, but would have personally chastised the publisher. In looking back at great-grandfather, we realize that his moral indignation was not always an emotion derived from prudishness.

Great-grandfather, it seems, regarded his town in very much the same light as he regarded his own home. The public square with its bandstand and benches and horse foundations had all the furniture of friendliness. Only a mean man could walk down Main Street in a hurry: for the average person it was slow progress because there were so many friends to stop and chat with.

Great·grandfather's Occupations

NOT LONG AGO, when a man's work gave him some certain aura, you could guess almost any American's profession simply by looking at him. Now that has become nearly impossible. Air pilots fly in business suits, farmers wear sport coats to town, and actors at last look like any other normal person. The uniform of one's occupation has become lost in present-day regimentation. It seems a pity, too, for there are yet those who are so proud of their occupations that they would still enjoy being identified with them by dress.

The uniforms of occupation are not the only thing that has vanished from the business world: many standard American professions have become obsolete. Trying to recall some, you might think of a few picturesque occupations like stagecoach driving or chimney-sweeping or town-crying. On the contrary, there were hundreds or thousands of major jobs which once occupied a goodly portion of the nation and which are now gone for all time.

Even within the past decade, hundreds of callings became obsolete. Even in the modern world of aviation, hardly a year goes by without witnessing the disappearance of some occupation. One of the most picturesque and American characters was the aviation barnstormer, whom we might pass by as an unimportant worker. Actually, there have been about five thousand professional barnstormers in America and their work was more important than even they dreamed.

After the First World War, when the airplane was regarded as nothing

314

more than a novel piece of war machinery, thousands of men returned to civilian life with the roar of motors still in their ears. With uncrated surplus OX-5 and Hispano-Suiza engines selling for two hundred dollars apiece, who could resist the temptation to build his own ship or buy an old Army "Jenny"?

For the next twenty years the country was treated to "air circuses" and passenger flights wherever there was an empty field and enough people to pay. The barnstorming birdman was born; wearing his cap backward, high laced boots, waxed moustache, and a scarf that trailed out behind him when in flight, he made a dashing picture, indeed. At night he often had to sleep in the field under the plane's wing, but by day he was the hero of young America.

Many people still recall the Gates Flying Circus and their method of advertising their show. When the group came to town, they unloosed rolls of toilet paper, which floated gaily across the sky and finally festooned trees and buildings, to tell the populace that an air show was to be seen at the fair grounds. With Gates there was always a special daredevil known as "Diavolo," who walked wings and actually stood atop the upper wing while the

Birdman 1920

315

plane looped. As each Diavolo finally plunged to his death, a new one took the name. Pilot "Duke" Kranz, who was the last Diavolo, is still active in the aviation world at the time of this writing.

The average barnstormer was regarded as a foolish daredevil, drunk much of the time. The poor fellow had sold his home and belongings to buy his plane and keep it in repair, and he inevitably sold his life in the bargain. Very few people realized that he was doing important work which the military forces should have undertaken at government expense. When the last great air show ended at Cleveland, Ohio in 1939, the souped-up motors and improvised plane designs for which the five thousand barnstormers had footed the bills were our most valuable military asset. They had reached a stage at which they could do little to make their ships go faster except saw a few inches off their wings each race day, and by then wings the length of ironing boards were lifting the nation's heaviest stock engines into the air. Those "crazy air devils" deserve a place in the nation's respect which has never been accorded them. And a military salute, too, for they are among the greatest of America's unsung heroes.

One of the quickest disappearances of any big business was that of the American natural-ice industry. Just fifty years ago there were some ten thou-

... a few inches off the wings each year

1939

316

sand men in America cutting natural ice during the winter months. They were a fabulous race, often farmer boys who found winter on the farm too slow and financially unproductive; others were drifters from river life or the lumber country who depended on picking up a winter's stake. Salaries included room and board, but so many blankets were ripped up and used for foot wrappings and warm undergarments that ice cutters were usually instructed to bring their own bedding.

Today, no record of the ice cutters, except an occasional anecdote about their rough living, survives. The icehouses in which they worked have vanished. Only a foundation or an abandoned railroad track marks their locations, but almost every pond and lake will produce some evidence of their existence. Icehouses were sometimes so big that clouds formed and rain fell within them. Often the railroad's busiest tracks were the ones which serviced the icehouses. The electric switch that starts your refrigerator machinery in less than five years blasted forever one of America's major industries and sent the ice cutter into an oblivion of Americana.

The first icehouses were farm root cellars. Pennsylvania farmers used to shovel snow and ice into their root cellars just before the thaw of spring; they found that, by packing a little meadow grass with it, the ice could be made to last into the next summer. By 1830 icehouses were standard farm equipment. The usual procedure was to build them of two walls with hay in between. Virginia icehouses were actually two separate houses, one built inside the other, with enough room in the vacant space for a man to walk. The sides and roof of both "houses" were thatched, and the ice placed in the inner house on a bed of straw.

In 1799 ice was cut from Canal Street in New York City and sent to Charleston, South Carolina by boat; it was welcomed with fife and drum and chopped up in drinks for city officials. It had melted considerably by the time it reached the dock down south, but the experiment was a success and the idea of exporting ice was born. In 1805, a man named Frederic Tudor from Boston sent one hundred and thirty tons of ice in the brig *Favorite* to Martinique in the West Indies. In 1815 he contracted to supply the Cuban government and by 1833 he had contracts with Madras, Bombay, and Calcutta.

To hint at the size of the American natural-ice business as early as 1847, we find Boston records showing 51,887 tons sent to coastal ports and 22,591 tons sent abroad. The returns for that year in Boston were far above the half-million-dollar mark. Multiplying this by the hundreds of other ice businesses, you may see that the industry was a major one for America.

The only evidence of the early ice cutter remaining may be his tools, which were sometimes made in the farm's forge barn. Even the later manu-

317

1910

*Ice-houses
so big that real clouds
formed inside!*

Ice-cutting at Lake Hopatcong, N.J.

Snow Warden

Snow Paving the road

factured tools are beginning to disappear now: the common ice tongs, ice saw and other paraphernalia of the ice cutter may already be seen in the antique shops. Natural ice for anything except skating will soon be past Americana. Even now we skate largely on artificial ice!

The ice and snow of yesteryear, one might think, should have inconvenienced the farmer, yet winter was a season to which he looked forward! Every hauling job waited for the first snow or ice because only then were the soft and uneven roads of yesterday really usable.

Instead of plowing the snow away as we do today, snow rollers packed it down and everyone traveled on top. One of the town's most important jobs was that of snow warden; he was the man who supervised "road packing" and, oddly enough, was responsible for covering the bare spots with snow. The whole northern country moved by sled in winter, and a bare spot on a snow-covered road became a frustrating roadblock. The snow warden's most tiring job was to "snow-pave" covered bridges so sleds could pass through. This, of course, explodes the theory that bridges were covered to keep them free of snow.

For every wagon a farmer owned, he once had about three sleds. Wheels were more for pleasure or light-carriage transportation: all heavy hauling was postponed until winter and moved over ice and snow. A few farmers improvised detachable runners to put beneath wagon wheels; just before the gasoline truck entered the scene, detachable runners were manufactured and sold by mail-order houses.

One road traveler who was never bothered by weather, good or bad, was the drover. And a most remarkable person he was. When one remembers that a farmer often entrusted his entire year's stock to his care, one realizes how

319

sober and reliable a gentleman the drover must have been. He was also one of the first American advertising men: his pung (sled) was so covered with signs advertising taverns or patent medicines that he seldom needed other identification.

Drovers who walked livestock from the farm to the city often found themselves guardians to a varied group. Cows and sheep and goats were comparatively simple to handle, but geese and turkeys made the drover's life difficult. The drover's dog is a forgotten animal, but it is said that his ability as a herder was amazing. While the drover slept, he depended upon his dog to guard his flock and warn him of any irregularity.

Among the feats of a drover was that of separating large droves into legal limits for crossing toll bridges. There seemed to be a standard fine of a dollar for any drove "of horses, jacks, mules, or oxen more than ten, at a distance less than thirty feet apart" over a wooden bridge. But it is doubted that a drover ever paid the fine, for he was usually the tollbridge keeper's best customer.

Tobacco drovers were the truck drivers of their day for those plantations without a river at their door. The commonest way of delivering tobacco from isolated farms to river docks was by "giant hogshead." This was a tremendous wooden barrel equipped with iron-bound "tire hoops"; a team of horses could pull such a hogshead of tobacco through jungle which no wagon might possibly navigate. Although the idea originated in the deep South, tobacco hogsheads were also common in New England. The hogshead was an old English measure of capacity (63 gallons of wine and 54 gallons of beer), but the American use of the giant hogshead for tobacco transportation enlarged

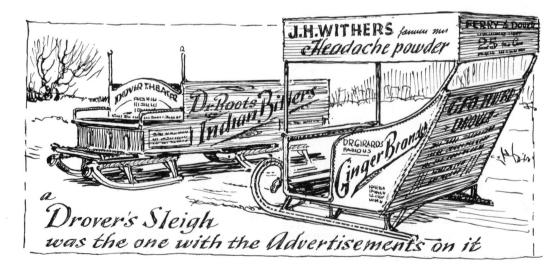

320

a Drover's Sleigh *was the one with the* Advertisements *on it*

Tobacco Drovers

-- a Giant Hogshead

its proportions to contain from 750 to 1200 pounds, varying in different states.

The drover had no standard identifying uniform, although many wore wide-brim hats and large capes. A staff to handle the animals was sometimes supplemented by a long pole with a red flag on it so that stagecoach traffic might be warned of an approaching drove. When railroads were young, locomotives had to be "escorted from one end of town to the other"; the town drover had the job of riding ahead on horseback with a red flag. Because that law had never been changed, freight trains moving about on the west side of New York's Manhattan Island were preceded by a man, horse, and red flag until only a few years ago.

The stage driver was more than a driver of horses like the English coachman; he was a power in the land. He carried political news from country to town and he was noted for the great kindness of delivering messages from farmhouse to farmhouse. A toot on the stagecoach horn would bring a farm wife to the door, where the driver might slow his horses to a walk and call out that "Netty had twins and she's doin' good," or other such news. Stagecoach drivers were second to sea captains in many ways and, like men of the sea, usually retired abruptly while their sons continued on the highways, "born to the box."

Children always associated a trip on the stage with an ocean voyage: such, indeed, was the common custom. The driver was referred to as captain, his crew always "got aboard," the inside of the coach was "the cabin," and the top was called "the deck." Most coaches were named after famous ships and

New Hampshire driver in winter—

322

3 sets of shoes and giant "over-stockings"

the summer headgear of drivers was often a sea captain's cap. Few people knew a stagecoach driver's first name and, although his constant imbibing of ale, brandy, and rum-and-milk must have had its effect, his dignity remained great and dominant. Young children were often entrusted to his care, and as soon as the coach had left town, the driver's word was as much law as that of any captain at sea.

The New Hampshire stage driver's winter dress identified him at once. Homespun trousers were tucked inside thin leather boots with fur-lined overshoes over the boots. Over these were worn Canadian hand-knit red stockings coming well up over the knees, creating the appearance of tremendously heavy legs. Incredible as it may seem, another light shoe was added, making three pairs of shoes in all! The driver's coats and caps were fur, and a red silk sash with tassels completed the costume.

Many of the early railroad brakemen, conductors, ticket men, and depot masters were former stage drivers. Benjamin Pierce Cheney, a prominent Boston railroad owner, founder of the rich Cheney Express, and chief owner of the American Express Company, began as a stage driver in New Hampshire between Exeter and Nashua. The rail lines soon had positions open for any stage driver who would accept, and the great American stage driver vanished into the complexities of the railroad business.

Another vanished knight of the road is the old-fashioned peddler whose home and shop was his wagon. He both bought and sold as he went, often selling his stock, horse, wagon, and all. Starting anew, with a few wares on his back, he invariably returned with a new horse and wagon and a tidy profit besides.

"Peddler" and "drummer" are typically American words. The ancient Scotch "peder" or foot-salesman became the "pedlar" of the New World. Although in England "peddlers" traveled only by foot and "hawkers" went only by wagon, anyone who sold wares from door to door in America became commonly known as a peddler. The drummer, or man who went about "drumming up trade," actually stemmed from the earliest time when drums were used to attract public attention, just as when church was called by a drum and public announcements were made after a drum call. The first American peddlers often carried a drum known as a "chapman's drum." The Yankee peddler was known to the townspeople of his time as a "chapman," a word which comes from the Anglo-Saxon "ceap" for trade, plus "man" (hence a "cheap-man"). The chapman who later won fame as a Yankee peddler often carried a drum and an American flag and boasted loudly that he sold only American goods. Actually, it was illegal for him to do otherwise, but he was a good salesman. The Connecticut statutes of the middle

The Peddler was an American Farm Institution

eighties said that "any petty-chapman dealing, trading or trafficking in foreign goods which are not the product of the United States, shall have his goods seized. One-half the value of the goods seized shall go to the State and the other half shall go to the informer."

The Yankee peddler was the original American who could "sell anyone anything." One of his claims to fame is his origination of the name "Nutmeg State" for Connecticut; this derived from the belief that the Connecticut peddler sold wooden nutmegs as real ones. Few people, however, know that nutmegs were famous in Connecticut on their own merits. The nutmeg was the most popular flavoring of the old days; it was even favored as a gift. Nutmegs were gilded and ribboned and given as presents, not only because of their worth, but because they were supposed to have great medicinal value. Some of the silver trinkets of colonial days which many people believe are snuff boxes were actually nutmeg-holders. The inside of the cover was often pierced to form a grater and served also as an opening to let the aroma escape. The *bon vivants* and fashionable dames of the period carried nut-

324

megs with them at all times as a sign of luxury. Because nutmegs were valuable and because they were easy to carry, it was always a convenient money-maker for the traveling peddler, who was often called a "nutmeg man."

American rivers have reversed their roles in the American scene during the past century, and with this change a great race of men has vanished. Today, rivers are often obstacles to travel, whereas yesterday they were the main means of inland transportation. At one time it was easier to push a cargo by flatboat with long poles for a few hundred miles than it would be to roll it on wheels over the then impassable roads. Before steam came to propel boats, the entire American river commerce depended upon the strength of river men, the likes of whom we shall never see again. In 1870 William Cullen Bryant wrote: "The keel-boatmen of the Mississippi were a remarkable race. . . . In strength they were absolute giants; in power of sustaining fatigue, without rivals in any age. If they had been classical in their exultation of physical power, they would confidently have challenged Hercules to combat, and, in our opinion, would have conquered that old Greek." The keel-boatmen have long since gone and only by folklore has their remarkable

of thousands of *Keelboats*, not one remains

75' long

River Men... a race of giants

325

Grindstone City

The
Ghost city of discarded
Grindstones

Grindstone
set in tree-fork

Water-can
on willow-stick

326

1860, Bucks County Pa.

size and strength been recorded. Mike Fink is to the river what Davy Crockett has become to the southwest, yet the story now is one of roughness and toughness rather than of the remarkable size and strength required for men actually to push large cargoes from town to town. One of the river stories concerns a giant of a river man who lived on an Ohio flatboat with his family of twelve children. After delivering a load of large grindstones to a pier, he decided to make some extra money and take them directly to the warehouse in town. He carried a stack of them on his back, while each of the children rolled one grindstone down the village street like a hoop.

Incidentally, grindstones as the average person knows them are something else from the past. They are often mistaken for, and are even sold by some antique shops, as millstones. Few old farmhouses have less than a dozen grindstones lying around the grounds or in the barns, but the greatest collection is probably at Grindstone City in Michigan. Buried along the shore there are hundreds of tons of good grindstones, discarded when new-type abrasives were developed.

Grindstones were first imported from England and later from Nova Scotia. America first quarried grindstones in Berea, Ohio, but by 1840 small mills appeared almost everywhere, grinding rock into serviceable grindstones to sell to the farmers. There were once about two hundred villages called Grindstone; only five remain.

The early grindstone man simply sold the stone and let the farmer make his own "grinding horse"; the first ones were turned by hand and therefore required two men to serve as operators. The more recent ones had a foot pedal. You can still buy foot-pedal grindstones, equipped with spring tractor seats, from a few mail-order houses. The first grindstones were placed in the crotch of a forked tree trunk; a can of water on a willow stick wiggled above, as the wheel turned, and splashed on the stone below. The later "grindstone man" was a big-city knife and scissor sharpener who carried his equipment on his back. The sketch of a grindstone man shows him also carrying a large advertising board: when he went into a house to collect knives or scissors, he naturally left his grinding stand outside and the sign told passersby that he was in the neighborhood and open for business.

The most famous "walking signs" were those of the more recent "sandwich men." You may still see sandwich men walking between their two advertising signs, but they are usually derelicts picking up money while otherwise out of work. New York once had agencies which hired groups of sandwich men and the scheme was always a popular part of any local advertising campaign. Restaurants and barber shops are examples of businesses which still employ sandwich men for advertising.

1750

Grindstones were sold unmounted

and made for 2 man operation

"I grind!"

GRIND
STONE
MAN

1850

The first one-man Grindstone was that of the town Grinder

328

Sandwich-men 1900

The barber shop of a century ago was not unlike that of today in its layout. The chair, however, was without arms and there was a separate stool for the feet. The barber's best advertisement was his array of shaving mugs inscribed with the owners' names. The ordinary customer hid under the anonymity of a number, but the town elite were represented by coats of arms, signs of their professions, and various embellishments in color and gold leaf. The whole array was a vivid advertisement of the barber's popularity.

Barber shops used to be museums of bric-a-brac; even today the small-town barber shop will often be filled with exotic plants and curious treasures. This custom stems from the time when the barber was also a surgeon, and the doctor's office was also a museum where stuffed animals were hung from the ceiling, skeletons were propped up in corners, and all sorts of strange things

329

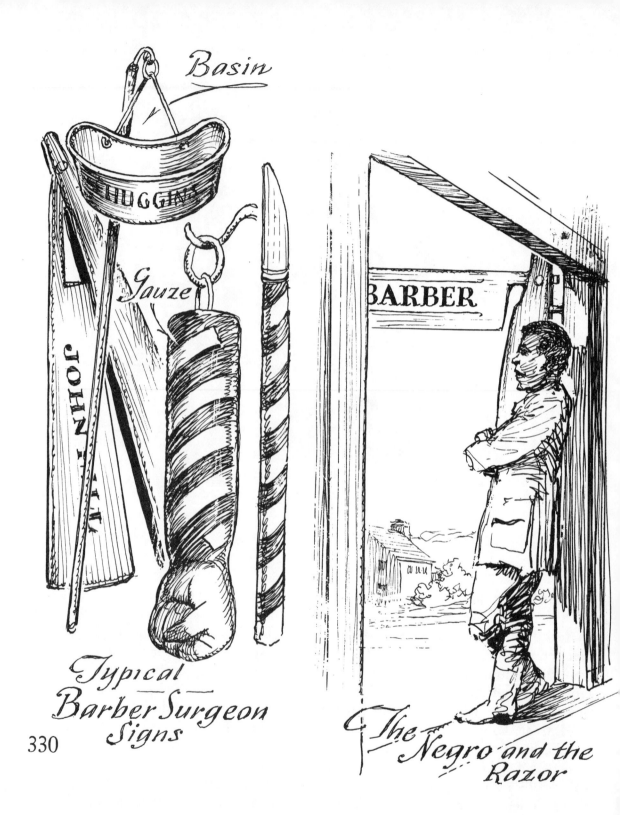

Basin

HUGGINS

Gauze

JOHN

Typical
Barber Surgeon
Signs

330

BARBER

The Negro and the
Razor

were to be seen sealed in glass jars. The first street signs of the barber did not advertise his hair-cutting, but rather his profession of blood-letting. The red pole with a spiraled white line represents a bleeding arm wrapped with white gauze. Another such sign was a barber's basin hung from a pole; the same basin used to catch shaving lather also caught blood from a patient who was being bled. The barber-surgeon profession began with a decree in 1092 stating that monks must not wear beards. "Barba-men" (from the Latin word for beard) were trained to shave monks and also to bleed them in time of sickness because their pans and cutting equipment were so similar. Unfortunately, they were often the same.

The earliest mention of barbers in America is in the *Archives* of Pennsylvania for 1702. It reveals that four barbers were fined for trimming people "on the first days of the week." Another early record is that of a Negro barber of Connecticut in 1730 who had no shop but made the rounds of the countryside in a wagon. The association of the Negro and the razor in American folklore has good foundation because until about 1820 Negroes controlled the profession of shaving and hair-cutting. As late as 1884, Chamber's *Encyclopedia of New York* said, "In the United States the business of barbering is almost exclusively in the hands of the colored population."

Typical of the small town was its attitude toward the unfortunate and weak-minded. It never tolerated a drunk, yet every town had its eccentrics who were good-naturedly passed off as "town characters." There is no room now for the hermits, the wanderers, the solitaries, and town do-nothings who were accepted a century ago. New Canaan, Connecticut harbored "Crazy Sam" who came out only after dark, when he yodeled until morning. Westerly, Rhode Island had the "Astronomer" who lived in summer on berries and in winter on nuts and grain; his ability to predict weather was reportedly unexcelled. He seldom showed himself, but he left strange messages scratched upon pumpkins. There were men who just "loathed the nearness of others" and became hermits in caves, in holes in the ground, or retreated into themselves. And great-grandfather tolerated them with the same patience and understanding that he would show to one of his own.

Most renowned of America's eccentrics was possibly Johnny Appleseed, who blamed his strange ways on an unhappy love affair. He was a religious man who wore few clothes and traveled barefoot. He always carried a Bible and a supply of apple seeds with him. On his head he wore a tin pan which he also used for cooking his meals. His real name was Jonathan Chapman and he was just another "touched" person who accepted the hospitality of yesteryear. But the kindness of the towns through which he traveled was more than repaid by his planting of apple seeds. After walking twenty miles

331

White water men

during one day in 1847, he stopped at the home of friends in Fort Wayne, Indiana to read his Bible to them and leave them the customary supply of seeds. There he died at the age of seventy-two.

You might say that the lumberjack and riverjack are still with us, but even they will be the first to admit that the old-timer at their work was a person entirely different from his modern counterpart. Timber is moved now mostly by rail and truck, but in the old days it was moved by river. Water continues to be a useful method of moving logs, but most log drives are tame ferry operations where the riverjack's work consists only of guiding the logs through calm water. The riverjack was once a "white-water man" who let the apprentice do his calm-water work and saved his acrobatic daring for the dangerous waters of rapids and swift rivers.

The only surviving white-water log drive in the east is still operating on the Machias River in Maine. Other survivors are the annual drives on the Clearwater River in Idaho and the Saguenay in Quebec.

A log drive takes about two weeks, and the moving force of melting snow is a power that is calculated and timed for weeks ahead. A riverjack might drink for the rest of the year, but when spring approached he became a quiet, sure-footed athlete. The old-time white-water man had a short life and he seldom found a wife to share his rugged existence, so the breed has nearly disappeared.

A century ago the riverfront of almost any town was crowded with logs. Each log had a name or initials marked on it and was waiting to be picked up by the owner who might take a month traveling downstream from the point where the log was cut. Of course, there was much argument over the ownership of many logs, and the log-viewer was called in to make his legal decision.

The title of inspector is recent: not long ago the word was "viewer." There were weight-viewers, fence-viewers, egg-viewers, gutter-viewers, and viewers of whatever needed inspection or supervision. Hardly a law was passed without a set of viewers to go along with it. From the beginning, viewers were seldom popular people; as years passed, viewing was embodied in a town ordinance for the resolution of personal disputes, and the government inspector became the "policeman" we know of today. If your neighbor put his fence on what you thought was your property, you called neither the policeman nor the surveyor, but the town fence-viewer. When he was on duty, the fence-viewer usually had two chainmen who carried the "Gunter's Chain" for measuring land distances, and he also worked closely with the hayward. The hayward was the man who impounded stray cattle and fined the owner. The similar words "strayward" and "straywarden" will not be found in the dictionary, but are still used in the Arkansas back country.

Another forgotten word is "wright." Millwright, shipwright, wheelwright, cartwright, and wainwright (wagon-maker) are words that have become people's proper names, but which have all joined the world of vanished occupations. The wheelwright began as an apprentice woodsman and

Settling a dispute.

Perch·pole or rod 16½'

fence-viewer.

Chainman *Gunter's Chain (4 rods or 66 feet long).*

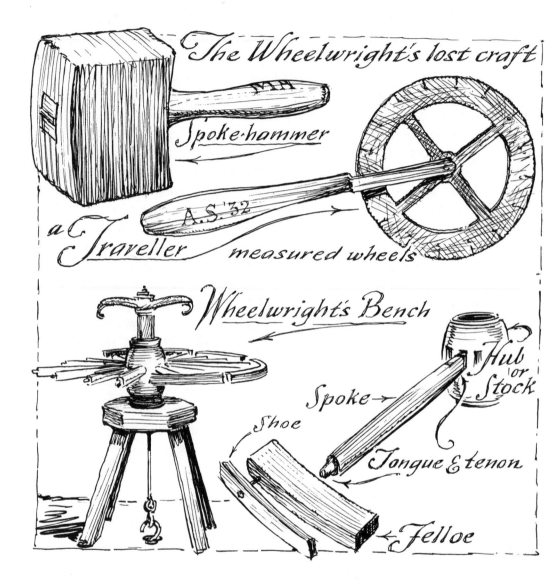

The Wheelwright's lost craft

Spoke-hammer

a Traveller

A.S. '32

measured wheels

Wheelwright's Bench

Spoke →

Shoe

Hub or Stock

Tongue & tenon

Felloe

334

became America's greatest wood expert. The spidery web of wheel that reached perfection during the Victorian age could not be made again. Its strength improved with age because its properly seasoned woods supplemented each other's merits to weld a unit as close to perfection as man has ever produced. Only well into the nineteenth century did the wheelwright use a circular iron tire; before that the wheel was shod only with strakes or curved sections over each spoke end. That enormous weights could speed over the rough roads of yesterday on wooden wheels much slenderer than modern bicycle tires and without any metal fastenings seems almost miraculous. Black or sour gum for hubs, oak or ash for spokes, hickory for felloes, beech or fresh ash for axles, oak for framing, and poplar for paneling were some of the many combinations of wood that made up a lasting wagon. Such combinations were the "secret recipes" of the old wheelwright, and he made every effort to keep them secret, as he did his methods of seasoning.

There is no need for anything but metal wheels today; when the world moved on dirt roads, however, a fine wooden wheel meant a great deal to the expert and almost every man was an expert. The "feel" and spring, even the sound, of a properly made wheel added to the enjoyment of yesterday's travel. But now all that is gone and wrights are practically extinct. Even the "smiths" who succeeded them in the iron age are on their way to oblivion.

A smith, the derivation of whose name is almost forgotten, is "a man who strikes." The meaning is derived from the word "smite," and the smith's tool was a hammer. Today we know only of the blacksmith and tinsmith. Not long ago, the whitesmith, working in lighter metals, was equally well-known. The blacksmith's shop, with doors open during the summer and a comfortably warm fire in winter, offered the country men a receptive atmosphere for gathering and gossip. The blacksmith ranked with the cobbler as a rural philosopher, but his hammer had more emphasis and the "mighty smith" became the greater legend.

The early farms all had their own forge barns, and it was almost unheard of for a farmer to have his horse's shoes made to order by a town blacksmith. The blacksmith's work was that of making such fine metal parts as hinges, guns, pots, or machinery. Only in later years, when specialization came into being and the gunsmith, the hingesmith, the tinsmith and other specialists opened their shops, did the blacksmith's art deteriorate to horseshoe making and the general rough farm smithing which we associate with the "village smithy."

335

In 1717 Jonathan Dickinson wrote: "This last summer one Thomas Rutter, a smith who lives not far from Germantown, hath removed further up in the country, and of his own strength has set upon making iron." From

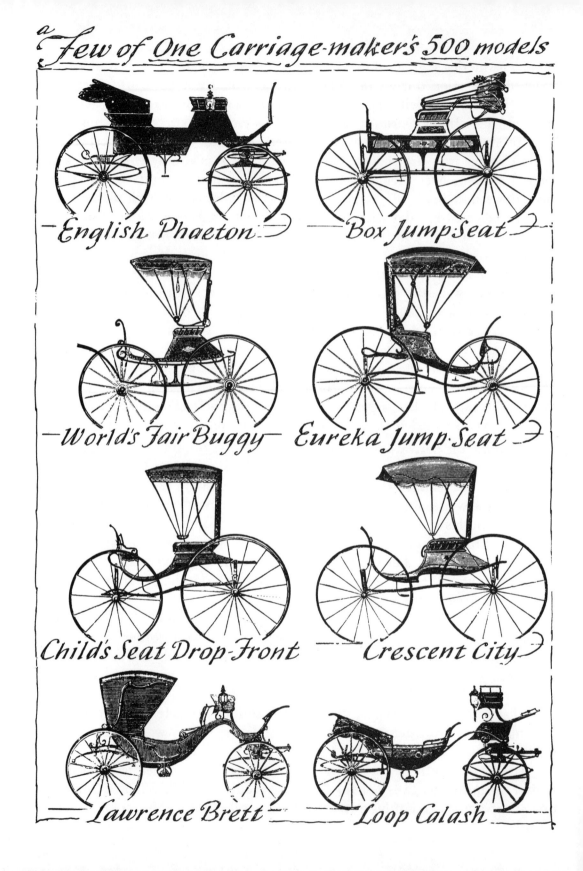

A Few of One Carriage-maker's 500 models

English Phaeton

Box Jump-Seat

World's Fair Buggy

Eureka Jump-Seat

Child's Seat Drop-Front

Crescent City

Lawrence Brett

Loop Calash

Doctor's Phaeton

Full top Cabriolet

Champion

Prince of Wales

Dayton Brett

City Coupe

Brewster Calash Coach

Coupe Rockaway

that early date, a number of German blacksmiths devoted a part of their time to mining and smelting iron in their own furnaces. Ore was melted in stone stacks about twenty feet high, often built by one man and standing undamaged today after two hundred years. The furnace was built into the side of a hill so that the ore, charcoal, and limestone could be hauled to the top by oxen and dumped into the stack. The process went on continually day and night for about nine months of the year.

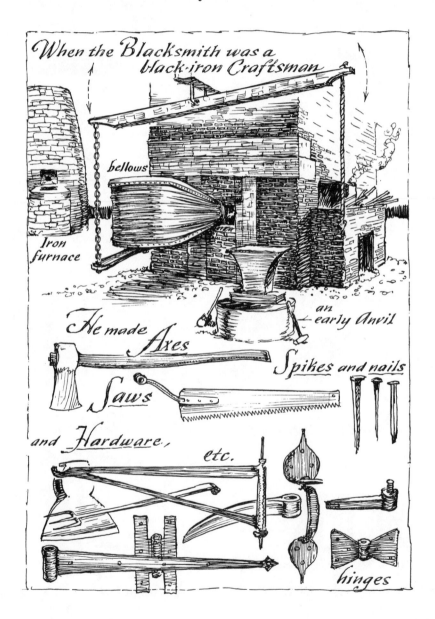

When the Blacksmith was a black-iron Craftsman

bellows

Iron furnace

an early Anvil

He made Axes

Spikes and nails

Saws

and Hardware, etc.

hinges

The amount of charcoal used to smelt iron was staggering, but the amount of wood used to make the charcoal was almost beyond comprehension. In 1840 the small town of Salisbury, Connecticut was using five thousand cords of wood a year in the manufacture of iron. This amount is hardly more than a mathematical figure, but if you visualize it in the form of one pile of wood in cord-width (4′ x 4′), such a woodpile would be over seven miles long. This, multiplied by the hundreds of iron-producing towns of that time, made a pitiful gap in the forests of America and cleared the farmer's countryside of every available tree.

When coke took over the work of charcoal, about ten thousand charcoal workers were left to find other employment. They were mostly Europeans who could speak no English and whose life of seclusion with their lonely charcoal stacks had turned them into a strange race of hermits. Like the others engaged in lost occupations, they had a rich history and suffered a sad disappearance.

With all the vanished occupations, a good deal of American tradition was shelved, for a man's work is reflected in his thinking as much as his thinking is reflected in his work. Great-grandfather not only built a business for his sons, but enjoyed evolving a philosophy to go with it and bestowed that upon his offspring as well. The inheritance of a principle, however, is like the inheritance of money: it needs constant and wise application lest it become lost.

Occupations are born quickly today and often die without achieving stature and character. It is then that a worker comes to resemble a discarded machine with nothing in the nature of business to leave to his children except money. The American heritage too frequently consists of nothing else.

His individuality, his church, his home, his town, and his occupation were the things great-grandfather most enjoyed bestowing. These things, he knew, were the ingredients of freedom. But freedom, while a heritage, must be rewon for each generation. These things were known to the American yesterday.

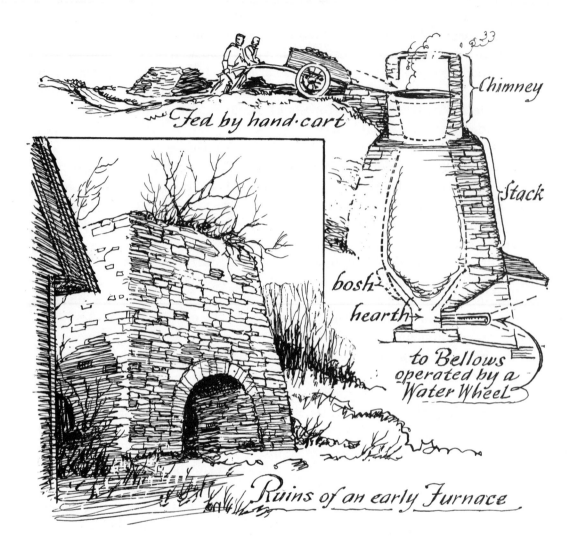

Fed by hand-cart

Chimney

Stack

bosh

hearth

to Bellows
operated by a
Water Wheel

Ruins of an early Furnace

340

Charcoal Burners often lived like solitary Animals

ᐧᐧin Sod-huts similar to their Charcoal Mounds

Charcoal making

a Lying Kiln — chimney

sod

about 35 cords

a Standing Kiln — 30 ft.

342

Postscript

THERE IS NO PLACE for nostalgia in a progressive world. The new school not only ignores nostalgia, but condemns it. The world of yesterday is becoming an isolated world of remembrances and echoes so forbidden that, to decorate the present with it, you must often do so with a sense of humor or belong to a select group. If this book is pessimistic about the present, and not merely enthusiastic about some of the past, then I have missed my objective. But such is the chance an individualist inevitably runs.

ERIC SLOANE

343